Expanding Democratic Space in Nigeria

I0113084

**Edited by
Jibrin Ibrahim**

CODESRIA National Studies Series

Expanding Democratic Space in Nigeria

First published in 1997 by CODESRIA

Copyright © CODESRIA

CODESRIA is the Council for the Development of Social Science Research in Africa, headquartered in Dakar, Senegal. It is an independent organisation whose principal objectives are facilitating research, promoting research-based publishing and creating multiple fora geared towards the exchange of views and information among African scholars. Its correspondence address is:

B.P. 3304, Dakar, Senegal.

ISBN   2-86978-068-0 (Soft Cover)

Reprinted in 2003

Cover art work: Alla A. Kleekpo
Typeset by Marie Therese Coron-Diouf, CODESRIA
Production Consultants: Foster & Phillips
Distributors: ABC, 27 Park End Street, Oxford OX1, IHU

CODESRIA would like to express its gratitude to the Swedish International Development Co-operation Agency (SIDA), the Rockefeller Foundation, the International Development Research Centre (IDRC), the Ford Foundation, the Canergie Corporation, the European Union, the Norwegian Ministry of Foreign Affairs and the Danish Agency for International Development (DANIDA), the Dutch Government and the Government of Senegal for support of its research and publication activities.

This book is dedicated to the memory of Claude Ake (1939-1996), one of our intellectual stars who has also played a major role in the struggle for expanding Nigerian democratic space.

Contents

Part One: The Expansion of Democratic Space
Theoretical and Empirical Issues

Part Two: The Babangida Administration
Checkmate or Impetus for Democratisation?

Part Three: Civil Society and Democratisation

Part Four: Liberties, Rights and Citizenship

Appendices

Preface

Much of the evidence in this book and the thrust of the theoretical argument is about the steady reduction of democratic space in Nigeria over the past decade. Although the country has a tradition of a strong civil society that has been consistently in the struggle for democratisation, democratic culture and politics have been declining rather than progressing. The state has been actively engaged in restricting the democratic potential of political parties, the media, trade unions, youth and professional organisations.

And yet, the expansion of democratic space is not just a dream of the authors. It is a collective reading of the march of history. Precisely because power and resources are being monopolised by an increasingly narrower circle, the struggle to expand access have been intensifying in the country. Precisely because civil society has been strong and relatively autonomous, the attempts cripple it have become more intense in recent years. It is the fear that popular and liberal democratic struggles would bear fruits that has been provoking the panic measures by those in power to block the access of others, eliminate dissent and destroy the capacity to struggle.

The notion that the central agenda in Nigeria is the expansion of democratic space was first articulated in workshops organised in Uppsala and Oxford in 1989 attended by among others Bjorn Beckman, Attahiru Jega, Gavin Williams, Yusuf Bangura, Adebayo Olukoshi, Raufu Mustapha, Akin Fadahunsi and Jibrin Ibrahim. It was first popularised by Bjorn Beckman's: 'Whose Democracy Bourgeois versus Popular Democracy' published in the *Review of African Political Economy* n45/46 of 1989 and in the collection edited by Rudebeck (1992). The debates also focused on recent developments in the Nigerian political economy that were promoting authoritarianism and resulted in the publication edited by Adebayo Olukoshi (1993) *The Politics of Structural Adjustment in Nigeria*. The twin programmes of structural adjustment and political transition to civil rule conducted by the military have been eroding development and democracy in the country, so a wide spectrum of interest groups have developed a concrete stake in contesting state policies and thereby striving for a better future. As Beckman (1992:148) has argued, many forces have a stake in protecting and expanding the democratic space in order that further advances for the society at large could be made.

It is the contention of the authors in this volume that popular organisations democratic movements, labour, the youth and students, women's organisations, etc. have a crucial role to play in the process. The Nigerian political class for its part has not played as important a role as has been expected. It has been unable to effectively combat the anti-democratic antics of the military.

It would be recalled that the political transition programme has been so long and convoluted, so tightly controlled and so manipulated under the Babangida regime, that it was clear the chances of successful implantation of a liberal democratic regime were very bleak. At the end of the day, the presidential elections held on June 12, 1993 were annulled by the General to the chagrin and the consternation of a large cross-section of Nigerian society. The events following the annulment were very revealing about the prospects for as well as the difficulties of expanding democratic space in Nigeria.

The immediate response to the annulment was a massive, broad based and national mobilisation against the regime's action and for democracy. A vigorous movement under the leadership of the Campaign for Democracy (CD) developed and it appeared, as Beko Ransome-Kuti, the leader of the CD said, that the organisation which had forty one affiliate groups, had been transformed from a small alliance to a position of 'determining the strategic direction of the democratic struggle in Nigeria' (African Guardian, 21 February 1994). In the Lagos Conference were the first drafts of the papers in this volume were presented and a human rights 'Round Table' organised, Chima Ubani, the General Secretary of the CD contended as follows in their position paper. The CD had succeeded in achieving better cohesion and coordination of the various groups seeking to expand democratic space and to empower civil society in Nigeria. A few weeks later, the same Chima Ubani published a letter 'CD : Setting the Records Straight (18 January 1994)', in which he confessed that the CD had been seriously affected by internal divisions that have weakened the cohesiveness of the organisation and the morale of its members and supporters Indeed, the Lagos Conference was the last occasion in which Beko Ransome-Kuti and Chima Ubani were publicly together as a joint team.

At the heart of the CD crises were revelations of a collaborationist relationship that had developed between the new military regime and some of the leaders of the organisation, in particular, its President, Beko Ransome-Kuti himself. More profoundly, the crises reflected the narrowing of democratic space within the organisation itself. As the opposition group to Ransome-Kuti asserted during the February 5 1994 Ibadan Second National Convention of the CD, 'democratic decision-making and collective leadership broke down, reducing the organisation almost to a one man show'. As the CD become more powerful as a democratic movement and appeared to be capable of being a major player in the game, its leadership became less willing to abide by the democratic principles it had been proclaiming and fighting for. The organisation became embroiled in factional struggles, it split and lost much of its appeal. At the national level, support for M.K.O. Abiola, the presumed victor of the presidential elections narrowed to his Yoruba ethnic base. There are no easy victories in the struggle for the expansion of democratic space. It is however instructive that mass organisations, democratic movements, professional associations, and even the political class have continued the struggle for democracy. *A luta continua*

Jibrin Ibrahim

Acknowledgements

The research leading to the publication of this book has taken a long time. The idea was initiated in 1989, it was developed into a research proposal at the Kano Workshop of January 1991 and the methodology workshop also held in Kano in September 1992. in December 1993, a major conference was held at the Nigerian Institute of International Affairs where the first drafts to the papers were presented. The Lagos Conference also included a workshop on human rights attended by the major human rights organisations in the country, as well as top scholars, journalists and other political activists. I therefore owe a lot to numerous people and institutions who helped and encouraged this effort through the years.

I am particularly grateful to Bashorun, former President of the West African Students Union, 1957, and the Nigerian Bar Association, the National Consultative Forum, Campaign for Democratic Alternative in the 1990's for his thought provoking keynote address to the Conference. And the following for their rich contributions to the debate Emma Ezeazu, Chima Ubani, Beko Ransome-Kuti, Chom Bagu, Nasiru Kura, Glory Kilanko, Osagie Obagwuna, Salihu Lukman, Ayesha Imam, Hajara Usman, Hamza Kwajafa, Steve Aluko, Tony Akika, John Odah, Peter Ozo-Oson, Bashir Kurfi, Cyril Obi, Baba Omojola, O. Kane, Kabiru Yusuf, Hauwa Mustapha, Oyerinde Olaitan, A. Hassan, A. Olugboji, Yahaya Hashim, A. Yusuf, H. Abdul, Adgbo Onoja, A. Olusanya.

The project benefited greatly from the position papers and participation in the debate by the following organisations : Academic Staff Union of Universities, Campaign for Democracy, Community Action for Popular Participation, Committee for the Defence of Human Rights, Constitutional Rights Projects, National Association of Nigerian Union of Journalists, Women in Nigeria and the Iron and Steel Senior Staff Association.

Finally, I wish to express my gratitude to : CODESRIA for funding this project, to the Nigerian Institute of International Affairs for allowing us use their facilities for the Conference and my colleagues of the Centre for Research and Documentation for their continuous support.

Jibrin Ibrahim

Contributors

Tanimu Abubakar is a Senior Lecturer in Literature in the Department of English, Ahmadu Bello University, Zaria. He took his PhD in Literature in 1987 on Black South African Prose and Politics, a topic on which he has just completed a book. He has published widely in literary journals in Nigeria and South Africa.

Issa Aremu is an Assistant General Secretary with the National Union of Textile, Garment and Tailoring Workers of Nigeria, an affiliate member of the Nigerian Labour Congress. He has a Masters degree in Labour and Development from the Institute of Social Studies, The Hague. He is a regular commentator on labour and social issues in Nigeria.

Bjorn Beckman is a Reader in the Department of Political Science at the University of Stockholm and is concurrently affiliated to Bayero University Kano. He taught at the Department of Political Science of Ahmadu Bello University from 1978 to 1987. He has published widely on Ghanaian and Nigerian peasant politics and is currently studying Nigerian textiles workers as well as structural adjustment and democratisation.

Femi Falana is a Lagos-based lawyer and civil rights advocate. He has defended scores of rusticated students, sacked workers and trade unionists and other civil rights advocates in numerous court cases and is an active member of the Committee for the Defence of Human Rights and of the Campaign for Democracy.

Jibrin Ibrahim is a Reader in the Department of Political Science, Ahmadu Bello University, Zaria. He has a doctorate from the University of Bordeaux on Nigerian party politics and has published widely in English and French on democratisation, pluralism and religious conflict.

Attahiru Mohammadu Jega is a Senior Lecturer in Political Science and Deputy Vice Chancellor at Bayero University, Kano. He took his doctorate at North-western University, Evanston, Illinois on the Politics of Irrigation in Nigeria. He is currently researching the role of professional associations in the democratisation process and is the immediate past President of the Academic Staff Union of Universities. He has published extensively in Nigeria and abroad.

Amina Mama has a D.Phil in Applied Psychology from the University of London and has taught development studies and feminist theory at the

Institute of Social Studies, The Hague. She has done substantial research and written publications on gender, ideology, race and violence.

Abubakar Momoh is a Lecturer in Political Science at the Lagos State University. His areas of specialisation are political theory and political economy. Momoh is completing his PhD at the University of Lagos on Nkrumah's political ideas.

Abdul Raufu Mustapha is a Senior Lecturer in Political Science at Ahmadu Bello University, Zaria. He has a D.Phil from the University of Oxford on politics and class formation in a Northern Nigerian village. He has published extensively on structural adjustment and agrarian change.

Adebayo A Olukoshi is a Professor at the Nigerian Institute of International Affairs and Research Coordinator at the Nordic Africa Institute. He took his doctorate from the University of Leeds on multinational corporations and industrialisation in Nigeria. Among other things he has researched and published extensively on the politics of structural adjustment in Africa.

Kole Ahmed Shettima is a Lecturer in the Department of Political Science of the University of Maiduguri. He is currently completing his doctoral dissertation on agrarian change in Sahelian communities in the North Eastern region of Nigeria at the University of Toronto.

Y. Z. Ya'u is a Lecturer in Electrical Engineering at Bayero University, Kano. He is also an ardent student of political economy and an analyst of the Nigerian mass media. Ya'u is an accomplished newspaper columnist.

Part One

The Expansion of Democratic Space — Theoretical and Empirical Issues

1

Expanding Nigerian Democratic Space

Jibrin Ibrahim

Introduction

Most contemporary African state traditions are built on legacies of autocratic chieftaincies, patriarchy, gerontocracy and imperial control. Independence did not reduce authoritarianism, in most cases, it increased it. In countries that followed the paths of both capitalist and socialist ideologies, political power was widely conceived as something that belonged to the state and its rulers. The people were supposed to produce and obey.

The question of establishing, broadening and maintaining democratic space has become a central issue on the African agenda precisely because the majority of Africans have been reduced to virtual outlaws, with little or no rights in their own countries. This has been done largely by their own governments. After suffering atrocities for a long period of time, the threshold of tolerance has been broken *all over* Africa and people are seeking ways to exercise some freedom from daily oppression. The result is increased agitation and popular demonstrations, strikes, protests, etc. aimed at the transformation of existing political systems.

Notions of popular sovereignty that see power as belonging to the people by right started taking roots in the mid-1980s. Since then, the question of a genuine democratic transition has imposed itself on the African, and indeed, global agenda.

Nigeria has a rich tradition of democratic struggles but post independence regimes in general and the military in particular have considerably eroded that tradition. The question of struggling to expand democratic space has now become crucial.

A History of Political Division and a Tradition of Democratic Struggle

Nigeria was one of few African countries which had a significant reputation for protecting human rights and civil liberties. In fact, one could talk of a certain democratic tradition in the country's political culture. This assertion is a paradoxical one, especially as military regimes have conducted Nigeria's affairs during most of its post independence life. Even these military regimes have been constrained to bottle up their authoritarian habits and conduct the nation's affairs in a fairly civil manner — until recently.

In the past, the first act of a military regime after a *coup d'état* was to suspend the constitution; but then, only the sections of the constitution that regulate partisan politics were usually suspended while the other sections, especially those that define the functions and powers of the judiciary and the human rights clauses, were left to function. As we shall argue·in chapter three, things have changed and the military no longer pretends to have any respect for the Nigerian Constitution.

Be that as it may, there is a rich but contradictory democratic tradition embedded in Nigerian civil society, although the pattern of primitive capital accumulation in the country and the impact of military rule have had devastating consequences on this democratic tradition. The democratic tradition in civil society is organised around a relatively fierce press, a fairly developed judicial system, a strong culture of trade union struggle and a political system based on disparate centres of power and governed by 'checks and balances' that delayed the rise of tyrannic regimes at the national level. The present conjuncture, as we shall see throughout this book, is a very difficult one for Nigerian democracy. That there are democratic assets is incontestable, but these assets have limitations and are confronted with dangers. To understand the present conjuncture, the colonial aspect of the Nigerian political system must be put in perspective.

During the years of 'self government' from 1957 to 1960 — and the years of the 'First Republic' from 1960 to 1965 — the situation was clear, or so it seemed. Nigeria had inherited the British Westminster tradition of liberal democracy. The Prime Minister of the epoch, Abubakar Tafawa Balewa, while commenting on the 'cordial relations' between Nigeria and Great Britain explained that 'their system of democratic government has now become part of our own heritage and we should be wise to maintain our institutions on the British model' (Oyovbaire 1987:4).

What then was this British model? It was certainly not the type of profound democratic political culture organised around a centralised Weberian administration found in the United Kingdom. It was a system of 'indirect rule' established by Lord Lugard, the British colonial administrator. It was based on a policy of non-centralised administration or separate government for 'different peoples'. This policy led to the evolution of certain structures and institutions which to a certain extent still characterise the contemporary Nigerian state.

Colonial rule introduced 'indirect rule' whose basic principle was 'divide and rule'. In the Emirates of northern Nigeria and in the Yoruba kingdoms of the south west, indigenous political structures were retained and often reinforced by the colonial administration as the primary level of government, while in the south east, as well as among some of the acephalus 'Middle Belt' societies, a new order of colonial chiefs known as 'warrant chiefs' was imposed. The system of 'indirect rule' had a profound impact on the evolution of Nigerian elites. In the north, traditional elites were fully involved in the administration of British imperialism thanks to the system of 'Native Administration' (NA), and were therefore allies of the Crown. Second, they had a pact with Lord Lugard to keep Christian missionaries and by extension, Western education, out of the Emirates. The result was that the pace of development of Western education in the Muslim part of the north was very slow and the few that were chosen for the western schools were all employed in the NA. Thus, virtually the totality of the elite in the Muslim north collaborated with colonialism and had a stake in it.

In the other parts of the country, Christian missionaries were given full freedom for proselytisation and virtually exclusive control of Western education. This resulted in a fairly rapid evolution of a Western educated elite, to the detriment of traditional ruling elites. The new elite, however, had limited chances of integrating into the upper echelons of the civil service even when they had high levels of education. With their high education and the frustration of being kept out, they naturally drifted into political agitation and adversary journalism, an argument that will be developed.below.

In the north, the British evolved a selection process to create a new educated elite to replace, or rather to work with, the Emirate aristocracy. Starting with the Kano 'Nassarawa' school in 1909, two new ones came up in 1913 at Katsina and Sokoto, and another in Maiduguri in 1915. In 1922 Katsina College (later Barewa College) was established which became the base for the creation of northern, Muslim and conservative leaders that later grew into what is widely known as the 'Northern Oligarchy' (Ibrahim 1991). The Nigerian democratic game therefore took off with these divided elites as actors whose theatre was also composed of institutions of division.

Nigeria was not colonised as a unified British territory. It was composed of three separate units — the colony of Lagos and the two Protectorates of northern and southern Nigeria, each administered separately. In 1914, the three units were united to constitute the colony of Nigeria with an internal division between the north and the south which continued to be administered separately. In 1938, the South was divided into two regions, the west and east. This last division followed the British 'discovery' of a Yoruba and Benin political tendency halfway between the centralised northern emirates and the 'acephalus' political organisation in the east — hence the origins of the so-called tripartite system. This system was formalised with the Richards Constitution of 1946 and five years later, Governor Macpherson's Constitution 'federated' the three regions by creating a central assembly in addition to the regional ones, devolving effective executive power to the regionally constituted elites.

The guiding principle of this tripartite federation was that each region had a 'majority ethnic group', which was to play the role of the leading actor — in the north it was the Hausa, in the west the Yoruba, and in the east the Igbo. In fact the whole process of Constitution making between 1946 and 1958 was an elaborate bargaining pantomime to find an equilibrium between the three regions, or rather, between the leading elites of the majority ethnic groups. No wonder the process resulted in the emergence of three major political parties.

In 1944, Herbert Macaulay and his nationalist friends formed the National Council of Nigeria and the Cameroons (NCNC), a nationalist, mass-based party composed of trade unions, ethnic associations and youth movements. After Macaulay's death in 1947, another politician with nationalist credentials, Nnamdi Azikiwe, took over the leadership of the party. The pan-Nigerian character of the party was compromised a year later with the formation of the Ibo State Union (ISU), an Igbo federation which was soon to take over control of the NCNC. The ISU itself was formed in response to the establishment in 1947 of the Egbe Omo Oduduwa, a pan-Yoruba ethnic association, by Awolowo and some of his (anti-Zik) friends. The Egbe was transformed into a political party, the Action Group (AG) in 1950.

In the north, the exigencies of the 1951 elections and the challenge posed by the rise of nationalism in the south precipitated the formation of a pan-northern party, the Northern Peoples Congress (NPC), from a regional cultural association — Jam'iyyar Mutanen Arewa. From that point on, the tripartite model of the politics of the First Republic was established, at least in the imagination of 'authoritative commentators' — an imagination that seems incapable of changing with changing reality. For example, in his book on the politics of the Second Republic, *Democracy and Prebendal Politics in Nigeria (1987)*, Richard Joseph persists in this tripolar tradition by reading the politics of the Second Republic from 1978 to 1983 as just another example of the persistence of tripolar politics.

Nigerian politics is not and has not been purely tripolar. Rather, it has been tri-tendential. The first tendency, it is true, is the tripolar one so characteristic of the politics of the First Republic, resulting from the domination of the political scene by the three major groups already referred to.

The second tendency is the bipolar one which is usually expressed during electoral periods. During the 1964 federal elections, political parties regrouped themselves in two blocs. The Government bloc, the Nigerian National Alliance (NNA) was composed of the Northern Peoples Congress (NPC), Nigerian National Democratic Party (NNDP), Mid-west Democratic Front (MDF) and Niger Delta Congress (NDC). The opposition, the United Progressive Grand Alliance (UPGA), was composed of the National Congress of Nigerian Citizens (NCNC), Action Group (AG) and Northern Progressive Front (NPF) which was itself an alliance of the United Middle Belt Congress (UMBC) and Northern Elements Progressive Union (NEPU). This regrouping, which took the form of progressive/conservative forces, actually reflected tactical manoeuvres of a multiplicity of political groups for better access to political power and the rewards it brings. This is why the composition of the alliances changed from time to time. The UMBC, for example, has had alliances at different times with the NPC, AG and NEPU. During the 1983 elections, this bipolar tendency took the form of Government groups composed of the National Party of Nigeria (NPN) and splinter factions from the five other parties and an opposition group of the rest, known as the Progressive Peoples Alliance (PPA).

After almost 30 years of shifting bipolar alliances, and a concerted effort by the Babangida Administration to institutionalise bipartisan politics as 'the Nigerian way' through the legal imposition of a two party system, bipolarity could be considered as one of the tendencies of Nigerian politics, even if it hides a more profound multipolar tendency.

Nigeria is not composed of two or three cultural groups but of hundreds of cultural and ethnic groups, the majority of which are dominated by the so-called majority groups. The third and perhaps the most important tendency in Nigerian politics is a persistent multipolarity which is continuously repressed by imposed bipolarity and/or tripolarity. Nonetheless it has managed to survive. None of the three regions of the First Republic represented a historic political bloc. Immediately after the Ibo State Union was formed in the east it was confronted by the Ibibio State Union. The anti-Igbo feeling in the Delta was so strong that in February 1966, Major Isaac Boro declared the secession of the 'Niger Delta Peoples Republic' in protest against Igbo leadership. This first formal succession attempt in Nigeria also resulted in the first declared civil war, the now forgotten 12-day war (Boro 1982).

Political differences in the west are more well known and need not be repeated here. In the north, many political poles exist. The dominant pole is rooted in the Sokoto Caliphate zone. It was this group that the British manoeuvred to place in power between 1946 and 1951, because they had cooperated so closely in the system of 'Native Administration'. The second pole in the same zone is the radical anti-aristocratic tendency that was expressed by the NEPU/PRP heritage. The third pole is the Bornu tendency expressed in the BYM and to some extent in the GNPP, while the fourth is the northern minorities tendency expressed in the Northern Nigeria non-Muslim League formed in 1950 and transformed into the United Middle Belt Peoples Congress in 1953. This movement formed part of the constituent groups that formed the NPP in 1978.

All these political divisions were violently repressed by the 'wazobia'[1] domination in the three regions, exacerbated by the Westminster Federalism of the First Republic evolving with the centre of political power held in regions rather than the centre, contrary to the British case. The refusal of the British to create more regions in 1958 when the Willink Commission affirmed that fears of domination of the 'minorities' by the 'majorities' were justified was virtually a disenfranchisement of at least 45 per cent of the population. The politics of the First Republic evolved in a contradictory manner, with the multi-polar tendency being simultaneously suppressed and supported. In each region, it was suppressed by one regional government but then encouraged and supported by the other regional governments, hence the elaborate system of shifting national alliances.

The domination of political power by the northern pole meant that a democratic change of government at the centre was virtually impossible, for the simple reason that internal regional democracy was impossible. In each region, the minorities were excluded. The Caliphate Oligarchy in control of the NPC could maintain perpetual control of federal power, although it was an aggregate minority even in the north, its base. This was due to the principle that the elite of the dominant ethnic group in each region had become the inheritors of political power. The north, with 54 per cent of official representatives, could always thwart shifting bipolar alliances by destabilising them.

The evolution of political structures and institutions in Nigeria was not therefore particularly democratic . The system of Native Administration which left vast powers — police, courts and prisons — in the hands of chiefs was a basic negation of democratic principles. The democratic process itself was systematically subverted by the system of 'wazobia' tyranny within the regions. Elections were so corrupt that they became farcical. In spite of these failures, however, the British policy of divide and rule which produced a multivariate framework of political structures and institutions prevented the evolution of a unified national oligarchic or sultanic leadership for a long time. In addition, the instability of the system and its ingrained 'fears of domination' encouraged the evolution of a culture of struggle for political survival and self assertion. It is against this background that a certain democratic tradition has evolved in Nigerian civil society organised around a relatively free press, a fairly well developed judiciary and a tradition of struggle by trade unions, students and professional associations.

The Role of the Media

The Nigerian mass media has a long and rich history. Its origins are rooted in the dialectic between missionary education and the colonial administration in southern Nigeria. The educational programme of the missionaries was based essentially on the three Rs — reading, writing and arithmetic — to provide the clerks, messengers, interpreters and teachers that colonialism needed. Sometimes, however, highly educated Nigerians emerged from the system by going abroad to extend their learning. Unfortunately, the colonial administration was unwilling to accept them into the so-called Senior Service. Even distributive trades and mining were blocked to the emerging African élite. This meant that only law and medicine were left to offer 'honourable' employment to them. Those who did not read these two disciplines tended to be pushed towards journalism — the other option.

Journalism developed rapidly. Commercial presses were one way of self-employment and journalism had the added advantage of being a political weapon against the exclusionary colonial system. The first newspaper established in Nigeria was *Iwe Irohin*, a missionary organ produced at Abeokuta from 1859. In 1862 the first 'agitational' newspaper, the *Anglo-African*, was established in Lagos. Its editor, Horace Campbell, was a mulatto conscripted into the colonial army from the West Indies. After his army career, he tried commerce but was confronted with colonial racism and commercial blockages, hence his conversion to journalism.

Since then, the press has developed rapidly as an instrument of political agitation by the educated and frustrated elite kept out of the colonial system. The *Lagos Weekly Record*, for example, complained in 1897 that it was in the most unenviable position of the British West African colonies, the worst feature of which was that the people themselves had little or no voice at all in the administration of their affairs (Omu 1978:149). Between 1862 and 1913 these journalist-cum-politicians, such as James Davies of the *Nigerian Times*, John Jackson of *Lagos Weekly Times*, Sapara Williams of *Lagos Weekly Record*, and E. D. Morel of the *African Mail*, became the pioneers of the struggle for public liberties as they fought against the excesses of the colonial laws, racial segregation, land alienation and taxes. Alarmed by this tendency, the Governor, Lord Lugard, convinced his Nigerian friend, Sir Kitoye Ajasa, to launch a pro-colonial newspaper, the *Nigerian Pioneer*, which operated from 1914 to 1936. The European Chamber of Commerce in 1925 also launched a pro-colonial newspaper, the *Daily Times*, the only one from that epoch still in existence.

The anti-colonial press received a boost in the early 1920s after the formation of the Nigerian National Democratic Party (NNDP) and its newspaper, the *Lagos Daily News*, and the campaigns for elections of that period of so-called proto-nationalism. The next phase was the arrival of Nnamdi Azikiwe in 1937 and his 'Elec-zikification' of both the press and politics in Nigeria organised around his *West African Pilot*. It was no accident that almost all the politicians of southern Nigeria during the First Republic, and many of those of the Second Republic, were journalists. In the north, since the totality of the elite were working with or for the colonial government, there was only one newspaper, *Gaskiya*, established by the government in 1939 and censored by both the government and the NA. This problem has persisted in northern Nigeria where the culture of an agitational press has still not developed, creating restrictions on the capacity of democratic forces to mobilise effectively.

After independence in 1960 the mass media followed the political process in evolving an express tripolar pattern.. This implied a political change from organs protecting the rights of citizens and of Nigeria as a nation, to instrumental organs for the defence of new regional ruling parties. Things did not change much until 1966 when a number of northern and western leaders were assassinated in the *coup d'état*. The result was that the media in the north and west became reoriented towards the fight against perceived Igbo domination. The *New Nigerian* in particular engaged in a campaign which former editor Mamman Daura called 'the defence of the interests of the Northern elite' (Daura 1971).

In spite of the draconian attempts by the state to control it, press freedom grew in Nigeria. In 1903, the Newspapers Ordinance was passed to control the press and in 1909 a Sedition Ordinance was passed to strengthen the first law. Journalists such as Herbert Macaulay were imprisoned several times under these laws. With independence, the anti-press laws were strengthened instead of liberalised. In 1962 an Official Secrets Act was enacted. (It was under this law that *Newbreed* and *Newswatch* magazines were proscribed in 1978 and 1987 respectively). The 1903 Ordinance was strengthened with the 1964 Newspapers [Amendment] Act and in 1984 the Public Officers Protection Against False Accusation Decree was enacted to establish finally that 'protection of public servants' rather than 'truth' should be the basic principle of journalism. Using these laws and often going beyond them, the government has imprisoned, detained, tortured, harassed and often sacked numerous journalists for writing things that are unpleasant to the state. Much more disturbing is the murder of Dele Giwa, a popular journalist, by a parcel bomb in 1986. This is the first case of murder in the 135-year old history of Nigerian journalism. In spite of all these problems, the Nigerian press remains fairly vigorous (*see* Ya'u in Chapter 6).

Two other forms of mass communication play an important role in the struggle for democracy in Nigeria : pamphleteering and literature. Political pamphleteering started as far back as 1908 when Herbert Macaulay distributed 1,000 pamphlets documenting maladministration at the Nigerian Railways and the role of Governor Egerton in 'wicked appropriation of land ... personification of prejudice ... and scandals' (Omu 1978:182). Pamphleteering developed as a complement to the press, usually used for sensitive issues that could not easily be printed in newspapers. Macaulay, for example, printed his pamphlet to side-track the 1903 Press Ordinance. Similarly, when in 1974 the late Tai Solarin could not get his stinging article 'The Beginning of the End' published in the press, he distributed it as a pamphlet. Solarin warned General Gowon to stick to his earlier promise to hand over power in 1976 or else it would be the 'beginning of his end'. The General refused to listen and was thrown out of office a few months later. The Nigerian left in particular has, over the past few years, developed pamphleteering into a fine art.

Finally, there is literature. . In his essay on the contribution of Wole Soyinka to the struggle for democracy in Nigeria and indeed in Africa, Alain Ricard (1988: 51) recalls Alioune Diop's 1947 prediction that African literature would become an institution like Parliament. Since then, parliaments have devolved, disappeared and sometimes re-appeared in Africa, but literature has remained: 'as the voice of public opinion — talking for those who are not military officers, big merchants or landlords, and who therefore need justice in their country'.

The works of Chinua Achebe, Cyprian Ekwensi, Wole Soyinka, Festus Iyayi etc. have done more for the struggle to liberalise the politics of Nigeria than the works of many political scientists and sociologists.

Struggles by Trade Unions, Students and Professional Associations

The dynamism of trades, professional and students unions in Nigeria is one of the clearest signs of the democratic drive embedded in its civil society. The ability of trade unions to carry out their basic functions of struggling to improve the material and social conditions of labour is itself an important aspect of the democratic struggle.

The Nigerian nationalist movement took its eland in 1945 after the general strike of that year. The strike was preceded by a mass campaign with the slogan that: 'in the hands of workers and not capitalists lies the freedom of the world' (Coleman 1986:257). By crippling the railways, postal and telegraph services among others, the strike virtually paralysed the colonial system and demonstrated its weakness when confronted with the popular will. Since then, the trades union movement, in conjunction with progressive movements and organisations, has consistently fought for the rights of the common worker. The general strikes of June 1964 and May 1981 were organised at critical periods of significant erosion of human and civic rights by the state.

The Nigerian state tried to completely destroy trade unionism in 1977-78 with a purge of 'Marxist' leaders. . The most prominent radical unionists were banned and a new central labour organisation, the Nigerian Labour Congress (NLC), was established. During the NLC elections, another generation of radical unionists under the leadership of

Hassan Sunmonu emerged. In addition, a common front was created between the NLC, the 'National Association of Nigerian Students (NANS) and the Academic Staff Union of Universities (ASUU) to organise popular struggles for improved conditions of life and to resist state repression. In 1986, for example, a mass protest movement emerged against the killing of demonstrating students in Zaria while in April 1988 another series of demonstrations were organised after an IMF-inspired increase in the price of petrol. In 1994, the Abacha regime once again took over control of the unions.

Nigerian students have played a very significant role since 1934, when they established the Lagos Youth Movement, the core on which the first nationalist party, the NCNC, was built. In the post-war years, the West African Students Union played a galvanising role in the independence movements. The 1959 'march on Lagos' of students of the University of Ibadan precipitated the press campaign against the 'Anglo-Nigerian Defence Pact.' Similarly, the spontaneous student demonstrations that followed the assassination of the popular General Murtala Mohammed in February 1976 helped in preventing the retrogressive Dimka-led coup d'etat.

In the case of the Academic Staff Union of Universities (ASUU), radicalisation was a product of the trade union struggles. Lecturers found themselves involved in the struggle to improve their conditions of work, enhance academic freedom and improve the quality of university education. Other professional associations, such as the Nigerian Bar Association (NBA) and even the National Association of Resident Doctors and the Nigerian Medical Association, have struggled for improved social services. Since the NLC's Worker's Charter of Demands in 1980 and NAN's Student's Charter of Demands in 1982, there has been a growing consciousness that specific economic and social demands could be met only if the frontiers of democracy are broadened.

The left has played a significant role in promoting the social and economic demands of the people. Olukoshi (in Chapter Nine) argues that the left itself has been transformed over time and has become much more committed to the promotion of liberal democratic rights. From the point of view of the state, however, there is a growing 'counter-consciousness' that the Nigerian bourgeoisie could only be protected by restricting human rights and tightening the frontiers of democracy. This accounts for the frequent ban orders, termination of appointments, detentions and other repressive measures that unions, professional organisations and their leaders have been subjected to. Increased repression is further reinforced by the difficulties faced by the Nigerian state in its attempt to impose the IMF-inspired Structural Adjustment Programme which is strongly resisted by Nigerian civil society — (Olukoshi 1993).

The Legal and Judicial System

We have already mentioned that law was one of the few respectable professions open to educated Africans under the colonial system. Being called to the bar was a ticket not only to a reasonably high income but also to respect. No wonder clans and villages taxed themselves to send a 'son of the soil' to Britain to study law. The result was that Nigeria produced so many lawyers that their influence went beyond the country's borders into other Anglophone countries.[2] For all these lawyers, most of whom were in private practice, to maintain their elevated place in society, the judicial machine had to operate in a fairly just and non arbitrary manner. The average plaintiff had to be convinced that the lawyer could make a difference in solving his problem otherwise they would have difficulty in paying for the service. Lawyers therefore had a corporate interest in the maintenance of due process, the rule of law and civil liberties. The fact that lawyers became a powerful pressure group, as well as the technocrats that drafted Nigerian Constitutions and laws, played an important role in maintaining this legal culture. In addition, they were able to guide subsequent military regimes to keep to the form, even if not to the essence, of judicial process. Military regimes were, for example, constrained to enact new decrees that would repeal or bypass existing laws that hindered their objectives rather than act in a 'might is right' manner. This legal fetishism often transgresses the course of justice and the spirit of the law but to a certain extent, legalism slows down political arbitrariness especially as until recently, no law or decree in Nigeria has been retroactive.

In the past decade, however, the principles of the rule of law have been increasingly threatened by the state. Decree no. 2 of 1984, still in vogue, allows the Chief of General Staff to detain citizens for extended periods without charging them to court. The decree suspends the important instrument of 'habeas corpus' that citizens could use to compel the state to produce detainees in court. It should be remembered that in April 1961, the three 'National Government' leaders; Ahmadu Bello, Michael Okpara and Tafawa Balewa met and decided to enact this type of detention law but resistance to their plans were too strong (*African Concord* 16.8.1988, p.16). It has taken the Nigerian state 23 years of 'effort' to be able to impose this repugnant law. The Nigerian legal system is, however, still in a fairly combative mood. In 1984, the whole legal profession rose against the suspension of due process and systematisation of military tribunals to 'persecute' rather than 'prosecute' politicians. They tried, with limited success, to resist the authoritarian excesses of the Babangida regime. The assassination of Dele Giwa, editor of Newswatch magazine, for example, has led to an important civil liberties case. Dele Giwa was said to have been interrogated and threatened just before his death by Col. Halilu Akilu, the Director of Military Security, and Lt. Col. A. K. Togun, Deputy Director of State Security, over a lead story he was preparing. In spite of the suspicious circumstances that surrounded his death, the Director of Public Prosecutions was unwilling to prosecute the two officers and a private lawyer, Gani Fawehinmi, decided to take the matter up in court. In a historic judgement delivered on 18 December 1987, the Supreme Court authorised private persons to prosecute criminal cases that have not been taken up by the Public Prosecution Department.

In recent years, the struggle by lawyers and other activists for human rights has assumed a sharper organisational focus. The Nigerian Bar Association (NBA) became more openly assertive of its commitment to the rule of law and democratisation until it became destroyed following protracted struggles by Government agents to take over its leadership in 1993. In 1985, an Association of Democratic Lawyers of Nigeria (ADLN), was set up and in 1989 a 'Committee for the Defence of Human Rights' (CDHR) was set up under the chairmanship of a medical doctor and human rights crusader, Dr. Beko Ransome-Kuti. One of the most significant developments in this regard was the formation in October 1987 of the Civil Liberties Organisation (CLO) which emerged to coordinate the struggle for civil liberties. In December 1988, the CLO published a report on Human Rights Violation in Nigeria as a working document to help in the fight against arbitrariness by the state and its agents. Another important organisation is the Constitutional Rights Project, established in 1990 to promote respect for human rights and the rule of law in Nigeria.

This brief overview of the Nigerian mass media, trades and professional unions, the legal system and human rights organisations reveals that the history of democratic struggles in Nigeria has not been limited to the formal political process. Nigerians have been forced to expand the terrains on which they struggle, and it is that spirit of expanding the democratic space that we wish to explore in this book. It is clear that there are a number of democratic assets embedded in the country's civil society and their force and relevance lies in the relative autonomy they have enjoyed from the state. This autonomy is frequently subjected to serious threats by the state but the capacity for resistance has been significantly high. The point should be made, however, that the preservation of democracy is not a simple function of assets and problems, it is also a question of historical will. Nigerians have demonstrated a will to preserve hard won democratic rights and if they are trained in the art of provocation, they are also trained in the art of compromise. The country could evolve towards an open regulative democracy based on the rule of law and the preservation of civil liberties rather than a dangerous and rigid 'democracy' composed of cabals representing authoritarian oligarchies. Numerous organisations are working towards this objective.

The Expansion of Democratic Space:
Citizenship and Human Rights

The success of the efforts towards democratisation will depend on the capacity of the African people to cope with a number of crippling challenges — that of imperialist control, that of the destruction of community by what we have called the Kalashnikov factor, that of excessive corruption and waste of resources, and that of evolving democratic systems that actually benefit the people (*see* Ibrahim 1995).[3] In the 1950s and 1960s, democracy was sacrificed on the altar of national unity and/or socialism before it was tried in most African countries. It is therefore wrong to assume that it had failed, it was never given a chance (Sithole 1994). After three decades of the negation of democracy, the current African conjuncture is characterised by increased popular struggles for the expansion of democracy and the consequent crumbling of authoritarian ideologies and practices. Some issues have been more or less resolved. Authoritarianism has failed in its promise to build the African nation-state and develop the economy. The military has· failed in its promise of imposing order and fighting corruption. The concentration of power in one party or one absolute president has failed to produce hegemony. The African people have shown that they are for plural democracy.

At the same time, we are witnessing the elaboration of new structures and processes of the neocolonial control of the African people and their resources under the Structural Adjustment Programmes imposed by the IMF and World Bank in collaboration with African governments who, despite protestations to the contrary, are re-invigorating the ideology of repression. This paradoxical situation sets a new research agenda of the development of new approaches, concepts and methods in the struggle for democracy based on consultation with popular forces and interest groups. The objective is the broadening of popular participation in responsible and responsive government in an environment in which citizens enjoy broad civil, political, social and economic rights.

Democracy is an all embracing concept and it grows and develops when there are movements working to extend it. It involves ideological factors, the normative belief that it is a desirable form of social and political organisation and institutional factors such as the constitutions, party systems and market structures. It also needs a strong and relatively autonomous civil society, a large space in which a network of non-state associations are involved in the articulation of faith, corporate interest and ideology.

Studies in social relations of gender have considerably broadened the debate on the expansion of democratic space by focusing on the immense space in which women are marginalised and subordinated (Imam 1993:20-34). The development of feminist discourse and struggle has also drawn attention to the ways in which human and civic rights are not gender neutral. Civic equality, for example, often translates as discrimination against women who have less time and resources to participate in political fora due to additional domestic burdens that tie them down and the non remuneration of much of the work they do (Phillips 1991:44). It means that women do not enjoy the same real rights, privileges, autonomy and power even when they have formal equality (Sow 1994:7). By taking politics into private, personal and sensual space, feminism has helped focus attention on issues such as access to resources, relative status and security which are fundamental to the democratic debate, but have often been ignored. The study by Imam (1993) on the seclusion of women in northern Nigeria, for example, reveals a major problem area that has so far not been taken into account in most political studies, including this one.

We have already referred to the 'wazobia' domination of minority ethnic groups as being one of the repressive legacies left by the British and exacerbated by subsequent post independence regimes. The struggles of minorities in Nigeria is increasingly being recognised as a legitimate democratic struggle. The success of the Movement for the Survival of the Ogoni People (MOSOP), in drawing attention to their marginalisation and exclusion at the world level since 1990, has sensitised Nigerians to the urgency of the minority question. With MOSOP and the Movement for National Reformation calling for a loose ethnic federation, it has become clear that:

> to survive as a nation-state, the country must restructure its political
> relations, vesting a substantial degree of autonomy in the component units
> (Naanen 1995:75)

The basic issue posed both in the federation of the First Republic and the subsequent over-centralisation of the country is that certain groups are always marginalised from power and resources and these groups need broad support in their struggle for expanded political space.

The construction of democracy therefore implies the continuous struggle against the privileges certain classes and groups enjoy because of their control of resources and/or power. The expansion of democratic space must focus not only on institutional and structural processes, but also on the empowerment of all marginalised groups. This includes ways of transforming their political, economic, social, psychological and legal conditions of powerlessness. The development of citizenship rights should be at the centre of the democratisation process, a return to primary sources in the debate.

Citizenship is an important notion because it defines the constitutive elements of the democratic state and spells out the relationship between state power and individuals. According to Malcolm Waters (1989:160), it spells out procedures and sets of practices defining the relationship between the nation state and its individual members. Citizenship implies not only the erosion of the arbitrary use (misuse) of state power but also the movement away from what has been called 'pro-forma democracy', in which 'formal citizens' are directed by so called mass parties, national single parties, national liberation movements etc. to act in particular ways defined and imposed by autocratic leaders. It seems to us that democracy should be about the rights of citizens to *live* their own aspirations and programmes.

The problem of citizenship is that although it sets out the conditions of formal equality, it also structures and institutionalises socially reproduced inequalities. Waters shows, for example, that in capitalist societies:

> Citizenship atomises society into multiple sovereign individuals and re-integrates them into a nation. Unequal class or status relations are denied and a structure and ideology of common objectives are superimposed (Waters 1989:174).

The State, however, intervenes to regulate the atomised individuals into labour markets that serve the interests of capital. In the former Soviet Union and Eastern European bloc, the existence of privileged individuals in the nomenclature and ruling party meant that:

> Dominating political interest groups are in principle able to dictate differential relationships between the state and individual members of civil society which constitutes virtual unequal citizenship. The substance of a 'partocratic' hierarchy of this sort is not merely political prestige, or

power, it is material. The three main political strata have differential access to the material resources of the state (Waters 1989:169)

In Africa, people have suffered the indignities of being forced to address themselves as citizens (in Zaire for example) or comrades (as in the Congo) in situations in which they enjoyed no citizenship rights and were being treated as subjects and in a very 'uncomradely' manner. The essence of the democratic movement is that people are struggling to give real content to some of these labels. In all possible instances, the frontiers of democracy should be broadened. The sense in which we use the notion of the expansion of democratic space is tied at one level to the reduction of the nuisance produced by those who control state power and economic power. At another level, it involves the struggle for concrete power gains by democratic actors. We are advocating that the individual and collective rights of citizens are taken seriously. In so doing, liberal and social democracy must be taken seriously.

Taking Liberal and Social Democracy Seriously

Modern democracy is based on the premise that all human beings are free and equal. It is a progressive principle for the organisation of society. It is true that democratic principles are not fully implemented in the societies that lay claim to it, so a gap exists between enunciated democratic principles and 'really existing democracies'. Liberal democracies have, on this score, a better track record than democratic centralist regimes. The problem with liberal democracy is that the capitalist economic model usually associated with it creates difficult conditions for the realisation of democratic principles. As Chantal Mouffe argues, however, there is no necessary relations between liberal democracy and the defence of private property and the capitalist economy:

> Political liberalism and economic liberalism need to be distinguished and then separated from each other. Defending and valuing the political form of society specific to liberal democracy does not commit us to the capitalist economic system (Mouffe 1992:2-3).

Economic equality and social justice empower people, so they must be brought into the main current of liberal democracy and the struggle for the expansion of democratic space. The rights of all peoples must be taken seriously.

Taking People's Rights Seriously

The expansion of democratic space develops on the basis of the empowerment of citizens as well as groups in society, be they ethnic, religious, regional or clan, etc. To put it differently, it means inverting the trend of the criss-crossing network of:

1. **Oppression** — the monopoly and misuse of power by a minority. We have to develop strategies that will enable citizens to monitor and push back the frontiers of authoritarianism.

2. **Exploitation** — unequal exchange in relations of production and in the market and monopoly of resources. We must struggle for a more equitable distribution of socially created wealth.

3. **Discrimination** — unequal rights and treatment on the basis of an incident of birth such as gender, religion, caste, language or ethnic group.

In so doing, we need to develop:

1. **Civil Rights** — The liberty of the person, freedom of speech, thought, movement, assembly, association and faith i.e. the maintenance of human rights and the rule of law and the empowerment of women, youth, peasants, ethnic and religious minorities and other subordinate groups.

2. **Political Rights** — The right to participate in political activity, voting and competition for political office. These rights are enhanced by the pluralism of political organisations, political parties, mass media, trade unions and professional organisations.

3. **Social and Economic Rights** — The right to economic welfare and security (health, education, living wage etc.) — this must include the prevention of the monopoly of public resources by a minority of central planners or 'free marketers'.

These are the essential variables around which the struggles for the expansion of democratic space are carried out. Struggles must be placed within concrete historical contexts as both the forces and issues in contention change over time. Nigeria is marked by, on the one hand, a long tradition of democratic struggles, and, on the other, a growing competence by its ruling class to subvert the said democratic struggles. These are the issues that are addressed in this book.

Outline of the Chapters

In chapter 2 Bjorn Beckman highlights the significant role played by interest groups in the construction of democratic space. He argues that significant expansion of democratic space has occurred, not so much in the strictly political arena but in the wider area of conflict resolution and interest representation in society. Nigeria has a rich associational life but so little democracy. There is nothing inherently democratic about associations but when they contest relations of domination within their domains, they help in the expansion of democratic space. In certain contexts therefore, the agenda of interest groups could be closely linked to broader national concerns relating both to welfare and to democratisation.

The focus of chapters 3 and 4 is the legacy of military rule on democratisation. Abubakar Momoh underscores the way in which the armed forces have militarised civil society and brutalised its psyche. He reviews the various transition programmes from military to democratic rule and shows how they have been truncated or aborted. In his own contribution, Jibrin Ibrahim analyses the depth of the militarisation of political life and the way in which it distorts constitutional developments and the political process. The central argument is that military rule has seriously eroded political assets in the country related to human rights, federalism and accountability of leaders. In addition, the military, under the tutelage of General Babangida, have perfected strategies for subverting programmes of transition to democratic rule that have been forced on them. The two chapters conclude that the military have become the major impediment to the expansion of democratic space in the country.

Chapter 5 treats the novel context in which the question of women has been posed on Nigeria's public arena. Amina Mama traces how women's participation has entered the political agenda even if it might have partly been a cynical attempt to get economic aid in an economic climate that has become increasingly sympathetic towards women's demands for greater equality. She introduces the notion of femocracy, an anti-democratic power structure which claims to exist for the advancement of ordinary women, but is unable to do so because it is dominated by a small clique of women whose authority derives from their powerful husbands, rather than any action or ideas of their own. The emergence of femocracy in Nigeria has led to a more prominent position for women's affairs but has not led to the expansion of 'feminist space' or improved gender equality.

Chapter 6 provides a detailed analysis of the ambiguous role of the mass media in the struggles for democracy. Ya'u traces the policies and practices developed by the state to promote a mass media that acquiesces to government positions. The focus is on how the Structural Adjustment Programme and the austerity it generates has led, on the one hand, to the erosion of good reporting and, on the other, to the promotion of radical pro-democratic media campaigns. The media is in the hands of the ruling class and subject to government control and manipulation but its plural nature provides a site for the struggle of ideas and interests so it is not as monolithic as it seems.

Chapter 7 by Kole Shettima traces the role of youth, and in particular, of the student movement, in the struggles for democracy, not only in the educational sector, but also in the wider society. The National Association of Nigerian Students has been the major player in this regard, acting as a vanguard in the struggle for social justice and democracy.

Chapter 8 by Attahiru Jega, the immediate past president of the Academic Staff Union of Universities, argues that intellectuals have under conditions of crisis played decisive roles in the struggle for democracy. Motivated by the bleak future emanating from persistent economic crisis, some academics have chosen the path of collaboration and opportunism while many others have been propelled into active involvement in democratic struggles in order that the conditions for intellectual work and socio-economic survival could be maintained.

Chapter 9 highlights the conceptions and role of the left in democratic struggles. Adebayo Olukoshi traces two different perspectives. The first is contemptuous of bourgeois political forms and of a democratic quest which draws its inspiration from liberal Western political traditions of multipartyism, promotion of human rights and the rule of law. The second perspective stresses the view that the democratic project cannot be advanced without taking its political dimensions, in particular liberal democratic issues, seriously. The Nigerian left tradition has been more interested in social and economic rights and rather dismissive of political rights. It was only in the late 1980s that economic austerity and hardship, coupled with increased repression and denial of rights, sensitised the Nigerian left to the necessity to struggle for liberal democratic rights.

Chapter 10 poses the issues concerning trades unions and democracy. Issa Aremu posits that democracy is restricted because of the existence of a very difficult labour regime characterised by restrictive laws and repressive state policies. Be that as it may, unions have been playing important roles in the country's democratic struggles. Trade unions, however, remain an arena in which much more needs to be done to expand internal democracy and maintain the larger social role played by them.

Chapter 11 takes on the issues around civil liberties, human rights organisations and the rule of law. Femi Falana argues that constitutionally guaranteed rights have always been inadequate in Nigerian laws and that there is a long history of state negation of the limited rights in the statute books. He contends that the colonial order of rule by force and violence has been maintained and indeed extended by a long period of military rule resulting in a clear reduction of the rule of law. When the tempo of military dictatorship increased at the end of 1983, human rights organisations sprang up to defend rapidly dwindling human and civil rights.

Chapter 12 explores the complexity of the relationship between universals such as democracy and citizenship and concrete perceptions of rights, in a context where different perceptions of injustice are anchored in a history of political domination and deprivation. Raufu Mustapha examines the contradictory relationship between citizenship and rights through a case study of Zangon Kataf, an area where authoctons and migrant residents have developed mutually exclusive identities and interests.

The appendices provide a detailed report of the Lagos Conference on the 'Expansion of Nigerian Democratic Space', written by Tanimu Abubakar, as well as the Conference Communiqué that was adopted by participants.

Notes

1. 'Wazobia' — a composite word from the verb 'to come' in the three major languages — Yoruba (wa), Hausa (zo) and Igbo (bia). It has become a symbol of the political domination of the numerous minority groups in the country by the majority groups.
2. Professor Arlot of the University of London in a lecture at the University of Bordeaux in June 1987 argued that Nigerian jurists were so predominant in the Bench and Bar of Anglophone countries such as Gambia, Tanzania and Zambia that the country could be accused of legal sub-imperialism.

3. This section of the chapter is a revised form of our conclusion in the chapter Democratic Transition in Africa: The Challenge of A New Agenda' in Chole and Ibrahim (eds.), *Democratic Processes in Africa: Prospects and Problems*, CODESRIA, Dakar, 1995.

2

Interest Groups and the Construction of Democratic Space

Bjorn Beckman

Introduction: Delusive Transitions

Dominant power groups — be it in a one, two, multi, or no-party context — keep regrouping themselves, splitting up, multiplying, striking deals, outwitting each other, regrouping again, reconciling and embracing, all surrounded by a deafening noise of national rhetoric. Those with special access (not just to guns) keep twisting the rules in favour of themselves and their friends, while faking constitutional legitimacy. Electorates are taken for a ride, again and again. It is all very depressing, inviting, understandably, and generating cynicism and apathy. Stout democrats keep calling the bluff, trying to untwist the rules, without illusions about immediate success but hoping that popular democratic aspirations may impress themselves on government and the powers that be in the long-run.

What support can such hopes draw from observing the actual social forces at work in society? Much more, I believe, than the miserable spectacle of 'transition' may suggest. Without belittling the importance of democratic party politics, we need to shift the focus to the wider arenas of conflict resolution and interest representation in society. This is where significant expansion of democratic space has been achieved in recent years, despite the continued oppressiveness of national politics.

Even substantial advances in the arena of electoral politics will have only limited impact in terms of democratising the state unless they are supported by advances in the constitutional regulation of conflict within a multitude of separate and overlapping arenas, including workplaces, schools, hospitals, market places, homes, and communities. Just as in national politics, these are arenas of ongoing struggles to restrain the arbitrary exercise of power and expand the sphere of constitutional rule, based on the recognition of conflicting interests. When writing the history of democratisation, these arenas should be explored for achievements and experiences, as can be documented, for instance, in the struggles by trade unions, professional associations, women and student organisations, but also in more fragmented arenas, less visible from the horizon of national politics, as in the contestation of patriarchal despotism in the peasant household and in the everyday resistance to arbitrary state violence and intimidation in roads and market places.

This chapter is about the role of organised interests in the construction and expansion of democratic space, from within the arenas where they are counterpoised, preoccupied with the rules that regulate the relations of domination, each seeking to pull the state on its side in that contest, and looking for allies outside its own immediate arena.

The establishment of the rule of law, in the sense of 'constitutionalising' conflict resolution, reducing the sphere of arbitrary rule, opening up the legal representation of interests and the recognition of rights of organisation, are all vital elements in the construction of democratic space. It presupposes an underlying 'social contract' — that is, a mutual understanding that 'if you abide by the rules, we will abide by the rules', implying the partial renunciation of the use of force. Yet, the contract rests on the balance of forces. The dominant party, be it the employer, the landowner, the authority or the state, will respect the new contractual legality only as long as its non-application can be forcefully contested from below.

Interest groups, especially in the context of the politics of structural adjustment, are commonly brandished as 'vested interests' and claimed to obstruct both the 'national interest' and the interests of less organised classes, such as the peasantry. This chapter also discusses if and in what ways the expansion of democratic space in the arenas of organised interests is of relevance for such wider interests. It also discusses the relevance of the internal — democratic — constitution of the organised interests themselves. It concludes by summarising the different ways in which interest groups contribute to the expansion of democratic space and by raising issues about their wider relevance for the transition to democracy.

So Much 'Civil Society', So Little Democracy?

Pluralist democratic theory suggests that democracy needs to be supported by a wide range of associations and other organised collectivities capable of articulating the interests of their members, moulding and constraining the power of the state. Their demands provide input for the democratic political process, being to some extent aggregated by political parties. Their approval or disapproval of what goes on in government contribute to accountability. Vigorous associational life is at the core of the current concern with 'civil society'. A country which is well endowed in this respect is expected to be favourably positioned for democratisation. Conversely, references to a 'weak civil society' are used to explain the failure of democracy, not least in Africa. Post-colonial statism (socialist or capitalist) is assumed to have retarded its development.

Nigeria has a rich associational life. The country bristles with organised interests at all levels of society, from village and community associations to specialised professional groups, including the associations of old-boys (and girls) from the most prestigious professional schools of the world, numerous and prosperous enough to rent luxury hotels for their annual conventions. Trades unions and employer associations, lawyers, doctors, teachers and students keep intervening dramatically in the public arena, contesting government regulations and policies and pursuing the demands of their members. An average market-place is criss-crossed by associations of traders, craftsmen, transporters and labourers, enforcing prices and rules of competition, negotiating with the police, the tax collectors and other agents of the state, occasionally engaging in violent battles, as in Minna in 1987 when butchers rioted and sacked the local police station after one of their leaders was found beaten, dumped and dead at a roadside. With massive internal migration, both rural-urban and rural-rural, home-town associations, ethnically based churches and other community groups are to be found all over. There is no doubt about the civic spirit of much of these associations, engaging in development projects, contributing to good causes, and even offering to supervise and enforce traffic regulations.

If Nigeria is so well endowed with associations, why so little democracy at the level of the state? There is nothing inherently democratic about associations. They can be organised on chauvinist and racist lines, with authoritarian and anti-democratic aspirations and modes of operation. Powerful landed and propertied interests, for instance, may organise themselves with the purpose of obstructing democratisation. Trades unions can be controlled by corrupt bosses who rule by intimidation, blocking attempts by the workers to organise themselves in defence of their self-perceived interests. Nor is there anything necessarily democratic about accountability. A military government, for instance, may at one level seem to exercise unlimited, personal and arbitrary powers. It may still be tied by a hidden mandate from organised formal or informal power groups to which it is accountable and in the interests of which it has to 'deliver'. The cancellation of the June 1993 elections, for instance, may well be an expression of such informal accountability.

So, what is it about organised interests that makes them' democratically relevant?

Contesting Relations of Domination

Associations become democratically relevant first of all if and when they contest relations of domination within their own fields of operation. Some associations are more prone than others to get involved in this respect. This chapter is primarily concerned with organised interests in a 'modern' sense, formally constituted in terms of a defined membership and with an internal constitutional process for electing leaders, rendering accounts, etc. These include in particular trades unions and professional associations. They differ from organised interests without such formal structure, for instance, social movements which are represented by activists without constitutional status and where membership is fluid. The distinction is not rigid. Formally organised interests may also claim to be part of and representing wider informal social movements, as in the case of trades unions and the 'labour movement', students organisations and the 'student movement', women's organisations and the 'women's movement', and human rights groups and the 'democratic movement', etc. Formal interest groups in this sense can certainly not claim to represent the entire associational life of a society. In discussions of 'the growth of civil society', however, they are usually given an important place.

This chapter deals primarily with the construction of democratic space within the professional arenas where such organised groups operate. These may be 'private' arenas, constituted by relations to other 'counterparts' than the state, for instance relations between workers and private employers. The state, however, is in most cases involved, not just as an employer in its own right, but in the political regulation of the relations between the private parties. The arena is defined by the nature of the interest and the relationships into which the group is obliged to enter by virtue of representing such interest, for instance, the relationship of labour to employers, tenants to landlords, producers to produce buyers, and students to school authorities. In each case we may identify basic underlying conflicts of interest that define the relationship: workers want better pay and job security, employers want to cut costs and raise productivity; tenants want low rent, landlords high; producers want high prices, produce buyers want low ones, etc.

Organised interest groups intervene in the regulation of these conflicts and develop a stake in the procedures by which the conflicts are resolved. Such procedures reflect the uneven power relations characterising the relationship. Employers assert their right to hire, fire and discipline workers on the basis of ownership and control over the means of production. Workers, in their turn, seek to enhance bargaining power, wages and working conditions by withholding their labour and other forms of collective industrial action. Farmers associations may organise sales boycotts and students may refuse to attend classes.

There is no scope within such asymmetrical power relations to resolve conflicts through a democratic process which would presume equal rights. However, a factory or a university can be more or less democratically constituted in terms of rights of organisation and expression and the extent to which workers, students and lecturers are given a say in decisions which affect them. Even if disciplinary rights rest with managers and authorities, the process by which such rights are exercised may or may not be organised in a way as to protect against arbitrary treatment. The scope and limitations of the disciplinary rights may themselves be subjected to negotiation.

Each such arena of conflicting interests can be seen as governed by a 'regime', a set of formal or informal rules and practices that define rights and obligations. We may speak of the workplace regime of a particular factory and a labour regime for a particular sphere of production, society or place. We may similarly speak of school, university or hospital regimes when referring to the way in which power and authority is structured in such institutions. These regimes may be more or less arbitrary (despotic) or constitutional, authoritarian or participatory, imposed or agreed. The extent to which the interests can assert themselves in the constitution and the operation of the regime will reflect the balance of power both in specific arenas and in society at large. That balance is not constant, it is continuously shifting, both as a result of circumstances (for example changing market conditions, state intervention etc.) and as a result of the efforts by the contesting parties (organisation, leadership).

As the regimes involve relations of domination (management, discipline, authority), they are potential arenas of democratic struggle because those who are being subordinated have an interest in changing the regime itself so as to enhance their say in the way in which they are ruled. This is what democracy is about. Struggles by workers against managerial despotism, for instance, are therefore part of the struggles to expand democratic space in society. The same is true for students contesting the authoritarianism of educational institutions and women's organisations contesting patriarchy at different levels of society.

Imposing the Rule of Law from Below

Central to the contestation of relations of domination in civil society is the struggle against the arbitrary exercise of power by those placed in a position of authority, as managers, landlords, teachers, heads of department, vice-chancellors, market supervisors etc. Much contestation takes place at an unorganised level by individuals and groups who defy authority that they consider to be illegitimate. This may itself be important in the disciplining of authority and the expansion of democratic space. Organised interests take a more direct part in the efforts to constitutionalise the relations of domination within their respective spheres of operation, with a view to regulate the exercise of authority and minimise arbitrary and personal rule. Having a say in the way one is ruled is closely linked to the establishment of recognised procedures for the regulation of conflict. In this respect democracy and constitutionalism are closely connected.

'Law and order' is often associated with the ideology of those who want to discipline and control subordinated groups. Historically, however, constitutionalism has also been the project of imposing the rule of law from below on those who exercise power. If left to themselves, the latter are likely to continue to rule as they deem fit, seeing themselves as responsible only to God or their own good will. Most managers, teachers and heads of families are convinced that they have the best interests of their 'wards' at heart. It is only when challenged that they will find virtue in constitutionalising their authority.

Organised interests, in their struggle to do away with arbitrary (despotic or paternalistic) forms of domination, enter into an implicit 'contract' whereby they agree to abide by certain rules if the other side makes the same undertaking. The contract imposes constraints on the exercise of power on both sides, including restrictions on the use of obstruction and non-cooperation by the subordinate party, as in the case of the regulation of the right to strike. The expansion of constitutional forms of conflict regulation is therefore as much a struggle for the definition and recognition of the 'legitimate interests' that are to inform such contract. As with all contracts, it is bound to reflect the differences in strength (resources, organisation, leadership, alliances, etc.) of the contracting parties. There is nothing necessarily 'fair' about it and the democratic content, in terms of influence, may be limited. Still, the contract may allow the subordinate party some element of legal protection on which to build the strength from which future, more advantageous, contracts can be negotiated.

In many instances, a formal set of rules may exist in the statute books, as required, for instance, by international conventions or as influenced by legal practices elsewhere. This is true of much labour legislation. But such rules are often of little consequence for the way in which authority is actually exercised. The Nigerian textile workers union, that Gunilla Andrae and I have studied closely, has fought hard for the recognition of such official labour rights in companies where they have been ignored or resisted by management, often with the collusion of government labour officers, police commissioners and other official guardians of the rule of law (Andrae and Beckman 1991, 1992). It underscores that the struggle for constitutional rule has to be waged from below and that formal rules have no more meaning than can be asserted and defended by the contending forces.

It also reminds us that the struggle for the constitutional regulation of conflict within relations of domination does not mean a renunciation of the use of force. Unless retaining the ultimate sanction of non-constitutional force, subordinate groups cannot expect their interests to be respected, either when establishing or seeking to uphold the new legality.

Representation, Recognition, Mediation

Interest groups provide means of representation in the regulation of conflicts of interest in society. But whose interests do they actually represent? Their democratic potential is frequently questioned on two grounds, one relates to the lack of internal democracy ('the iron law of oligarchy', 'labour aristocracy', 'boss-rule' etc.); the other concerns their lack of autonomy in relation to the other party of the conflict ('co-optation', 'incorporation', 'yellow unions'). 'Representation' is complicated by the need for interest groups to be 'recognised' both in law and by the other parties to the conflict and that they tend to perform a 'mediatory' role. The tension between representation and mediation underscores that interest groups themselves are contested territory, and not just by internal forces. The way in which they are constituted within the arena where they seek representation and in relation to the state are all objects of struggle.

The constitutional practices and processes inside the organisations themselves are of obvious importance, including the way in which problems of succession, accountability, divisions, minority rights etc. are handled. All of this involves struggles for the construction, extension and protection of democratic space. Interest groups may be seen as laboratories for practices and values of importance to society at large, contributing to the formation of experienced democrats, an essential asset in the development of democracy. Conversely, the anti-democratic practices and values characteristic of many interest groups undercut the ability of the latter to serve as a democratic force in society.

Interest groups that are weakly organised in terms of internal democracy may still perform a democratic function by expanding constitutionalism and the principle of representation within their sphere of operation. It presupposes, however, that they have some reasonable claim to represent the interests of their members, as defined by the nature of the conflict, the issues at stake, and the lines pursued by the leaders.

The question of representation and the democratic role of interest groups is complicated by the problem of recognition. An organisation needs to be recognised by the other party in the conflict. Some may be able to force recognition by virtue of the militancy and perseverance of their members. Often, however, recognition is granted without any showdown because the other party has an interest in seeking accommodation, hoping to ensure greater co-operation by granting benefits to the organisation and its leaders. Co-optation may be crude and corrupt or more subtle. Interest groups may even be turned into instruments used by the dominant party for administering its domination. In some cases, interest groups are even created and maintained by the dominant party, as in the case of so-called 'yellow', management-sponsored, unions.

Recognition is thus double edged. It is necessary to obtain it but it may also be a means of control, undermining the democratic potential. The rules regulating the establishment and recognition of interest groups are therefore an important area of contest. The right to represent somebody else is regulated in law. There is no natural right to fall back on. The right to strike, for instance, as a means of collective industrial action organised and enforced by a union, conflicts, as neo-liberals remind us, with the right of the individual to freely negotiate with the employer. The right to strike assumes the authorisation of the union to act on behalf of its members. The balance struck between these conflicting principles is an outcome of historical struggle and the balance of forces, varying from one context to another.

The element of recognition and external authorisation prevents interest groups from being 'pure' expressions of the aspirations of their members.

This is where the issue of mediation comes in. As 'society' (the state, the other party) agrees to 'recognise' an organisation, authorising it to be the 'legitimate' representative of a particular interest, it also reinforces its role as middleman or mediator in the regulation of conflict.

Frontiers in the Expansion of Democratic Space

The frontiers of democratic struggles are constituted within different arenas, from places of work to national politics. Contestation at one level creates the preconditions for what happens at another. For instance, basic rights at the workplace, such as rights of organisation and representation, have to.be secured at the level of national legislation as well as in confronting local employers and authorities. Rights that are specific to one arena will overlap with and depend on more general rights. The right not to be discriminated against on the basis of religion, race or gender, for instance, is clearly more basic to democratic rights than, say, the right to strike or to organise a picket line to prevent others from taking your work when on strike. The more specific right, the one to strike, however, may be critical to upholding the more general ones. While it may be possible to envisage a widening range of arenas, reaching out like concentric circles, 'democratic relevance' does not necessarily grow with the range of such circles. An organisation which dabbles ineffectually in 'national democratic politics' may contribute less to democratisation than one engaged in transforming relations of domination in its own immediate arena of operation.

Our primary concern, however, is with tracing the way in which struggles at different levels connect, how they prompt and reinforce each other. Seemingly narrow conflicts, as over the appalling quality of food in the students' canteen, may take on a wider democratic significance due to the linkages between local and national power relations. If, for instance, the wife of the Vice-Chancellor is a food.contractor who supplies the canteen, issues of corruption and nepotism become mingled with the politics of warring local and national power factions that seek to control the universities for their own purposes. Such linkages help to explain why the authorities often react violently, seeing students as proxies for forces with sinister motives which are out to destroy them. The victimisation of students and lecturers seen as instigating them, generates additional national political linkages, leading to contestation in courts, engaging civil rights lawyers and arousing solidarity actions both from other students and other organised interests, sympathetic to the cause of the students or anxious to teach the state a lesson.

As events 'get out of hand', the authorities respond by sending in the police and army into the campus, closing down the universities and sending home the students. While intended to diffuse the tensions, such collective punishment not only generates new resentment but also ensures that the controversies are disseminated in society as the students return home to their villages and towns. Wide media coverage also highlights the issues of civil rights, social justice, and democracy, not least in reaction to the efforts by the authorities to portray the students as destructive, irresponsible, selfish and unpatriotic (Beckman and Jega 1994).

In a joint study with Attahiru Jega on organised interests and democratisation the following interconnecting frontiers of significance to the expansion of democratic space were identified (Beckman and Jega 1994):

1. **Rights of organisation**: the right to exist, hold meetings, elect representatives, and voice views, without risking interference and victimisation.

2. **Rights of collective bargaining**: the right to be recognised by authorities/employers, etc. as representing the members for the purpose of negotiating on their behalf, including entering into legally enforceable agreements within their spheres of operation.

3. **Rights of participation in management**: in the institutions that constitute the immediate arena of operation, restricting personal and authoritarian forms of rule and promoting internal structures of representation.

4. **Upholding the rule of law**: within these institutions, including transparency of transactions and the accountability of those placed in authority.

5. **Institutional autonomy vis-à-vis the state**: (for example free collective bargaining, 'academic freedom') as to maintain the integrity of institutional processes and to restrict the domain of authoritarian state power.

6. **Participation in public policy**: rights of representation and consultation in the development of policies which directly affect the members of the organisation in the capacity that defines them as members, for example as workers, teachers, students.

7. **Solidarity with other organised interests**: in the defence of their organisational rights, including entering into formal and informal alliances for mutual support.

8. **Participation in political alliances**: in defence of democratic political rights and freedoms in society at large, resisting and challenging authoritarian state power.

9. **Providing a platform for wider popular demands**: a 'people's tribune' in the absence of democratic means of political representation under authoritarian rule.

Incorporation, Disengagement, and Democratisation

The post-colonial world has been characterised invariably by the incorporation of organised interests by state and one-party structures. Their disengagement from such more or less repressive arrangements is part and parcel of economic and political liberalisation. Rising new cadres, resentful of the way leaders have compromised the organisations by allowing themselves to be tied to the state, are in the forefront in the demand for autonomy. Most of the democratic frontiers identified above, however, suggest some form of state involvement not just as an obstacle to autonomy but also as a facilitator. Basic organisational rights require state legislation and enforcement. Collective bargaining, while a matter between the parties concerned, normally also presupposes some state legal backing. Similarly, organised interests seek to engage the state on its side when demanding participation, democratic practices, accountability and transparency in workplaces and institutions.

The state is profoundly involved in structuring the regimes that govern the arenas where organised interests operate, apart from being a contesting party in its own right as an employer of labour and producer of public services. Organised interests that contest relations of domination in their respective arenas will therefore inevitably come up against the state. They will have a stake in political solutions which facilitate the pursuit of their interests. Such solutions are not necessarily democratic. Interest groups may accept corporative deals which award them privileges of access to state resources in exchange for political support for an authoritarian government or for not joining the political opposition.

So when does interest group politics link up with and reinforce wider democratisation? The link-up is affected by changing policy conjunctures which cause corporatist solutions to be undermined. In the Nigerian situation, we have seen how organised interests seek to enhance their autonomy *vis-à-vis* the state in a situation where the latter is increasingly unable or unwilling to deliver or protect the benefits originally associated with the corporatist arrangements. Organised interests take advantage of the decline in state power to advance their own bargaining capacity.

The contribution made by organised interests to the expansion of democratic space in Nigeria needs to be situated in the context of this shift in the balance of forces, both global and local, and the related restructuring of state-interest group relations. It is a precarious process where opposition to economic liberalisation encourages interest groups to disengage from the state in defence of their 'special interests', while reinforcing their commitment to political liberalisation as the best possible framework for enhancing autonomy and bargaining power. The process has opened up alliances between organised interests that operate in widely different arenas in defence of organisational rights against state encroachment as well as in support of wider democratic demands.

Whose Interests? Special Interests Versus the People

Organised interests, trades unions and professional associations in particular, are often attacked from both neo-liberal and radical democratic perspectives as representing 'special' or 'vested' interests that make up only a tiny segment of the population and whose narrow, self-interested pursuits are either irrelevant or even positively harmful to the concerns of the majority — peasants, small producers and traders who have no effective organisations of their own. In the neo-liberal perspective, such 'vested interests' are linked to a notion of an inflated and parasitic public wage economy which is biased against the rural sector and obstructs the development of such private entrepreneurship which could give work and income to the unemployed and marginalised (World Bank 1989, 1991; Beckman 1992, 1993). The radical democrats, on the other hand, feel that the prevailing democratic agenda, sponsored by local alternative elites and foreign 'donors', focus on segments of a 'civil society' which are largely middle class and fails to address the relations of oppression facing the lower classes, rural and urban, and the problems of democratic advance at that level (Mamdani 1990, 1992).

Peasant communities and the urban poor face their own democratic frontiers which cannot be subsumed under those of the organised interests discussed here. The latter, however, may be of lesser or greater relevance for the former. The Nigerian experiences of the past decade suggest the interest group agenda can be closely linked to broader popular concerns, relating both to democratisation and welfare. Even special and elitist organisations such as university lecturers and students, may be seen as giving voice to popular aspirations when, for instance, resisting the imposition of school fees and educational levies and defending the 'right to education'. They have also spearheaded wider popular protests against military dictatorship in the absence of other democratic channels. While some of the conflicts of interest are real and important (for example wage earners vs. peasants), the special interests groups may still function as the vanguard of a wider process of democratisation from which those 'outside' have much to gain, not the least from the advancement of the rule of law in the regulation of the relations between state and society.

Part Two

The Babangida
Administration —
Checkmate or Impetus for
Democratisation?

3

The Legacy of Military Rule over the Democratisation Process

Abubakar Momoh

Introduction

The theme of this chapter is rather deceptive as it assumes first that military rule is already in existence and second, that the military in government has bequeathed some legacy of democratisation worthy of examination or study. The task will then be to demonstrate to what extent or degree this has left a legacy in Nigeria's history. Posed in this way, the legacy could be negative or positive. The misleading nature of the topic is that it seems to suggest either that we are concerned with how the military disengages from politics or how the military, while in government, helps to democratise institutions and structures from the state to civil society. The components of the former will include all the repressive apparatuses and the latter will include all interest and associational groups.

However, in both the assumptions and representation, we believe there must be a need for establishing a genealogy, a basis of coalescence or even the interpretation of these elements. Unless we explicate in a less unambiguous and problematic form the functional and heuristic value of each of those elements, the task we set ourselves will become cumbersome if not difficult to pursue.

Scholars like Oyovbaire (1987:175) have argued that the 'military made a tremendous contribution towards the democratisation of the Nigerian political process and this radicalises the political system'. Agbese and Kieh (1992:13), however, argue that from the civil war to the oil boom, the military have made the state fragile, causing fractional struggles amongst the bourgeoisie and provoking a crisis of accumulation. In addition the military's appetite to rule has been established, as exemplified in Gowon's extension of the transition to civil

rule earlier scheduled for October 1976. This chapter examines the
hypothesis that there are in-built mechanisms in military culture that
makes its democratisation processes truncated, less enduring and prone to
failure. If the military perceives its role in society as 'custodian guard'
and 'praetorian', why must it rule? Has it also in the process of rule
acquired the values that create friction and crisis for the civilians viz.,
corruption, avarice, greed, ethnicity, etc.? Is the assumption and
argument for dyarchy not rooted in this logic? That is a situation where
the military either rules along with civilians or institutionalises itself as a
professional group as an alternative to the civilians. How was the army
politicised, or how did it become conscious of politics and hence of
power?

Unlike in Britain, in which since 1688 there has been no military coup
and yet there is political discussion in the military in the form of public
opinion and lobby, in Nigeria the military is assumed to be insulated
from political participation or discussion and hence politically naive —
yet it seizes power frequently. What is the myth about military ethos,
commandism, respect for its own internal constitution and the violation
of the constitution of the state? Has this anything to do with the relative
weakness of the civil society or the army's monopoly of the instrument
of coercion? To discuss these questions, first we look at the role of the
military as a colonial creation, second, the problem of constitutionalism
and the state, third the military in its relation to civil society, fourth, the
attempts at military disengagement from politics in 1976 and 1979, and
finally Babangida's attempt at democratisation.

The Nigerian Military and Colonial Heritage

Colonisation was brought about by the use of violence and superior
weaponry. To sustain it, the apparatuses of violence had to be created,
especially in response to resistance by Africans. The first British formed
armed unit of Nigerians was the 'Clover's Hausas' in 1862 — also called
'Hausa Militia' and later 'Lagos Constabulary'. It was made up of 100
Hausa slaves, said to have run away from their masters to seek refuge
with Lieutenant Clover. The second unit, established in 1886, the 'Royal
Niger Company Constabulary', was created to protect British trading
interests. They formed the core of the 1st and 2nd battalions of the
Northern Nigeria Regiment, created in 1900. Sir Ralph Moore raised the
'Oil Rivers Irregulars' between 1891 and 1892, renamed the Nigeria
Coast Constabulary with headquarters at Calabar.

This constabulary formed the nucleus of the 3rd Battalion of the
Southern Nigeria Regiment of the West Africa Frontier Force (WAFF).

The WAFF was established by Frederick Lugard in 1897. It was made up of all the colonial troops in West Africa. In Nigeria, the WAFF was constituted into the Northern and Southern Nigeria Regiments. However, after the amalgamation of 1914, they were renamed the Nigeria Regiment of WAFF. The regiment provided a standing army for dealing with any issue requiring military intervention and provided a leverage for Britain to effectively establish its stamp on West Africa after the Berlin Conference. It also reduced British expenditure incurred in having to deploy the West Indian regiment. The ordinance establishing the Nigeria regiment of WAFF came out in 1892 and incorporated the British Camerouns. On June 7 1956, the Nigeria regiment of WAFF was renamed the Nigeria Military Force, Royal West African Frontier Force. Earlier, King George V had added the prefix 'Royal' to WAFF (Ukpabi 1987; Achike 1980).

Before independence, there were only 15 officers in the force who were Nigerians, the rest were British. In 1956, there were over 300 British NCOs, this fell to 80 in 1960 and to 21 in 1964. Between 1946 to 1958, 62.25 per cent of Nigerian indigenes came from the north; 37.5 per cent from southern Camerouns, eastern and western Nigeria. At that time the northern population was put at 54.5 per cent, against the 45.5 per cent of the rest of Nigeria including southern Camerouns. However, the most senior Nigerian officers as at 1960 were mostly easterners with the Ika-Igbo, constituting 61.3 per cent. At the first military coup in 1966 it was 65 per cent with the rest of the country accounting for 35 per cent. The Hausa, with its vocal leader Abdullahi Magajin Musawa, advocated equalisation of the officers corps in the army, while leaders of the Yorubas and Igbos argued that the other ranks were dominated by the north.

The problem of illiteracy led the British to pursue a recruitment programme based on growth. They favoured the north, and allocated them a quota of 50 per cent while the east and west were given 25 per cent each. However, the majority of the soldiers from the north were recruited from the middle belt. According to Tanko Galadima, the northern advocacy for quota in the military was to allay fears of domination if a section of the country was under-represented. However, quota recruitment in the military did not guarantee ethnic balance.

The colonial military was used to fight colonial and imperialist wars, quash internal insurgency etc. Gutteridge (1975) records that most of those recruited were illiterates and non urbanites. But their military training at Sandhurst, Aldershot, etc., their use in civil-political matters to overthrow the *de facto* and *de jure* government of Patrice Lumumba in the Congo crisis and above all the conscious promotion of the use of the quota system in recruitment into the army by the British and the post independence governments created a political consciousness in the Nigerian military which appetised their interest in political power. In all military recruitments and appointments, the Nigerian was now made to believe he was filling a political power balance.

While Ruth First is therefore correct in saying that the military is part of the colonial vestige, she should have added that it was one of the most backward legacies left behind. There are two reasons for this. First, as Fayemi (1992) argues, the army was never involved in the anti-colonial struggles. In fact, the army actively participated in repressing the nationalist ideal. Second, in the neo-colonial era, the role of the army has been one of consolidating the interests of metropolitan and local capital in the process of accumulation. Added to the seriousness of this, is the situation where, because of the weak material base of the emergent bourgeoisie, violence or the apparatus of repression was needed for social appropriation and capital accumulation in the neo-colony. As an apparatus of repression the military has also been concerned about its own share in the accumulation process.

The State and Constitutionalism

At independence, the Nigerian military saw itself as serving politicians who only yesterday they had hounded and repressed on the instruction of the colonial masters. However, the neo-colonial state still required the military to play the same role. Welch (1987:1) argues that: 'Those who support the government by coercion pose the closest, clearest threat to its continuation'. Adekanye (1992:1) poses the pertinent question and puzzle 'who will guard the guardians themselves?' Hutchful (1991) notes that the process of institutional transfer was uneven and lopsided in favour of repressive state apparatuses, with the representational organs of the state emerging last on the eve of independence. The attitude created, as it relates to law and due process, was to place 'emphasis on criminal rather than civil law'. He further contends that:

> ...the colonial state failed to instil the notion of the legitimate purposes and limits of state action of acceptable procedures for gaining and maintaining power (Hutchful 1991:185)

This approximates Dudley's (1973:13) idea of disequilibrium in 'constitutive' and 'regulative' rules causing instability or dysfunctionalism within the political system. One problem with these arguments is that they do not appreciate the sociology of a neo-colonial state, and are unable to locate the military as part of the contradictions of the state. The issue is not simply one of borrowed or invented political order impacting on a new social order. If it were so, how could we explain the incessant military coups in South America with their highly developed states of the latifundia.

To appreciate the nature and character of the state, we need to understand its social and material context. For as Nzongola Ntalaja (1987:74) surmises:

> The institutional materiality of the state, or its material framework of institutions and social practices, does not exist in a vacuum. It is a foundation of the social division of labour, and it is intelligible only with reference to the state's relationship to the economy and the social relations of production that the latter implies. For the state is above all a condensation of social relationships, the cohesive force of a conflict-ridden society, a force for order, and ultimately a relation of power between antagonistic social classes.

In this sense we can talk about a military fraction of the bourgeoisie, taking over and using power. This has two implications. First, it shows that there is nothing sacrosanct about the social category of the military because it is made up of human beings and is as divided materially as the rest of society. Second, it shows that whenever the military is in power, it governs on behalf of a particular class. Any form of military dictatorship represents a dominant class interest or at least a dominant fractional class interest, otherwise it cannot last longer than the minute it came into being. But this is a contradiction of a secondary nature, the fundamental one being that of the military-civil contradiction.

The Military and Civil Society

If we reflect on the civil society discourse from the point of view of liberal democracy, we shall see that Marx himself acknowledges the formal freedom that political form gives the human person from the bondage of pre-civil society/capitalist states. Ibrahim (1986:48) argues:

> The minimum response of progressive forces must be to struggle for the establishment of a genuine liberal democracy for the country. This is the best atmosphere in which they can mobilise and organise the masses for a more fundamental social and economic transformation of the country. It is important to realise that although liberal democracy is associated with capitalism, its provisions are never willingly granted by the ruling class.

Sandbrook (1988:24), although making a case for a schematic transition to socialism, identifies the elements of liberal democracy as regular and free elections in which politicians stand and contest elections on the platforms of political parties, adult suffrage, and guaranteed and protected political and civil rights. Stephan (1988:3-5) identifies three polities in military politics viz.: civil society, political society and the state. He states that:

... in any given polity these three arenas expand and shrink at different rates, interpenetrate or even dominate each other and constantly change.

He identifies civil society with social movements or associations, he defines the political society as that arena which is prepared to contest and take over power. The state is the legal, bureaucratic and coercive organ that structures relations between civil and public power. Stephan argues that the role of civil society is to resist and dislodge from power authoritarian regimes, and it is the duty of the political society to take over power, through elections. A notion of democracy cannot be nurtured by a regime which represses its people, rules by decree, insulates and immunises itself from the laws of the society, etc. This brings into question the role of the civil society from which the state is supposed to derive its powers.

According to Mamdani (1990:48), in the course of the struggle for independence, popular movements and forces were demobilised by the emergent nationalist elites and incorporated into the liberal project, signalling their defeat:

The defeat was not only political, it was also ideological. In fact, out of this defeat was borne an ideological inversion, from a popular rooted conception, nationalism was turned into a state ideology.

Even within the context of the state, and its developmentalist objectives, civil society, it has been said, has been unable to raise voluntary associations to achieve state objectives. However, this does not explain the renewed upsurge in action for democracy in Africa, such as militant trade unionism and intellectual and students associations.

The salient point here is that once the military lives above the civil society and refuses to see itself as one interest group among many, and so far as the civil society has not developed parallel power structures, 'people's power', in order to diffuse or neutralise the army, military rule will continue to be an albatross around the neck of developing countries. More importantly, if the mythical garb of professionalism is retained by the military, it cannot democratise its structures so as to learn to appreciate the nuances of civil rule. It can only continue the cyclical game of musical chairs with its 'yoyo' effect. The military must know that democracy is not about consensus politics or the absence of conflict, rather it is the institutionalisation of the conflict process through procedures and rules, learned and nurtured in order that they endure.

Instability, therefore, is the surreptitious disequilibriation of the attempt to institutionalise conflict.

This should constitute the basis of a democratisation agenda by all associational and interest groups in civil society against the militarist and authoritarian state. This task is not about interest group counter-hegemony or leverage in terms of closer access to state power and domination over the rest of civil society, rather it is one of waging a struggle that would ensure that the values of liberal democracy are enthroned leaving the 'political society' for those who are interested in political power via the defined route and rules. Therefore the paranoia about the two traps of 'parochial imaginary liberation and bureaucratic appropriation' (Bayart 1986:119), in this context, becomes misplaced and unfounded, as indeed it would have amounted to reverting to the original sin — the military guilt.

Disengagement or Democratisation

The Nigerian military has not proceeded on a democratisation programme in the way we have conceptualised it above. Indeed, the military homogenises itself and pursues a 'disengagement' drive, while civil society, especially within the political arena, pursues the project of 'democratisation' as taught by the military. The military seeks a transition to civil rule rather than to democratise. In both form and content, the latter is more all-embracing and more far-reaching than the former. Recent writers on the military have been very pessimistic about a coup-free Nigeria, or Africa. Hence the new cliches: 'no farewell to arms' (Welch 1987), 'the post military-state in Africa' (Adekanye 1985), 'the Praetorian Trap' (Dare 1991) etc. All the best known experts on military disengagement in Nigeria are very pessimistic, but with due modesty it should be pointed out that much of their solutions and indeed their analyses are limited to the institutional/structural level. The issue of disengagement or demilitarisation, (complete military withdrawal from government), is in our view a one-sided, endogenic disposition of an interest group. Because civil society does not determine or control what happens within the military, reforms in the nature of the democratisation process are never carried out thoroughly. For transition to civil rule to be democratic, the military must subject itself to the control and moderation of the civil society.

Adekanye (1984:214) identifies three approaches to military disengagement viz.: the counter coup inspired approach, the military-turned-politician and the constitutional revolutionary model. He argues that the Nigerian experience falls within the third model. To him the military returns to barracks if first, there are pressures from the civil population, second, there are internal military squabbles occasioning a handover to civilians third, when the military itself disengages voluntarily. Finer, cited in Dare (1991), had argued that military disengagement occurs when:

a) The leaders shall sincerely want his (sic) troops to quit politics.

b) The military should be able to establish a regime capable of functioning without further military intervention and assistance.

c) The successor regime should be acceptable to the armed forces; and

d) The military itself should have sufficient confidence in its leaders so as to return to the barracks on order.

Huntington (1968) sees the necessary conditions for nurturing and implanting democracy as the establishment of national unity and political authority, and the achievement of equality. However, as we shall argue, the greatest antidote to military rule and the most effective means of democratising society is the creation of an active civil society. This is the arena that requires, and that can facilitate, the expansion of democratic space. We shall now profile the various attempts at a transition to civil rule by the Nigerian military.

The Gowon and Obasanjo Experiments

When General Yakubu Gowon assumed the reins of power in July 1966, he promised to hand over power to civilians within six months. However, the civil war broke out shortly after and Gowon rationalised that '... the Nigerian Armed Forces will not hand over power in Chaos...' (Agbese and Kieh 1992:12). Prominent politicians who served in his government during the civil war, notably Chief Obafemi Awolowo, resigned as a symbolic demonstration of a commitment to democratic rule. As a result of pressures and condemnation from civil society, Gowon had to announce on October 1, 1970 the 'nine point programme of transition to civil rule in 1976:

1. The re-organisation of the Armed Forces.

2. The implementation of the National Development Plan, and the repair of the damage and neglect of the war.

3. The eradication of corruption in national life.

4. The settlement of the question of the creation of more states.

5. The preparation and adoption of a new constitution.

6. The introduction of a new Revenue Allocation Formula.

7. Conducting a National Population Census.

8. The organisation of elections and the installation of popularly elected government in the states and centre.

9. The organisation of genuine political parties.

As Dare (1991:16-19) argues, the nine point programme was vague and had no specific dates for handover of power. This battered the credibility of the regime and led civil society, especially trade unions, the intelligentsia and students to begin to agitate for Gowon's departure. This atmosphere led to the publication of an article by Tai Solarin entitled 'The Beginning of the End', which predicted the downfall of the Gowon regime. Gowon became desperate and unleashed repression, cornering a section of the political class including Nnamdi Azikiwe who anchored an intellectual argument on Gowon's behalf for diarchy.[1] After the boom of the oil economy and the expanded accumulation process that followed, the bureaucrats and civil servants were given enormous powers. This was done in the regime's desperate search for credibility. The nine-point programme was implemented piecemeal and half-heartedly. Meanwhile, top military officers began to make conflicting statements as to whether the military would handover power to civilians or not. Finally on October 1, 1974, Gowon announced that the original date of handing over in 1976 was no longer realistic because:

> It would indeed amount to a betrayal of trust to adhere rigidly to the date. It was clear that those who would lead the nation in the return of civilian rule, have not learnt any lessons from past experiences. Consequently, it would be utterly irresponsible to leave the nation in the lurch by a precipitate withdrawal which would certainly throw the nation back into confusion (Agbese and Kieh 1992:13).

This was a huge setback for the popular forces in civil society who had been struggling for democracy.

The authoritarianism of the Gowon era was exemplified by the mindless civil war in which Nigeria was plunged, culminating in the killing of no less than one million Igbos. The militarised civil society it created and its negative fall-out led to a substantial increase in armed robbery in the 1970s. The press was gagged and brutalised, as the case of Amakiri showed, students and teachers were equally repressed. Accumulation and squandermania continued, the indigenisation decree was introduced which gave a leverage to the Nigerian national bourgeoisie, yet and quite contradictorily, the policy consolidated the stranglehold of the multinationals over the Nigerian economy (Turner 1976). There were several scandals — the scania bus, the cement armada, etc. The objectives of the Second National Development Plan, which in part promised 'a free and democratic society...' were jettisoned. Rather than rehabilitate the widowed, orphaned and destitute victims created by the civil war, the bourgeoisie rehabilitated their pockets. Rather than talk of abandoned human beings the bourgeoisie begun to quarrel over the control of so called 'abandoned property'.

It is hard to see how the creation of states by Gowon actually democratised the Nigerian society, as Oyovbaire (1987) argues, as it was a programme which was undertaken essentially for political expediency. The Murtala/Obasanjo transition has received some attention in the literature, unlike the truncated and still-born Gowon transition. The Murtala regime indicted Gowon thus:

> After the civil war, the affairs of state, hitherto a collective responsibility, became characterised by lack of consultation, indecision, indiscipline and even neglect. Indeed, the public at large became disillusioned and disappointed by these developments. This trend was clearly incompatible with the philosophy and image of a corrective regime. Unknown to the general public, the feeling of disillusion was also evident among members of the Armed Forces whose administration was neglected but who, out of sheer loyalty to the Nation, and in the hope that there would be a change, continued to suffer in silence (Maiden Broadcast by Murtala Mohamed).

The Murtala regime drew up a political timetable for a return of power to civilians by October 1, 1979. It was a programme in stages (Owolabi 1992):

Stage One: The state creation review panel to report by December, 1975 and the creation of new states to be completed by April 1976.
: Constitution drafting committee to submit a draft by September 1976.

Stage Two: Local government elections without party politics.
: Setting up of Constituent Assembly; partly elected and partly nominated to consider the draft constitution by October 1978.

Stage Three: Ban on politics to be lifted in October 1978 with the formation of political parties.

Stages Four and Five: Federal and state elections.

Although the Murtala/Obasanjo transition programme procedurally accomplished the major elements on its timetable, it ended up consolidating the economic and political power base of some fractional interests. Several avenues for this were created. The indigenisation decree was reviewed, the Land Use Decree introduced, the first major debt was acquired and jamboree projects embarked upon. And the national bourgeoisie continued to pilfer from the rentier state.

The process of democratic expansion was contrived. The Constitution Drafting Committee (CDC) was elitist, made up essentially of professionals and the business class. Its report represented metropolitan and local business interests in what is euphemistically referred to as a mixed economy. The Osoba and Usman radical Minority Report on the Constitution was scarcely given a mention. The CDC condemned socialism as 'foreign' (Osoba 1978). The Constitution itself made bourgeois rights enforceable and social welfare needs non-justiciable. The local government reforms undertaken, rather than creating room for democratisation, merely decentralised electoral structures for elite recruitment. The five political parties that were recognised vacillated on the political spectrum between the right, the centre and even to populist positions. The Supreme Military Council vetted the Constitution, registered the political parties and regulated the process of the transition. The Federal Electoral Commission (FEDECO) took orders from the SMC. In the end, FEDECO was accused of partisanship and interest in the military's own candidate for the Presidency (the National Party of Nigeria's candidate). Little wonder that a link was also established between some factions of the ruling class and the military in the coup that ousted Shagari (Othman 1984).

The acid test of Obasanjo's democratisation was at the level of civil society. The government banned the central labour union, the Nigerian Labour Congress, formed by Nigerian workers after the Apena Cemetery declaration. The trade disputes decree of 1977, which prescribed 'no work — no pay', reviving the memory of the civil war repressive Gowon Decree, was re-introduced and given teeth. Following the Adebiyi Tribunal Report, strong radical unionists such as Michael Imoudu, Wahab Goodluck etc. were banned from trade unionism.

For demanding campus reforms, improved welfare and for resisting the hike in feeding costs, Obasanjo ordered the killing of 13 students in Nigerian higher educational institutions. Their apex union, the National Union of Nigerian Students (NUNS), was banned, their president, Segun Okeowo, and several other leaders were incarcerated. Several university lecturers were also sacked, supposedly because they supported the students. The press was gagged, *Newbreed* magazine was banned and several other pressmen were arbitrarily detained. Obasanjo founded the Ita-Oko Prison on an island in the Atlantic, a prison which is similar to

Robben island in all its ramifications. It was an illegal detention camp, where several people disappeared, unknown and unrecorded.

Many Nigerians were disqualified from active political participation, including civil servants and other professionals. The Nigerian Advance Party, which laid claim to the socialist ideology, was denied registration even though it met all the requirements for registration. It should be acknowledged that Obasanjo did hand over power to a civilian government. However, the Obasanjo regime could be said to be the prime initiator of the country's current debt-trap. Under Gowon, Nigeria's external debts stood at US$478 million in 1970 and increased to US$560 million in 1975. However, under Obasanjo, it shot to US$3,969.1 million in 1978. During his period in office, Nigeria took loans it had no need for and most of the money was spent on jamboree projects like Festac 77.

The Babangida Experiment

The downfall of the Shagari civilian government has been well documented (Falola and Ihonbvere 1984; Adamolekun 1985). The most serious and significant reason for the overthrow was the threat to the interests of the bourgeoisie as a result of the inability to manage the country's economic crisis. This was an organic outflow of the Obasanjo era, which now coincided with the cyclical crisis of World Capitalism in the early 1980s, a cover up for which was found in the so-called 'oil-glut'.

When General Muhammadu Buhari's group took over power and set up a neo-fascist regime in January 1984, they began to repress the Nigerian people in an unprecedented manner (Dike 1990; Olukoshi and Abdulraheem 1985; Ekwe-Ekwe 1985). They introduced the Constitution (Suspension and Modification) Decree No.1 of 1984 which suspended vital sections of the Nigerian Constitution, especially Chapter IV of the 1979 Constitution, and gave military decrees superiority. Other decrees were the Federal Military Government (Supremacy and Enforcement of Powers) Decree of 1984 which ousted all powers of civil courts and proceedings against decrees or edicts (of state governments). The Public Officers (Protection Against False Accusation) Decree No.4 of 1984 sought to shield public officers from press attention. Decree No. 2 of 1984 was also promulgated and directed at politicians. By that decree, the Chief of General Staff could arbitrarily throw any of them into detention for a period of six months if they were deemed to have committed. '...acts prejudicial to state security....'

Although Babangida repealed Decree No. 4 of 1984, he promulgated more decrees and consolidated the state security decree by giving powers to the CGS to detain anybody for as long as he pleased.[2] Babangida established the Political Bureau in 1986 with the basic objective of searching for a suitable philosophy of government for Nigeria. After broad consultation, the bureau recommended socialism. This was in spite of the fact that its membership was elitist and hand picked. Babangida rejected that recommendation. He opened the debate on whether Nigerians wanted the government to take the IMF loan and the people returned a resounding NO verdict. Yet he proceeded to pursue the pernicious and imperialist-inspired IMF Structural Adjustment Programme (SAP). The Constitution Review Committee was also made up of Babangida's appointees and close to one-third of the members of the Constituent Assembly (CA) were either his direct appointees or indirect benefactors. The Armed Forces Ruling Council set up a small presidential committee under General Paul Omu and expunged some major recommendations of the CA which were inter alia; that military rule should be declared criminal and that particular presidents should be held liable and accountable for their economic misdeeds. The transition timetable, which effectively started with the recognition of the two political parties in March 1989, signalled a bad omen as their finances, secretariats, manifestos and constitutions were drafted and decreed by the government rather than by their members.

The Political Transition Programme (PTP) was to be aided by an Economic Transition Programme (ETP). It started in June 1986 and was to have terminated in June 1988. However, the government reneged on this promise and imposed the SAP, under which the country is still suffering. Nigerians soon began to doubt Babangida's commitment of handing over power to an elected regime. The continued implementation of ETP through the instrument of SAP created deteriorating social conditions and hardship. The people were forced to resist. In the month of May of every year since 1988, there has been anti-SAP demonstrations in the country. These struggles created structures for the civil society to resist the Babangida regime at the political level, especially after the annulment of the June 12, 1993 elections. Also, it became easy to see the link between a delayed PTP, insincerity in its pursuit and accumulation.

The response of the state was predictably authoritarian, finding outlets in more decrees, and the use of the coercive apparatuses of the state against civil society, co-optation and consequently, shifts in handover dates. Babangida then started consolidating himself through the legal instrument. Decree No. 9 of 1990 insulated three categories of military officers from civil action in court viz.: the President and Commander in Chief of the Armed Forces, the Chief of General Staff and the Military Governors. Decree No. 16 of 1986 eroded university autonomy and increased government supervision of universities. Decree No. 17 of 1986 disaffiliates senior staff unions from the Nigerian Labour Congress. Decree 37 of 1986 empowers Military Governors to deduct special levies from workers' salaries without prior consultation with them. Decree 47 of 1987 prohibits students from taking part in demonstrations and protests and those found guilty are liable to five years in jail or a fine of N50,000 or both. Decree 25 of 1987 disqualifies and bans specific Nigerians, especially politicians and civil servants, from taking part in partisan politics and elections. Decree 25 of 1990 legalises the open ballot system, a relic of stone age democracy.

Decree 38 of 1990 instructs the National Electoral Commission (NEC) to ignore any court order, actions or judgements relating to the transition programme. Decrees 52 and 55 of 1992 oust all powers of courts from interfering in the transition to civil rule programme. Decree 53 of 1992 restricts the powers of the National Assembly in 29 out of 38 subjects. And Decree 54 of 1992 composes the National Security and Defence Council and confers absolute powers on Babangida. Decree 13 of 1993 gives the National Electoral Commission (NEC) unsurpassed powers over elections as a result of the dissolution of the two political parties in November 1992.

Following the annulment of the June 12 election, Babangida repealed Decree 13 of 1992, Decree 53 of 1992, dissolved the NEC, set up a new NEC and established the Interim National Government. Decree 35 of 1993 empowers the military to confiscate and prohibit the circulation of any publication that undermines 'state security'. Decree 43 of 1993 requires all existing newspapers to re-register afresh, with a view to weeding out perceived anti-government press.

Precisely because of the military's disposition, Nigerian civil society has been militarised and its psyche brutalised. And Babangida, in spite of his ideas of being a perceptive liberal (Olagunju, Jinadu and Oyovbaire 1993), had been a very mundane survivalist in his tactical manoeuvring of the transition to civil rule programme. Co-optation, 'settlement' bribes and fraud were used with repression. Fawehinmi (1991), documents that between 1961 and 1991 there have been 164 ouster laws promulgated, covering 216 sections of the statute books. Under Babangida's rule alone, from 1985 to 1991 there were 20 ouster laws (decrees). Babangida was not concerned about democracy, rather, he was obsessed that the military should not allow itself to be stampeded or humiliated out of power. He was conscious of history, yet too devilish in intents and precepts to achieve his goal. The entire transition programme was full of booby traps, occasioning the shift in military disengagement or handover date four times (from 10 October, 1990, to 10 October, 1992, to 2 January, 1992, to August 27 1993). And yet the transition remained interminable and became engulfed in simulated and premeditated crisis. The hidden agenda thesis has been proven and the initial pessimism and scepticism which spectators and commentators anticipated have come to light. It has been argued that the political transition programme was a safety valve for the prolongation of military rule and the faithful implementation of the Economic Transition Programme (ETP) under the SAP, and that has been achieved (Momoh 1992).

Babangida democratised neither the transition process nor civil society. The institutional and statutory instruments put in place to facilitate the PTP helped to consolidate and defend Babangida's dictatorship. What happened to civil society? We have mentioned the numerous decrees that technically excluded a large majority of Nigerians from political participation. The 13 political associations formed by Nigerians were dissolved and two government parties were imposed on the people. And quite arbitrarily, political aspirants were disqualified and their right to a hearing in civil courts was denied. Tribunals were constituted to hear and try cases from civil to criminal matters. Hence the transition to civil rule also had a tribunal constituted for it.

The executives of the political parties were dissolved at will, election primaries, in both parties at both Gubernatorial and Presidential levels, were tampered with by government through supervision and monitoring. Anybody who criticised the government's action was stigmatised as anti-government, or an extremist. He or she was hunted and clamped into detention. Human rights activists who attempted to 'expand the democratic space' by clamouring for multi-partyism, social rights and ,basic freedoms, including the right of Nigerians to decide and choose what form of government, political economy and person they wanted, were persecuted. Recurring names in this regard include Gani Fawehinmi, Beko Ransome Kuti, Femi Falana, Baba Omojola and Segun Maiyegun among others.

Trade unions were banned or subordinated. The Academic Staff Union of Universities and the National Association of Nigerian Students were banned and unbanned twice by the regime. In 1990, seven registered unions were proscribed. These were the Metallic and Non-Metallic Senior Staff Association, the Printing and Publishing Association of

Nigeria, Air Transport Services Employers of Nigeria, Nigeria Mining Employers Association, the Association of Furniture, Fixture and Wood Workers Employers of Nigeria and the Electricity and Gas Workers Senior Staff Association.

The Nigerian Labour Congress was completely subordinated when its rightful President Ali Chiroma was prevented from gaining entrance into the NLC Headquarters and the Personnel Director of John Holt, Mr. Michael Ogunkoya, was imposed as Sole Administrator. He handed over the NLC to a career trade unionist, Paschal Bafyau, in violation of the NLC Constitution. The press was gagged and repressed. No fewer than 35 media houses have been sealed off under the Babangida regime, with nine of them formally banned. Between March 2 and August 23, 1993, it was said that some 274,000 copies of magazines were seized by government agents. And no less that 65 journalists have been in and out of detention for the same period.

The implementation of SAP under the ETP, and the co-optation and 'settlement' policy of the regime has led to the emergence of new patterns of accumulation and a new SAP 'political class', mainly located in and identified with government. Unfortunately, a lot of them are from the intelligentsia and it is doubly tragic that many of them are political scientists. Since 1986, all the Annual Conferences of the Nigerian Political Science Association have been devoted exclusively to the transition to civil rule programme. The Association's communiques have not spared the insincerity and deceit of the Babangida junta from condemnation. Issues contested include the way and manner the theoretical argument for the imposition of the two political parties was put forward, the open ballot system (and its modified version) and the adoption of Option A4 system of candidate nomination (which produced two millionaire Presidential Candidates). The political scientists who served the regime, to say the least, scandalised the discipline and the profession.

Conclusion: Which Route to Democratisation?

Babangida's 'stepping aside' from government on 26 August, 1993, was a demonstration of the will, resilience and determination of Nigerian civil society, especially the 42 affiliate members of the Campaign for Democracy[3] and other ordinary Nigerians and card carriers of both political parties who became disenchanted with the demobilising role, the double speak and insincerity of the regime, of the political class (both executive and legislative), of traditional rulers, and some sections of the business community and metropolitan capital.

The action of civil society, i.e. its non-political wing, has shown that true democracy rather than mere transition to civil rule can only be created by popular will. Already the CD has called for and has been campaigning for a Sovereign National Conference. Indeed, the broad alliance formulation of CD encompasses varying interests and groups from the left, through the centrist to the liberal wing of the political spectrum. It shows that people's popular power is the only enduring solution and check to military usurpation of power. Unless the military as a social force is convinced by 'force of example' that it does not have a monopoly on the use of force, and that 'people's popular will' is superior to their force, we may not get out of the game of musical chairs that political power has become.

This conviction can only come through the democratisation of the instrument of violence and its social and popular use for establishing counterhegemony. For the sake of emphasis and at the risk of repetition, it should be stated that our model of democratisation goes beyond the formalism and rituals of party politics, elections and power transfer. Democratisation must permeate civil society at its interface with the state.

From our analysis, it can be safely concluded that the military has left negative imprints on Nigeria's democratisation process. The military must be seen and made to see itself as a professional interest group just like academics, journalists, etc. although their professional calling makes them rooted in the structure of the repressive apparatuses of the state. They should be re-socialised to see themselves as part of civil society rather than as a force above it. This is possible. After all the military were human beings first before they became what they are today.

Notes

1. At the Samuel Jereton Mariere Inaugural Lecture at the University of Lagos held on October 27, 1972, Dr Nnamdi Azikiwe recommended: 'A civilian based parliamentary democracy invigilated by the Heads of the Armed and Security Forces'. See his *Democracy With Military Vigilance*, Nsukka, African Broco, 1974.

2. For details, see Chukwemeka Gahia, *Human Rights in Retreat*, Civil Liberties Organisation, Lagos, 1993.

3. The Campaign for Democracy (CD), a front that brought together numerous organisations on the platform of the struggle for democracy played a major role in bringing down the Babangida regime.

4

The Military and the Programme of Transition to Democratic Rule

Jibrin Ibrahim

Military Stumbling Blocks to Democratisation

The military has ruled Nigeria for 25 out of the 34 years in which the country has existed as an independent entity with an enormous impact on the country's culture and institutions. The argument of this chapter is that military rule ultimately impacts negatively on society by generalising its authoritarian values which are in essence antisocial and destructive of politics. Politics in this sense is understood as the art of negotiating conflicts related to the exercise of power.

The pace and character of the so-called 'programme of transition to democratic rule' have been dictated by military fiat. Authors such as Harbeson (1987:2) have questioned the assumption that African military regimes are distinct and distinguishable from civilian regimes. He argues correctly that many civilian regimes in the continent are as authoritarian and hierarchical as military regimes. This argument is, however, short-sighted because while civilian regimes are indeed often authoritarian, their authoritarianism often functions as a tactical instrument rather than a world view or value orientation. Military regimes are not only authoritarian in a structural sense, but also in their values and their politics they are bred in a subculture that believes power could be wielded and conserved on the basis of the force that resides within the military institution itself. This is a value system that is committed to the destruction of politics as a cocktail of bargaining, negotiating, force and compromise. These values notwithstanding, military culture in Africa has generally led to the decomposition of political processes and ultimately resulted in the antithesis of the military dream of the forceful imposition of order as seen in the anarchic situations in Somalia, Liberia, Rwanda, to name but a few.

Military regimes have succeeded in permeating civil society with their values — both the formal military values of centralisation and authoritarianism and the informal lumpen values associated with 'barrack culture' and brutality that were derived from the colonial army.[1] The contemporary Nigerian elite has been acquiring a lot of 'barrack culture' over the past few years. Many of them starch and press their clothing in a very military style. The army barracks has become a major social centre for sports, discotheques, consumption of alcoholic beverages, gambling, prostitution, mammy markets etc. At a more significant level, there is a decline in civility and a rise in violence in social interaction. In terms of governance, the most devastating impact of the military has been to spread the myth that they have a useful political role as an institution that can use its 'monopoly' of force to prevent chaos. It will be recalled that since the Gowon era, the military regimes have used the 'impending chaos' argument to postpone promised democratisation. The military institution itself is under stress and almost collapsing with its only basis for a tenuous unity being its determination to stay in power and its hostility to genuine democratisation (Hutchful 1993).

Elections have meaning for most people only in a democratic context because they lead to the choice of decision makers by the majority. Nigeria has a long history of electoral rigging and fraud that has frustrated the wishes of the people to choose those who exercise political power. The country's political class used 'democracy' as a tool to take over the political economy during the First Republic. The groups of Nigerian political entrepreneurs who took power in the middle of the 1950s used it to enrich several people from resources controlled by the state.[2] After over three decades of this process, a neopatrimonial bourgeoisie built on the pillage of state resources has emerged.

It was not only the military that introduced corruption, authoritarianism and antidemocratic tendencies into Nigeria's body politic. From 1954, all the regional governments were involved in big corruption scandals. To cite only a few examples, in 1957, the Forster Sutton Commission found that Nnamdi Azikiwe had placed public funds in his private bank, the African Continental Bank. In 1963, it was the turn of the Coker Commission to reveal that, in the Western Region, Awolowo had appropriated public resources for his own personal use. Many works have been published on what used to be called corruption in Nigeria and which now goes under the more cosy formulation of 'sharing of the national cake'. In the north, for example, the £900 required to register the Northern Peoples' Congress was paid by Kano traders, under the aegis of Ibrahim Gashash, who kept the party's certificate of registration with his bank, as one would do with any other collateral for loans. In return, Gashash was named Minister of Lands and Survey in 1954 (Tahir 1975:84, 439 and 440). Indeed, it would appear that in all the regions, political entrepreneurs took over the control of political parties, a strategy which enabled them to embark on primitive accumulation of capital (Ibrahim 1991). During the successive military and civilian regimes, the extraction of public resources for personal use increased significantly. The relatively large size and scope of the Nigerian economy, coupled with the 'manna' from petroleum, contributed to this.

Nigeria was transformed into a neopatrimonial state based on the promotion of booty capitalism (see Medard 1991). The neopatrimonial bourgeoisie is parasitic and predatory and has no interest in transparence, in accountability, in the existence of political opposition or in the culture of public debate that democracy breeds. The interest of individuals, factions, cliques etc. within the neopatrimonial bourgeoisie is to secure, maintain and expand their access to state resources while trying to exclude the access of others. This ruthless struggle for access fuels the increasing instability of the state. As the bourgeoisie does not have a real autonomous base for accumulation, the struggles do not take place at the level of the economy. Primary sociological categories of an absolute nature such as sect, religion, tribe, ethnic group, language, etc., are the most effective instruments. The political economy that has evolved is therefore not very supportive of a democratic culture.

As mentioned in the first chapter of this book, during the First Republic, regionalism and tribalism totally blocked the parliamentary system. So much so, that it became clear that the ruling parties at the regions and at the centre were not willing to allow another party to win and take over power. An equilibrium of regional tyrannies was maintained for some time until everything ended in civil war. During the Second Republic, there were fewer problems of regionalism and ethnicity but the Hobbesian battles for power increased. Religion and the control of political parties were the main areas of conflict. The nomination of candidates became a particularly serious problem. The majority of candidates had to use party thugs to ensure their victory. Indeed, the Second Republic, just like the First, ended in a situation of non-declared civil war. In the interminable transition to the Third Republic under the Babangida and Abacha regimes, the level of thuggery, acid throwing and even assassination of political opponents has been worse than the preceding cases. The level of violence is then used by the military to justify the 'necessity' for a sultanic leviathan.

It was in this context that the utility of elections in deciding who governs were considerably reduced. Some analysts have even argued that elections serve no useful purpose since all the parties get involved in electoral malpractices. The report of experts prepared by the Nigerian Institute of Policy and Strategic Studies just before the 1983 elections, showed that elections could not be conducted without massive electoral fraud because the parties in power were not ready to allow others to come to power.[3] The report also showed that only the 1959 and 1979 elections were held without systematic rigging and that those two elections had one point in common: they were held in the presence of strong arbiters, the colonial state and the military, who were not themselves participants in the elections and who desired free and fair elections at those instances. The specific legacy from the military is therefore neither corruption nor authoritarianism, much as they took both to new heights. The military legacy is the fabrication of a political culture oriented towards the imposition of a command and control structure on the political process that is destroying the residual democratic values that have managed to survive.

The Military Legacy

Military regimes have played a major role in eroding civil relations and banalising an authoritarian political culture in Africa. Central to the logic of this culture is greed. The military has realised that access to posts of power guarantees enrichment through private appropriation of public resources. The history of the repression and exclusion which the African people have been subjected to has been motivated mainly by the desire of ruling groups to protect avenues of corruption. The result has been a steady reduction in democratic space and values. Almost all the military regimes which took power after overthrowing the first generation of politicians on the continent declared that they took power in order to fight against corruption. It has turned out that each military regime has become more corrupt than the regime from which it took over power.

The Nigerian military is today the major segment of the power elite. They are the most wealthy people in the country and they occupy the summit of most powerful organisations in the country's polity and economy.[4] It is thus not surprising that they have made a significant impact on the political life of the country. The military power elite in Nigeria has always claimed that they were playing a role similar to the one played by Cincinnatus (Oyovbaire 1987:178). In Roman mythology, Cincinnatus was the model par excellence of human selfless service and civic consciousness. He had been invited by the representatives of the people in a period of national decay to carry out a fundamental civic responsibility — to repair and reconstruct the decomposing institutions, structures, and norms of the society. Having brilliantly carried out his civic duty, he scorned the glory of power and appeals for him to remain as ruler, and left the scene.

In contrast to the mythical Roman hero, the soldiers in power in Nigeria have found it increasingly difficult to relinquish power. In January 1966, General Aguiyi Ironsi, who had become Head of State after the coup d'etat organised by the 'Five Majors', declared that he was a temporary impartial arbiter accepting the responsibility of power only for the short time that was necessary to reorganise the world of civilian politics which would then take back the power that belonged to it. It was for that reason that he was advised not to take a political title like President or Prime Minister but to restrict himself to being a temporary Head of State. The three other military regimes that succeeded his regime more or less remained faithful to this idea. A discernable political culture evolved in Nigeria — one that delegitimated military rule, except as short 'corrective' regimes intervening at moments of political crisis. Consistently, when military regimes were settling down as 'natural rulers', Nigerian civil society has arisen, fought for the departure of the military to their barracks and insisted on a return to democracy. A certain form of professional political ethical code was thus imposed on the Nigerian military by civil society — that they could organise occasional military coup d'etats for the resolution of acute political crisis, the reorganisation of structures and institutions and the organisation of elections, but they should not try to perpetuate their rule.

Within the military itself, a resistance to this culture gradually developed. The Gowon regime sought to perpetuate its rule but the Murtala coup led to the acceptance of the agenda of civil society and eventually to the Second Republic. The Buhari regime that ended the Second Republic sought to impose a clearly military value system — that discipline and force, applied in a military manner could resolve the numerous problems confronting Nigeria. The Buhari regime was a sincere attempt to militarise Nigeria and Nigerians abhorred it. That created the conditions for the emergence of the Babangida regime which consciously and deliberately broke with the tradition of the 'impartial arbiter'. General Ibrahim Babangida took the title of 'president' and clearly embarked along a trajectory of personal, as opposed to military, rule.[5] For example, he dissolved and reconstituted the ruling military council at will and informed his military colleagues of his decisions rather than consult with them in the official decision making bodies. He was, however, obliged to pretend to remain within the said political culture and even stated that a 'military regime is an aberration' and that he had no intention of staying in power beyond 1992, one of the years during which he promised to hand over power to civilians (*West Africa* 20/4/87).

The Nigerian military has significantly transformed the country's body politic. In the first place, the military have entrenched the culture of public corruption established by earlier civilian regimes. This is a major change in the country's political culture — in the past, corruption was corruption — unethical or illegal advantages procured through official positions. Gradually, the military became power drunk and started believing they could banalise corruption and use their 'monopoly of force to prevent Nigerians complaining about it. The turning point in this regard was Gowon's attempt to prevent the swearing of affidavits containing accusations of corruption against leading members of his regime.

Under the Babangida and Abacha Administrations, what used to be known as corruption has become the art of government itself. There is a complete prebendalisation of state power and virtually all acts by public officials involving public expenditure or public goods of any kind leads to the appropriation of state finances or property by officials. The routine operations of government are being subjected to prebendal rules. It is widely known, for example, that officials of state governments and parastatals have to pay, as they put it, 'up front' a percentage of their statutory allocations to the Presidency, Ministry of Finance and Central Bank officials before their allocations are released. They, in turn, simply take their own personal shares 'up front' from so called government coffers. Contractors who used to bribe officials for government contracts have been completely sidelined. The President, military governors, ministers etc. simply allocate contracts to their own front companies, and they don't even have to pretend they are doing the job because nobody can dare pose questions.

The country's major resource, petroleum, is now allocated to individuals who sell their allocations to petroleum companies. Custom officers have been reported to have refused to release equipment imported by government because they had not been paid their percentage 'up front'. All the major drug barons arrested by the Agency set up to fight against the narcotics business have been released, or rather, allowed to escape, by their captors and most of the captured drugs have 'disappeared' from government security depots as the anti drug squad becomes the major pusher. There is even a major struggle between different military and security agencies for the control of the lucrative 'drug prevention' business. The military have succeeded in transforming corruption from a deviant activity by public officials into the 'raison d'être' of the Nigerian state. Second, the military have succeeded in destroying Nigerian federalism, sacrificing it on the altar of overcentralisation. The military are structurally incapable of running a federal system because their unified command structure is incapable of accepting that a state government, which they consider to be hierarchically subordinate to the federal government, could have domain over that which it is sovereign, which, as is generally recognised, is the essence of federalism.[6] Nigeria's geopolitical realities have been completely modified. The tripartite structure which had become quadripartite with the creation of the mid-west in 1963, has changed drastically as a result of the multiplication of states whose number now stands at 30. The multiplication of states has produced a Jacobean effect that strengthens the centre by eroding the autonomy of the regions. Nigeria thus finds itself now with a so-called federation that is for all practical purposes a unitary state with some limited devolution of power to the states.

This tendency was reinforced with the decision by former President Babangida on October 1, 1988, to scrap Ministries of Local Governments and establish a Directorate in the Presidency to directly finance and control local governments. The Abacha Administration, which took over from Babangida, has gone a step further, insisting not only on determining the criteria for the appointment of state commissioners and local government caretaker chairpersons, but also insisting on a right of veto over those chosen. It is the height of ridiculousness for the President of a so called federal country to seek to control appointments in the 589 local governments in the country.

The heritage of centralisation established by the military is so strong that it has permeated the civilian political establishment. As far back as 1986, the Nigerian political class seems to have accepted the silly idea that the First Republic failed because the Westminster System produces a weak Prime Minister and that the solution is a strong Executive President who could act in a decisive and unhindered manner (Ibrahim 1986). This resulted in the disastrous allocation of enormous powers, hitherto held by the regions or the cabinet, to the President or the Governor in the 1979, 1989 and 1995 constitutions. The military succeeded in making the civilian politicians accept the principles of military government as a basis for Nigeria's 'democratisation'. The political class forgot that Nigerians had accepted federalism as a guarantee that would help reduce the fears of ethnoregional domination and that these fears could only be allayed if the federating units had real powers that could guarantee people some autonomy in their local operations.

The result was that Nigeria's heritage of a federal and parliamentary tradition, both of which tend to encourage the dispersal of power, were replaced not by the American style presidential system, but by an excessively centralised executive system that centralised power in one person, thus opening the gates, not for the over acclaimed American system, but for the worst form of Jacobean dictatorship. Nigeria has certainly not developed its own military Cincinnatus. Instead, it has created the conditions for the rise of absolute dictators whose totalitarian ambitions are very difficult to contain.

The Military Legacy and Party Politics

The centralising features that the military has imposed on Nigeria have resulted in the extensive use of public law as an instrument for the control of the political process. The single most ominous impact of the military legacy on Nigeria's political process is the imposition of a state command and control system on political parties and party politics. The military seem to believe that good politics is non-party politics and both the 1976 and 1987 non party local government elections were presented as strategies to initiate wholesome politics before parties messed them up. Both the Gowon and Murtala regimes tried to steer the country towards a zero party or one party system with the clear intention of establishing more effective state control over the political process. When these attempts were rejected by civil society, the military used the national unity argument to popularise the idea of the necessity of imposing conditions for the registration of parties.

The immediate result of this was that the definition of a political party was changed from what it was in the first Republic, an organisation formed by a number of people to propagate certain ideas and contest power, to an organisation that is recognised by the state to contest elections. Sections 201 of the 1979 Constitution and 219 of the 1989 Constitution specifically limit the definition of a political party to an organisation recognised by the state to canvass for votes. The law forbids any organisation not so recognised to canvass for votes. More importantly, both on the juridical and political levels, parties were no longer considered as popular organisations that aggregate and articulate interests and opinions but as corporate entities that are registered with the state. This meant that the political significance of parties were no longer determined by popular support, as is the case in all democratic countries in the world, but by administrative fiat.[7]

Thus in the run up to the Second Republic, of the 150 parties announced about 50 of them were fully constituted as parties, but only 18 were able to feel that they had any chance of meeting the imposed conditions and submitted their applications. The·state recognised five of them. The Constitution also banned independent candidates from contesting elections. The naiveté that underscored these decisions was that if regional, ethnic, religious, extremist etc. parties were disallowed, then the people and forces that they represent would somehow disappear. This is the same argument that was used in many African countries to justify the establishment of one party regimes. The tragedy is that as more 'national' parties are imposed in the various countries, ethnic and regional tensions have increased, as more and more people have felt they were being excluded from the political process. The 1979 Constitutional provisions wiped out the right of minorities, who believed they had specific local problems, to form parties to articulate these problems. The concerns that had led to the popularity of parties such as the Bornu Youth Movement, United Middle Belt Congress and the Niger Delta Congress in certain regions during the First Republic were thus disregarded. In addition, the Constitutional provisions for the establishment of offices nation-wide meant parties must necessarily be big and rich, because of the large financial outlay necessary to establish the party infrastructure. Parties with non-mainstream ideological positions were also excluded by administrative fiat. The democratic ideal that a small poor party representing popular interests could develop into a major party was thus excluded.

The 1979 Constitutional provisions also created the basis for the elimination of internal party democracy. The fact that parties were parties because they were recognised by the state meant that party leaders were party leaders not because they were popular with their grassroots members, but because they were so recognised by the state. During the Second Republic, politicians ceased trying to persuade their rivals that they should lead, they simply expelled them for antiparty activities by using money, thugs, and sometimes the police.

The role of party officials became more important than that of party .members because they decided on nominations for electoral posts as factions developed in all the parties, the state became the arbiter that decided on which faction was the 'genuine' representative of the party. The state, however, through the courts and FEDECO, was less than neutral in its decisions. In the GNPP and PRP factional crisis for example, the factions that represented the majority of party members and the elected legislators of the parties were declared illegal and the minority factions were recognised. The frustrated and alienated members were reduced to negotiating with other parties to work out deals for electoral purposes. Many popular politicians were thus denied the right to contest elections. The logic of democratic politics is that parties try to get popular candidates to improve their electoral chances. The logic of the Second Republic was that powerful and rich political entrepreneurs sought to exclude popular candidates from their parties so that they could get an undeserved nomination.[8]

Interminable Democratic Transition as a Ruse for Military Dictatorship

In 1985, General Ibrahim Babangida carried out a palace coup d'etat against the Buhari regime under which he was serving. He was able to carry forward the military project of destabilising the political class and imposing a militaristic conception of politics on the country. In addition, he pushed forward the transformation of the military into a virtual ruling class:

> The military regime have capitalised on the structural adjustment programme to strengthen its control over the political process, contained and domesticated the civilian faction of the bourgeoisie, imposed its 'hegemony' over the pattern of political and economic reproduction and actually laid the foundation for the continuation of military rule beyond the ongoing transition programme. (Ihonvbere 1991:23)

The military faction of the bourgeoisie was henceforth leading not only in wealth, but also in the control of the politico-administrative apparatus of the state.

General Babangida fabricated the most antidemocratic programme of 'a return to democratic rule' in the history of Nigeria. He was like a voluntarist architect, designing a plan for a complete transformation of the Nigerian body politic. His programme covered a long transition period, during which a group of political scientists drew up a programme of 'political crafting' that was supposed to create a new democratic political culture.[9] There were two aspects to the plan. The first involved the resolution of the country's economic and socio-political problems through institutions such as the Directorate for Social Mobilisation, the Centre for Democratic Studies and the Structural Adjustment Programme that would turn Nigeria into a genuine democracy operated by honest people with a sound economy. The second aspect was the political transition programme itself, which had a series of elections that would eventually culminate in a handover to an elected civilian administration. The handover date was, however, a mirage which was postponed from October 1990, to October 1992, to January 1993 and finally to August 1993 when Babangida's military colleagues finally eased him out of power.

General Babangida was indeed like an experienced trapeze artist determined to use his political skills to complete the patrimonialisation of Nigeria's political culture. He had ensured that only the most rapacious political entrepreneurs that had looted the nation's wealth and had no commitment to the people's welfare were in a position to contest for power. The method he used involved an elaborate process of political engineering in which the popular forces were successively excluded from the transition programme through arbitrary and ever-changing rules and corruption was entrenched as the only instrument for the acquisition of political power. The method he used relied on taking the logic of the controlled party to its logical conclusion, fabricating parties that resembled garrisons.

The Garrison Conception of Political Parties

The military closely supervised the design and implementation of the transition programme to ensure that it was in conformity with their world view. They used university intellectuals to produce the drafts and brought in military officers to fine tune the programme. After the Political Bureau drew up the programme, for example, it was handed over to a nine-man committee chaired by and with a majority of military officers for the drafting of the Government's position.[10] The committee charged with drawing up a white paper on democratic transition was said to have worked in close consultation with critical elements of the armed forces and the military administration (see Olagunju *et al.* 1993:165).

The first concern of the soldiers and their intellectual friends was to destabilise the country's political class. The military was conscious that previous military attempts to control the political process had been derailed by politicians. In 1986, the military junta announced a ten year ban on some old politicians. In September 1987, the ban was extended to the totality of those who had held political office in all proceeding civilian and military regimes and in 1989 the ban was extended to all those who had been heads of the various transition agencies. A new breed of 'grassroots politicians', 'untainted' by multiparty politics, were to be created. The idea was that grassroots persons elected in the 1987 non party local government elections were suitable material for the formation of the new breed parties. When, however, these local government councillors started consulting nationally in an attempt to form a nation wide grassroots party, they were destabilised by the Government which summarily dissolved all local government councils. The military and their friends rejected a multiparty framework and proposed a two party system with both parties requiring state registration. To determine the two political parties to be registered, the National Electoral Commission (NEC) and the government imposed expensive and virtually impossible preconditions that only the upper section of the bourgeoisie or old politicians with established networks could have afforded or met. In three months, the parties were to establish well equipped offices with at least three paid staff in all the 435 local government areas in the country. In addition, they were to supply 25 membership lists of their parties comprising the names, photographs and personal details of at least 200 members from each local government in the country (making at least 87,000 individual membership files per party) to the NEC. For good measure, prospective parties were to submit their applications with a registration fee of 50,000 naira. In spite of these draconian measures, 13 parties were able to submit their files before the deadline.[11] In a broadcast to the nation on October 6, 1989, the Head of State in a perfect Catch 22 scenario used the argument that the 'impossible' preconditions had not been perfectly adhered to as a justification to refuse to register any of the parties. The political parties, he said, had:

> failed to comply with key conditions in the guidelines such as documentation on members, declaration of assets and liabilities of individual members of the national executive committees [...] most of them (parties) had operated underground prior to the lifting of the ban on politics on 3rd May 1989 [...] (and) had deep roots in the party politics of the First and Second Republics. There were very strong indications of the wealthy individuals in the executive committees of the associations that confirm fears that they were being hijacked by moneybags.

The idea that a mass party should know all its members and have files on them is a very military one. To control the political process, the military were ready to deny the reality of democratic parties who had differential levels of commitment, such as members who would want to register and sympathisers who might not bother to register but might vote for the party. In addition, the whole idea of democratic elections is that attempts are made by candidates to transfer the loyalty of voters from one party to another, so adherence to parties is never a rigid bureaucratic issue. No democratic party in the world can give exact and detailed information on all its members at any point in time, so when the military and their intellectuals insisted on these conditions, one cannot but be suspicious of their motives. Their insistence that the politicians of the Third Republic could not have contacts or connections with old politicians was clearly mischievous. Similarly, the rule that wealthy people must not play a major role in the parties or use their money to win votes, at a time when their economic policies were creating a tiny minority of excessively wealthy people in a sea of mass poverty, was nothing short of pure mischief.

The government eventually decided to dissolve all the 13 registered parties. One of the closest political advisers of the military admits that the parties were dissolved because none of them met the vision and objectives of the military administration (Olagunju *et al.* 1993:214). The military wanted 100 per cent control over the parties.

The next step they took was to create two new parties, allegedly for the 'ordinary people' the Social Democratic Party and the National Republican Convention, with the former leaning 'a little to the left of centre' and the latter leaning 'a little to the right of the centre'. The task of overseeing and coordinating the institutionalisation of the two parties was given to a transition committee under the chairmanship of another military man and former Chief of Air Staff, Ibrahim Alfa (Olagunju *et al.* 1993:215). It was under his military direction that the government drew up the manifestos and constitutions of the two parties, and decided to fund and staff them, before calling on individuals (as opposed to organised groups) to sign up. As Anthony Enahoro said:

> My judgement of the two bodies is that they are military government parastatals being paraded as political parties for the benefit of the outside world (1992:56).

In an interesting response to this development, former military Head of State General Obasanjo, delivered a stinging rebuke to General Babangida for using gimmicks to cling to power although he ended up with the 'normal military' vision of order and discipline as the most important elements of parties:

> Those who call the two government created parties parastatals are even being generous. Parastatals at least have effective and accountable chief executives, who can enforce *order* and *discipline*. The same cannot be said about the government created parties. And yet they are the vehicle through which it is hoped that a stable democracy will be nurtured. We delude ourselves (my emphasis) (*Newswatch* 23/11/92).

What was clear from the transition programme was that the military government had decided to define and apply each 'democratic' step on behalf of the people. They were determined, and had the capacity, to stamp their world view on the so called democratisation process.

Apart from imposing manifestos and constitutions on the two parties, excessive powers were given to government appointed Administrative Secretaries to organise their takeoff and to exclude undue radicals, socialists, anti-Structural Adjustment Programme agitators as well as alleged ideological and religious extremists from them. In addition, Decree 48 of 1991 gave the National Electoral Commission (NEC), established by the Military Government, wide ranging powers to disqualify any political aspirant whose action was 'likely to disrupt the process of grassroots democracy' and the law was amended with Decree 6 of 1992 which widened these powers by absolving the NEC of the duty of explaining or giving reasons for disqualification. This law enabled the NEC to disqualify 32 aspirants who had already won their party's nominations for the Senatorial and House of Assembly elections in July 1992. In October 1992, the government sacked elected party leaders and appointed caretaker committees to run their affairs. In the spirit of the times, one of the chairpersons, Air Vice Marshall Shekari, was a retired military officer. The caretaker committees were directed by the NEC to reregister party members with the provision that they should not accept more than 2,000 members in each ward (Tell, 18/1/1993). This level of arbitrariness by the NEC was indeed scandalous.

The Hidden Agenda:
Elections Without Choice or the Choice of the Military'

The politically acute Nigerian press discerned after two to three years that General Babangida had a hidden agenda which involved using the so called programme of transition to civilian rule as a ploy to cling to power for as long as possible. While launching the Political Bureau in January 1986, General Babangida had announced that power would be handed over to a democratically elected civilian regime in 1990 and the Report of the Political Bureau confirmed this date. However, he clung to power until August 1993, when he was finally pushed out of power by his equally ambitious military colleagues.

At every twist and turn of the convoluted transition programme, President Babangida's government tried to create conditions that would make the process collapse. The National Electoral Commission was established in 1987 to manage the political parties and the elections under the leadership of a respected retired professor, Eme Awa. When the government realised he was not amenable to manipulation, he was removed and replaced by a more pliable professor, Humphry Nwosu.

The most dramatic aspect of the transition was the commercialisation of the nomination and electoral process through the use, or rather abuse, of the open ballot or queuing system in which the secret ballot was disallowed and voters queued up in public behind the party symbol of their 'choice'. The political parties and elections would henceforth operate on the principles of the Garrison parade. The open ballot debate was initiated by Ahmadu Kurfi who proposed queuing as an antidote to rigging, fondly calling it the Fatima Principle.[12] Kurfi argued that a close examination of the history of electoral fraud in the country revealed that they were all linked to the manipulation of the ballot and that by eliminating the ballot and making people queue up in public, the instrument for cheating was eliminated. While it was indeed true that ballots have been used extensively in electoral fraud in Nigeria, Kurfi underestimated the two other, even more traumatic methods used to cheat in elections, preventing candidates from submitting their nomination papers, as was frequently done during the First Republic and rigging by 'official FEDECO declaration' as was the case during the 1983 general elections.[13]

Over and above the technical details of 'secret ballot rigging' the most serious problem with the open ballot system was its fundamentally antifree choice, and thus antidemocratic character. When it was proposed, the Sultan of Sokoto, Ibrahim Dasuki, had complained about its antidemocratic character, citing possible problems such as that of virtually denying wives and peasants the possibility of benefiting from the secret ballot to vote against the candidates of their more powerful husbands and patrons respectively (*Citizen* 15/10/1990). He was later proved right, but unfortunately for him, he had, for whatever reasons, recanted and claimed that he was misquoted. Most informed opinion in Nigeria was against the open ballot but the government went ahead to implement it in 1990 and the transition intellectuals went out of their way to defend it. The direct effect of the system was that candidates paid people to vote for them and party aides could directly observe and ensure that people who have been 'bought' joined the queue of the aspirant who had paid for their vote. Much has been written in the press of the naira notes sandwiched in bread slices given to voters already in queues to make them shift to the rival queue.

The NEC Chair, Humphry Nwosu, once complained that Nigerian voters were corrupt because they would take money from one candidate and vote for another. What a tragedy that Nigerian citizens were denied even this meagre right to frustrate their wealthy enemies. Not surprisingly, the state governors that were elected in 1991 were known to be some of the most corrupt and notorious elements in the society. They included a well known cocaine dealer and somebody who had been found guilty by a Judicial Tribunal of bankrupting a state-owned National Supply Company by stealing its resources. They were political entrepreneurs who had decided to invest in the political game to make more money. It has been estimated, for example, 'that no serious presidential candidate spent less than 50 million naira ($2.5 million) for his or her campaigns.[14]

The open ballot has been described by Nwosu as Nigeria's unique form of democracy, its own innovation just like the Americans, British and Japanese have theirs. After the first 1992 presidential primaries, however, he complained that the system was 'riddled with wealth, falsification of figures, threats and favouritism' (*Newswatch* 23/11/93). It was a pity that it took this professor, described by the Nigerian press as a crack political scientist, so long to discover something so obvious. But then, it is doubtful if the 'transition professors' actually believed the silly things they were saying and doing while in office.

From the primaries for the 1990 local government elections, the garrison political parties started revealing their paramilitary character. They became embroiled in squabbles over who was allowed to be a genuine party member, that being the qualification necessary to participate in rigging. The general principle was that the faction that succeeded in 'capturing' the party executive issued party cards to its clients and made sure possible supporters of its rivals were not officially registered as party members. A lot of squabbles developed over determining 'genuine party members' and the issue of party cards became a do or die issue because it was used to rig nomination of party candidates. In a manner reminiscent of communist parties and in direct contradiction to the tradition of democratic parties, belonging to the faction became a central precondition for belonging to the party.

In addition, after successfully crossing the party Rubicon, nominees had to have security clearance from the state to be recognised as genuine nominees. It was not enough for candidates to rig their nomination, the soldiers in charge of state security had to declare that the candidate was suitable before he/she was allowed to contest for any election. It was the worst travesty of democracy in Nigerian history. The level of manipulation was so high that all prospective presidential candidates had to see President Babangida personally and seek his blessing, as it were, to contest. He encouraged many of them to go ahead and it is generally believed that he gave a lot of them a lot of money to contest, so that he could turn around later and accuse them of unethically using money to influence voters.

The NEC played a major role in managing the 'hidden agenda' by creating excuses and confusion in the electoral process. In March 1992, for example, Nwosu argued that the October 1992 handover date was unrealistic because that would necessitate an election during the rainy season, a great difficulty because people would have to queue for hours during torrential rains. A few days later, he came out to announce that it was necessary to hold the National Assembly elections in July, in the middle of the rainy season, because people were behaving as if only the Presidential elections mattered *(Tell* 22/4/1992). By holding the legislative elections in July, and refusing to conduct the presidential elections at the same time, they created conditions for a one sided diarchy controlled by the military.

Most of the elections were characterised by what former governor Bola Ige called 'free style rigging that made the occurrences of the Second Republic appear sluggish and amateurish' *(Guardian* 12/10/1992). The first set of leading Presidential candidates for the two parties were disqualified by NEC for using money and rigging the primaries. The adoption of the 'Option A4' method was purportedly designed to resolve the problem of undue influence from moneybags. The idea was to organise primaries through a series of elections from the ward level through the local governments and states to the national level. However, by multiplying the number of times and places of elections, the costs of transport and feeding etc., skyrocketed, thus making the nomination open to the highest bidder. Not surprisingly, the 1992 presidential primaries were characterised by massive rigging and falsification of figures.

In a last ditch attempt to get the General to hand over power, the two parties virtually nominated close personal friends and business associates of President Babangida as their presidential candidates M.K.O. Abiola for the SDP and Bashir Tofa for the NRC. After a lot of procrastination by the government and determined protest against another postponement by the people, presidential elections were finally held on June 12, 1993. The candidate of the SDP won neatly in an election that was surprisingly generally considered free and fair. The elections were above all a referendum in which Nigerians voted to oust Babangida, but he would not take no for an answer. He cancelled the elections and tried to initiate yet another round of 'political crafting'. There was so much mass protest against the cancellation that he had to leave power in haste and hand over to an incompetent and powerless civilian without any mandate, creating the basis for yet another coup d'etat in November 1993 by his former second in command, General Abacha.

The 'new' Abacha Administration seems to be determined to keep to the Babangida policy of perpetuating military rule while using the ruse of an interminable transition programme to keep the democrats and politicians occupied. A Constitutional Conference was convened in the second half of 1994 and it was supposed to finish its deliberations in December 1994. It did finish, but later reconvened in early 1995, an obvious strategy to prolong its assignment and delay the process of power transfer. However, the conference proposed that the military junta should hand over power to a democratically elected government in January 1996. Since the conference took that decision, the military has refused to let them sit again and has also refused to commit itself to any hand over date.

Conclusion

Nigerian civil society has a strong political culture oriented to the struggle for the democratisation of society. For almost 30 years, civil society has been resisting the consolidation of the military as a ruling class from which succeeding generations of the country's rulers are drawn. The military, on the other hand, has succeeded in introducing a military political counter culture of a controlled 'garrison' democracy in which the state and those who control it, (soldiers for most of the life of the postcolony), decide on the individuals and parties that are allowed to rule in the brief interregnums between long periods of military rule. The military has even succeeded in recruiting leading, hitherto liberal, members of the political science community to propound the mischievous and palpably opportunist argument that the military leadership has been inducted into mainstream liberal democratic and federalist ideology and that:

> The belief in and commitment to this heritage provide the rationale and justification for military intervention as the last bastion of democracy in this country (Olagunju, Jinadu and Oyovbaire 1993:32).

The military has not only destroyed Nigeria's federal system, its has played a major role in eroding the country's democratic assets. Be that as it may, a powerful movement for the promotion of human rights and for multiparty democracy is growing in the country, a movement which may yet be able to confront and destroy the ambitions of the military and their friends.

Notes

1. The term 'barrack person' in Nigerian English or 'dan bariki' in Hausa suggests someone who is uncouth, uncultured, rough and violent.
2. For the means used, see the classical article by S. Osoba, 'The Nigerian Power Elite: 1952-1965' in P. Gutkind and P. Waterman, *African Social Studies: A Radical Reader*, Heineman, London, 1977.
3. National Institute for Policy and Strategic Studies, *Roundtable Meeting on the 1983 General Elections*, Kuru, 1983.
4. We include the large crop of retired army officers in this category.
5. Traditionally, military rule always begins as collegiate rule among a section or faction of the military. However, the culture of unified command and authoritarianism invariably leads to the emergence of one man dictatorship as numerous examples such as Mobutu, in Zaire, Kountche in Niger and Eyadema in Togo have shown.
6. The other entity incapable of operating a federal system, for the same reason, is a communist state, in which the Leninist theory of organisation is incompatible with the federal idea of certain areas of exclusive competence for the regions or states.
7. During the First Republic, there were about 150 parties in the country but only about 10 were politically significant. The party system was much more democratic than what we had in the Second Republic.
8. See Ibrahim (1991) for a detailed analysis of factionalism and the politics of exclusion within the National Party of Nigeria.
9. The three major Professors of Political Science that 'crafted' Babangida's diabolical democratic transition that never was, have recently published a book of self justification. See T. Olagunju, A. Jinadu and S. Oyovbaire, *Transition to Democracy in Nigeria: 1985-1993*, Safari Books, Ibadan, 1993.
10. The chair was General Paul Omu, other members were Brigadier Diya, Commodore Kanu, Brigadier Mamman, Air Vice-Marshall Imam, Professors Nzimiro, Elaigwu and Aliyu with Alhaja Okunnu of the Cabinet office as secretary. See Olagunju *et al.* (1993:163).
11. It was political farce at its worst. Nigeria ran out of photographic materials and polaroid films in the stampede to produce photographs of their members and emergency imports had to be made and people were paid to have their photographs taken etc. The parties had to hire lorries to carry hundreds of thousands of the hurriedly prepared membership files to the NEC.
12. Fatima is the name of his wife. Kurfi was FEDECO secretary for the 1979 elections and has written a book on the 1959 and 1979 general elections. The article in question is: 'The Fatima Principle: Antidote to Rigging', *New Nigerian*, April 15 and 16, 1986.
13. There were elaborate anti-fraud safeguards during the 1983 elections and much of the rigging was done by disregarding the real returns and simply declaring fabricated results at FEDECO collation centres.
14. For some detailed examples of the types and scale of the expenses incurred, see 'The Money Game', *African Concord*, 21 September 1992.

5

Feminism or Femocracy? State Feminism and Democratisation

Amina Mama

Introduction

The constitutional and legal status of women and women's participation in all levels of governance have long been taken as key indicators of the general level of a country's democracy, usually on the basis that since women constitute a historically oppressed and marginalised group and at least half of most national populations, their level of political representation and participation is crucial. This is as true of African countries as it has been in Western Europe and North America.

In Africa, national liberation movements called for and relied upon the active participation and support of women at all levels of the anti-colonial struggle. The manner in which women participated has differed from country to country, but all such movements involved women in one way or another. The degree of their involvement has often been taken as an index of how progressive a movement was, something which has become increasingly important for those seeking to secure the support of the international community over the last decade or so. It is fair to say that the exigencies of engaging in national liberation struggles — which in some cases have involved waging full scale war against occupying forces — required women's active involvement, whether or not the struggle included a commitment to women's liberation. In any case, a great many African women identified national liberation as being in their interests as women, and participated wholeheartedly through their own organisations or through the movement itself, in the various ways that have been amply documented (Jayawardena 1986; Abdel-Kadr 1988; Urdang 1979, 1989; Russell 1989; Organisation of Angolan Women 1984; Mba 1982; Walker 1982; Staunton 1992).

During the post-colonial period, it has increasingly become incumbent upon independent states to display a commitment to improving the status and participation of women. A cynic might be forgiven for suggesting that with independence, African governments have found it expedient to exploit the gender question so as to receive economic aid in an international climate that has become increasingly sympathetic towards women's demands for greater equality. The fact is that despite the virtual absence of a mass-based women's movement in most African countries, the majority of African states have, for one reason or another, begun to profess a gender politics that is usually couched in terms of encouraging women's integration into development. The WID paradigm, as it has been dubbed, has come under attack from feminist scholars who have rightly pointed out that it assumes women have not been contributing to development, and in so doing, ignores women's work and denies the manifold ways in which development strategies have themselves contributed to women's marginalisation and oppression (DAWN 1988). The actual situation of women and the steps being taken by African governments in the name of increasing women's participation in development vary widely across the region, throwing up interesting questions about the relation between gender politics and democratisation.

In the present era of democratisation, it is both theoretically and politically important to assess the changes in gender politics accompanying the transition away from military and civilian dictatorships, and towards civilian and multiparty forms of government. One may ask, for example, whether multipartyism affords better opportunities for the liberation of women than one-partyism? Or whether civilian regimes necessarily grant greater political space to women than military regimes? What space do transition programmes provide for the realisation of women's political ambitions?

Research in the area of women and the state in Africa has so far addressed itself to the effects of the colonial and post-colonial state on women, for the most part noting the ways in which both have enhanced male power over women, and the way in which the state has been primarily a vehicle of male elite interests (Parpart and Staudt 1989). Others have highlighted how women have struggled to defend and advance their individual and collective interests under the changing conditions of colonialism and post-colonialism (Mba 1989; Tsikata 1990; Amadiume 1987; Mann 1985). A great many studies have empirically examined the ways in which legislation discriminates against women, the ways in which national and local development strategies have advanced male interests over women's interests, enhanced male domination in the formal economy as well as in the home, and excluded women from governance. In accordance with all the evidence demonstrating the role of the state in the oppression of women, efforts aimed at improving the situation of women have also targeted the state, for example by calling for legal reforms.

Attention lately has been turned to considering why the state affects women in the ways that have been specified. There is substantial agreement in characterising post-independence African states as patriarchal, but this is variously attributed to the fact that the colonial regimes that they are derived from excluded women, to the nature of precolonial African culture, or it is ascribed to the actual processes of state formation. One commentator puts it this way:

> Women have neither played a significant part in the creation of the modern state system on the continent, nor have they been able to establish regular channels of access to decision-makers. State policies toward women have, as a result, exhibited varying degrees of discrimination and coercion (Chazan 1989:186).

Given the widely made observation that women played a key role in many of the region's national liberation movements, this appraisal raises a further question: did all the women and women's organisations active in the independence struggles simply opt out of public life once independence was achieved, or were they disenfranchised? Nowadays, even if all states discriminate against women, do women simply allow this to happen, or is there more to the picture than Chazan suggests? Are post-colonial states a site of gender struggles, and if so, what form do these struggles take? Even if we agree that post-colonial states discriminate against and are coercive towards women, can we still say that women play no significant part in the state? More pertinently, can we say that women have played no significant part in the changes that have recently swept away a number of long standing dictatorships, and threaten to remove the remaining autocracies?

Whatever the specific role of women in contemporary African states, it is increasingly clear that gender cannot be left out of our analyses. Furthermore, instead of limiting ourselves to considering the impact on and exclusion of women, a more fruitful approach may be to consider the ways in which state formation and state practices are all gendered, and to analyse the involvement of women in these processes and practices.

It seems fair to suggest that now, several decades into the post-colonial epoch for most African nations, women are likely to have gained in political experience, regardless of whether men have elected to include them in the state or not, especially if the state has continued to be a major perpetrator of sexist discrimination. Perhaps African women's political maturation has been most visible at international fora. African women not only hosted the Nairobi Conference at the end of the UN Decade for Women (1975-1985), but were highly articulate and active in both the governmental and non-governmental organisations that participated in the Decade. Locally, too, African women have been engaging in political action, both within and outside of the state. The African community subsequently pioneered efforts to carry out the Nairobi resolutions. By the end of the decade, several regional structures had been put in place: the African Training and Research Centre for Women was set up in 1975, designed to be a focal point for women and development activities in the ECA secretariat. The ACTRW was to be supported by the African Regional Coordinating Committee for the Integration of Women in Development (ARCC) and by subregional organs in the five ECA Multinational and Operational Centres (MULPOCs).

By the end of the UN Decade, 51 African countries had set up national machineries with a mandate to promote the full integration of women into development and to eliminate discrimination on grounds of sex. These have taken various forms, the most prominent being the Ministries set up in, for example, Côte D'Ivoire. Others have established women's bureaux, departments or divisions within Ministries (Uganda's Ministry for Women and Development, Youth, Sports and Culture), or commissions, committees or councils, such as the Ghanaian National Council for Women and Development set up in 1975. In countries with political parties, the women's wings of the ruling party may have acted as the national women's structure, as Tanzania's Umoja wa Wanawake Tanzania, formed in 1962. Finally, in a number of cases, non-governmental organisations have succeeded in acting as the main vehicles for women's development, although in recent years many of these have been eclipsed, or taken over by governments, as was the case with the Sudanese Women's Union. How successful these regional and national structures have been is a subject for debate. It is now clear that international structures can go no further than their component governments in any matter. In order to consider the efficacy of the regional structures for the advancement of women, the situation prevailing within national structures for women must first be known.

In a number of states, individual women have capitalised on the internationally favourable climate and their positions as wives of Heads of State to assume powerful new roles, often arrogating to themselves the right to represent and lead women. The First Lady phenomenon, as it has been dubbed, has reached new levels of prominence, begging a number of questions regarding the democratic character of this form of gender politics, and its likely impact on ordinary African women. The First Lady Syndrome was conspicuous in the early days of Kenyan independence, and following Siyad Barre's seizure of power in Somalia; The wives of both Heads of State wielded a great deal of public influence and amassed vast fortunes for themselves. More recently, African First Ladies have developed organisational proclivities. In Ghana, for example, the government structure — the National Council for Women and Development — has been effectively eclipsed by the December 31 Women's Movement, founded and run by Mrs Nana Agyeman Rawlings, and is now far more prominent nationally and internationally than the official structure for women's development.

It is these post-colonial developments in African gender politics that I hope to address by posing the question: feminism or femocracy? ·Feminism is defined as being the popular struggle of African women for their liberation from the various forms of oppression to which they are subjected. Just as the oppression of women takes many forms — psychological, cultural, economic and political — so to does the struggle for women's liberation. The term itself has been variously defined,[1] but common to all such definitions is the idea of women organising autonomously to defend collective interests or to combat forces identified and defined as inimical by women. In Nigerian history, struggles that could be defined as feminist include, the mass uprisings of women that occurred in eastern Nigeria during the colonial period and the collective organisation of Egba women to oust chiefs (Mba 1982; Amadiume 1987). More recent examples include the collective mobilisation of Ogbarefe and Ekpan women against the oil industry in 1984 and 1986 respectively (Turner and Oshare 1993).

Feminism is here counterpoised to the idea of a femocracy — an antidemocratic female power structure which claims to exist for the advancement of ordinary women, but is unable to do so because it is dominated by a small clique of women whose authority derives from their being married to powerful men, rather than from any actions or ideas of their own. Femocracies exploit the commitments of the international movement for greater gender equality while actually only advancing the interests of a small female elite, and in the long-term undermining women's interests by upholding the patriarchal status quo. In short, femocracy is a feminine autocracy running in parallel to the patriarchal oligarchy upon which it relies for its authority, and which it supports completely. It is worth distinguishing femocracy from the dual-sex system that anthropologists have delineated (Okonjo 1981; Amadiume 1987) for several reasons. The most obvious of these is that in such systems, the female political structure is one that owes its authority to women, rather than to the power wielded by one's spouse. Furthermore in the traditional dual systems that have been outlined, even male councils were elected or otherwise mandated by the people of the community, rather than having seized power by the gun, or by electoral fraud.

Given that women have succeeded in establishing femocracies in a number of African countries, it is incumbent upon us to ask the question: can a femocracy result in changes in gender relations, or improve the prospects of ordinary women? Can femocracy be democratised? More generally, can state structures act as vehicles for ordinary women's struggles, or do they only serve the femocracy? In what follows, a case study of Nigeria is used to address these questions.

Gender Politics of Military Vs Civilian Rule

In discussing the Nigerian situation, one cannot avoid starting with the militarised character of the Nigerian state. Nigerians have now probably endured more years of military dictatorship than any other African country, with the catastrophic exception of Somalia. The military have ruled for 24 of the 34 years that have passed since independence, and her seventh set of soldiers are currently in power. With the exception of one assassination, and one hand over (discounting the most recently thwarted transition programme), all have been ousted by the same mechanism that brought them to power: military coup d'etat.

At first glance, this is easily seen to be a highly patriarchal set-up because of the exclusively male nature of the upper levels of the Nigerian military. Nonetheless, it is worth digressing briefly to point out that military rule is not necessarily exclusively male. Military rule as practised within liberation movements has often advanced the interests of women, encouraging their participation as freedom fighters as well as supporters, as was the case in Zimbabwe's ZANU, Mozambique's FRELIMO, the Angolan MPLA and the Eritrean EPLF, to name only a few. In Nigeria's own history, several women stand out as having been military leaders themselves: women like Amina of Zazzau who led her troops on wars of conquest, or Queen Kambassa of Bonny who is acknowledged to have pioneered the militarisation of the Bonny state (Awe 1992:30-35). In addition to these, highly successful women like Iyalode Efunsetan Aniwura of Ibadan were rewarded with high-ranking titles during periods of military rule in nineteenth century Yorubaland

(Awe 1992:55). In theory, it would be possible for a military government to include women at the highest level. Nonetheless, today's Nigerian military apparently owes no allegiance to these antecedents, having started out as an all-male colonial force whose primary responsibility was to ensure the subjugation of the population. Elsewhere it has been noted that the British saw the creation of an all-male army as a key step in exercising their hegemony over the societies they sought to dominate (Mies 1986).

Military rule may not necessarily be completely male-dominated, but in Nigeria it does appear to be so. Given that no women have ever ascended to the top echelons of the Nigerian army, it comes as no surprise to find that women have played no significant role in central government during the seven military regimes. But have the few years of civilian rule allowed for greater participation of women in government? Mba (1989) points out that women appear not to have fared any better under the few years of civilian government. She reminds us that at independence, the northern region was so virulently opposed to women being given the vote that only women in the former southern regions were enfranchised. Nonetheless, men in the former northern region insisted on being given seats on behalf of the disenfranchised female population as well as themselves in the first House of Assembly. Hajiya Gambo Sawaba, one of the exceptional few northern women activists, was repeatedly harassed and assaulted for participating in politics, and for joining hands with southern women to campaign for the vote (Mba 1982; Shawalu 1990).

Although General Gowon supported the idea of women being given the vote in the 1973 discussions about returning the country to civilian rule, (a handover which never occurred), northern men mounted such vocal opposition to this that he found it necessary to backtrack, finally declaring that in the north, only 'educated women' should vote, a move which provoked further outcry, this time from women's organisations. It was not until 1979 that the Obasanjo military regime, backed with all the coercive powers of a dictatorship, was able to introduce universal suffrage for women (Draft Local Government Edict No. 189, 1976). As Mba points out, this was probably not due to any particular commitment to women's liberation, but an almost incidental development that occurred during the drafting of the Local Government Electoral Regulations (Mba 1989:76).

In the rest of the country, women threw themselves into politics both before and after independence, generating a history ably documented elsewhere (Mba 1982). Nonetheless few women have been allowed to play any significant part in government. Although this may be partly a result of the military having dominated the state for so long, the fact is that in Nigeria, military rule has always involved significant civilian participation, and so could have involved more women, had those in power been of a mind to do so. As it was, the first woman commissioner was Flora Nwapa — also Nigeria's first women novelist — who was appointed in 1970 by the civilian administrator of East Central State during the military government of Yakubu Gowon. She was followed by Dorothy Miller in North Central State, Folake Solanke and Ronke Doherty in Oyo State and Kofoworola Pratt in Lagos State (Mba˜ 1989:72).

The Gowon administration (1966-1975) was supplanted by a military coup led by General Murtala Mohammed, who was in turn assassinated within a few months of taking office, to be replaced by General Olusegun Obasanjo, who was to rule from 1976-1979 and to usher in the civilian Second Republic. The policies of these regimes were not significantly different from their predecessors in their gender politics, continuing the almost complete exclusion of women from government. None involved women at the federal level or on any of the major commissions they set up. At state level, however, it became unofficial policy to appoint one token woman commissioner out of about ten per state, usually to advise on social welfare or education. During the first set of local government elections under Obasanjo, in which women across the country ran as well as voted, six women were elected in the northern states (including Gambo Sawaba in Zaria's Sabon Gari District), eight in Anambra and a handful in Lagos and Oyo states. All in all, the total number of women elected amounted to no more than a minuscule minority of the 299 local government councils.

When it came to electing the highly elitist Constituent Assembly, only one woman, Chief Janet Akinrinade, was elected, perhaps as a result of her status as a powerful businesswoman, while four others were appointed, making the total up to 5 out of 250, that is, less than 2 per cent women. The Constituent Assembly was to approve the Draft Constitution produced by the Constitution Drafting Committee, a 50-man body set up in 1975, with not a single woman on it. Little wonder then, that the Draft Constitution too had no provisions for women. This was challenged by one of the four women on the Constituent Assembly, Abigail Ukpabi, who was supported by other women members, a vocal few thus succeeding in passing a historically significant amendment to the Constitution, outlawing sexual discrimination in customary or Islamic law for the first time in Nigerian history:

A citizen of Nigeria of a particular community, ethnic group, place of
origin, sex, religion or political opinion shall not by reason only that he is
such a person be subjected either expressly by or in the political
application of any law force in Nigeria (Proceedings of the Constituent
Assembly of the Federal Republic of Nigeria, Official Report, Vol.
III:2334-2343).

When the ban on political associations was lifted on September 21, 1978,
a few women rushed to announce their political intentions as eagerly as
the men (see Mba 1989:79-82). Since political associations were subject
to the requirement that they were not formed on the basis of ethnicity,
religion or sex, women soon discovered they would be better off
operating under the auspices of the national political parties which
emerged. However, here they did not fare very well, since women's
wings largely confined their activities to registering women voters and
campaigning and dancing for their parties. Amongst northern women
politicians, Hajiya Gambo Sawaba and Hajiya Laila Dogonyaro stood
out, as did the rivalry between them. Gambo Sawaba joined the Great
Nigerian People's Party (GNPP), while Laila Dogonyaro ran on the
ticket of the conservative National Party of Nigeria which eventually
won the elections. Bola Ogumbo achieved the highest position of any
woman when she was selected as running mate to the late Aminu Kano,
presidential candidate of the radical People's Redemption Party.
Nonetheless, a great many women were active in party politics, more
visibly so at local and state levels. Shettima (undated) points out that of
the five parties registered for the 1979 elections, only two had particular
provisions for women: the GNPP manifesto proclaimed that they would
make it compulsory for employers with more than 20 women employees
to have child-care centres at their places of work, and the NPN declared
that it was:

...committed to the development of our womenfolk on an identical base
with menfolk to enable them to realise the innate qualities in themselves.
Our womenfolk will be actively encouraged by the NPN to come forward
and play a full part in public life (cited in Shettima, undated:1)

When the Second Republic (1979-1983) came into being, led by
President Shehu Shagari, a northern former schoolmaster, the record
continued to be poor. At Federal level there were three women Ministers:
of National Planning (Mrs Oyegbola), Education (Mrs Ivase) and Internal
Affairs (Chief Akinrade). Despite these first steps, the power houses
retained a scornful attitude: the Speaker of the House of Representatives
declared that women were not fit to head committees. In any case, very
few had been elected to the decision-making bodies: 17 women contested

for the 450 member House of Representatives and only three won, whereas of the five women who had contested for the 95 member senate, only one was victorious.

Regrettably, we cannot conclude on the basis of this track record that Nigeria's civilian regimes have adopted a significantly more favourable position than the military with regard to involving women in public life. However, the poor civilian track record cannot be taken as indicating that Nigeria's military rulers have been more democratic. Elections, albeit first at local government level and under military rule, and later to the Constituent Assembly, the House of Representatives and the Senate offered a democratic space in which women could participate. Given time and experience, the fortunes of women at the polls could only have improved. This was not to be so.

The return of the military through the 1983 coup d'etat led by Generals Buhari and Idiagbon, saw women once again excluded from Federal levels of government. As usual, no women sat on the Supreme Military Council. There were no women ministers, and there were no women in the senior ranks of the increasingly powerful National Security Organisation (NSO). The civil service, a channel through which women could hope to ascend to decision-making levels of government, was severely weakened under this regime. It is in this context, and in the light of the generally coercive and repressive character of the Buhari-Idiagbon regime, that the existence of three women permanent secretaries, and General Buhari's proclamation that there should be one woman commissioner in each of the 19 states must be viewed. The same regime launched the notorious War Against Indiscipline (WAI) which effectively licensed all manner of harassment, including the specific humiliations visited upon women. Women working as petty traders and single women were singled out to be accused of 'indiscipline' and 'moral laxity', while working mothers were blamed for delinquency and the wives of civil servants and military officers held responsible for corruption. Regional variations in gender politics have continued to persist, but extremely misogynistic values and actions have continued to be tolerated across the society.

During this period, the military governor of Kano State issued an edict banning single women, an action which led to a spate of marriages of convenience and mass evictions by local landlords refusing to accommodate unmarried women any longer. Women in Sokoto State have been repeatedly charged with immorality and subjected to punitive measures, while more generally, the practice of female seclusion has been increasing rather than decreasing, with more complete forms of veiling appearing for the first time. In Lagos state, market women and street hawkers came in for regular harassment, limited only by the existence of strong market women's organisations.

Ousted in 1985 by a 'coup to end all coups' led by General Ibrahim Badamasi Babangida, the Buhari-Idiagbon regime will, not go down in history for its progressive gender politics. With the Babangida regime, the steady picture of military and civilian exclusion of women from top levels of government alters somewhat. At first glance, little appears to have changed. There were no women on the new Armed Forces Ruling Council, or at ministerial level, although the practice of appointing women as state commissioners continued. There were no female state governors. At the local level however, a proclamation was issued to the effect that one in four local government councillors should be women. Disappointingly, when local government elections were held in 1987, only two out of 301 women were elected as chairs of local government, actually a decline on previous local government elections. This can be interpreted as indicating a setback in the electorate's gender politics, possibly the result of the high levels of contempt for women generated during the War Against Indiscipline.

Many of the subsequent activities of the Babangida regime fall under the programme purportedly designed to effect a transition to civilian rule. Here we see that two women were included in the Political Bureau, one of whom was Mrs Adefarasin in her capacity as Head of the National Council of Women's Societies. That these women were tokenistic, and the Bureau was itself weak, is affirmed by the fact that the Armed Forces Ruling Council chose to ignore the modest recommendation that women be allocated a mere 5 per cent of the legislative seats in all three tiers of government. The reason given was this: since the government believed in equality of the sexes, no affirmative action would be necessary to ensure women's participation (Shettima, undated).

Women in Nigeria (WIN), a radical organisation constitutionally committed to the elimination of the gender and class inequalities in Nigerian society, was one of the organisations the Political Bureau commissioned to hold consultative workshops and make recommendations. In response to the demands of secluded northern women in particular, WIN called for 50 per cent representation of women on the basis that women constitute half of the population (WIN 1989:3), and for social and economic recognition of women's domestic and reproductive labour. WIN also called for an amendment to the 1979 constitution to enable women to confer privileges and rights on their husbands and children; an amendment was directed at section 24(2)a

which allows men, but not women, to confer citizenship on their spouses
and children (WIN 1989).

Yet Babangida's regime is likely to go down in history as one in
which women gained prominence. This was not because it had radical
gender politics, but because his wife engaged in highly publicised
activities, and ordered other wives of the military oligarchy to replicate
her example. Mrs Babangida's impact on the body politic ought to be
assessed against the extreme marginalisation of women in the Nigerian
state and national politics under both military and civilian regimes, which
I have documented in the preceding pages.

The Emergence of Femocracy

Mrs Maryam Babangida was not an activist of any kind until her
husband's seizure of power in 1985. After attending primary school in
Asaba and secondary school at a convent in Kaduna, Miss King as she
was then, gained secretarial qualifications in Nigeria and the USA and
met her husband, then Captain Babangida, in 1965. Four years later they
were married, the converted and renamed Maryam continuing her career
as a housewife for the 14 years that followed. In 1983, when her husband
became the Chief of Army Staff, she too benefited by becoming
President of the Nigerian Army Officers Wives Association, as the
custom ordained (*New Life* 4, 1990:8). It was in this capacity that she
first began to see herself as a leader. When she accompanied her husband
into State House as wife of the Head of State after the successful coup,
Maryam Babangida embarked on a short career which was to mark the
emergence of a new phase in the history of Nigerian First Ladies: she
opened an office of her own and by astutely wielding her influence, she
soon became a prominent figure in public life. A brief look at her
predecessors indicates how different her approach to her position as wife
of the Head of State was.

General Buhari's wife, Hajiya Sefinatu Buhari, was courted by her
husband from the age of 14, married at 18 and remained a shy and
retiring woman committed to a conservative reading of Islam. Hajiya
Hadiza Dawaiya, as the most senior of the four women married to
President Shehu Shagari, assumed the position of First Lady when her
husband became President, but remained out of the public eye. General
Obasanjo was not known to have a wife while in office, and Mrs Ajoke
Murtala Muhammed was not in place long enough to wield much
influence as a result of the brevity of her husband's rule. Mrs Victoria
Gowon married her husband during the civil war. Although their
wedding was a prominent social event, and Mrs Gowon became known

for accompanying her husband on his tours and generally being supportive, her input was unremarkable, being largely in accord with conventional notions of a good wife. Mrs Victoria Nwanyiocha Aguiyi-Ironsi was similarly unremarkable. During the first Republic, Prime Minister Tafawa Balewa's wives were kept in full-time seclusion, and none of them ever accompanied him on his duties, or performed any public function. It is therefore in comparison to her recent predecessors that Maryam Babangida features so prominently.

Mrs Maryam Babangida, already a powerful public figure, grew increasingly prominent through the Better Life for Rural Women Programme (BLP) which she launched in 1987. Initially under the auspices of the Directorate of Food, Roads and Rural Infrastructure (DFRRI), BLP was launched at a workshop on rural women held on 13-16 September, 1987, in Abuja. The idea of focusing on rural women was not new. Long before BLP, WIN described rural women as the backbone of the nation's food production and the most exploited section of Nigerian society (WIN 1985). Internationally too, the plight of rural women had attracted the sympathy and aid of donor organisations as well as the support of an international women's movement seeking to include and articulate the concerns of the most exploited groups of women in the so-called Third World (see for example DAWN 1988). More locally, other sources credit Professor Ogundipe-Leslie (a former WIN member), with the idea of focusing on rural women during her mysteriously brief tenure in the Presidency during which she worked for the Directorate of Social Mobilisation (*African Guardian* 16/11/92:24).

Whatever the source, rural women became the professed target of the Nigerian First Lady's programme. BLP soon evolved beyond DFRRI. Following the Abuja seminar, attended by the wife of the Chief of General Staff, Mrs Rebecca Aikhomu, the wives of other military service chiefs and women from 304 local government areas, the wives of all the military state governors, were called upon to set up Better Life committees in each state. They were instructed to familiarise themselves with rural women's problems and link them with the appropriate government agencies and to initiate and monitor programmes. Governors' wives were to encourage rural women to 'become more active and useful to themselves, their families and their environment at large' and the method of doing this involved training and income generating (Daily Times, Special Publication 1990; Tongo 1990:10). It was therefore through military governors' wives, who automatically became the Chairpersons of the state level BLP committees, that Mrs

Babangida sought to implement the goal of 'mobilising rural women for development'.

In addition to the Chairperson, each state was to have a coordinator/director-general to head an office in the state level DFRRI offices, and an advisory board comprising whichever women were commissioners, DGs, heads of parastatals, High Court judges or deputy general managers. There was also to be a committee in every state, comprising all the above and representatives of existing women's organisations. Each state committee was instructed to form seven implementation subcommittees, and it was these that were to advise, organise and mobilise rural women wherever they deemed it necessary (Tongo 1990:9-10).

The second high-profile event took place a year after the launch. The first Better Life Fair was held in Tafawa Balewa Square, Lagos, in September 1988. Here women from women's organisations and many of the rural cooperatives that had been formed were bussed in to central Lagos to exhibit their products. Attended by the Head of State as well as the wives of the military elite, and a good many other eminent women as well, it was a highly publicised jamboree. At the end of it all, the Federal Government announced that it would set up a National Commission on Women and Development. This was something that had been lobbied for by women's organisations over a great many years, but which was now established by a military decree (No.30) 'in recognition of the commitment of (the) government to the ideals of the Better Life for Rural Women Programme' (Tongo 1990). The National Commission on Women and Development (NCW) was thus irrevocably linked to the First Lady and the BLP, conceptually as well as structurally, a point returned to below.

The second BLP fair was held on March 12-19, 1990 in the new national capital, Abuja, and focused on 'Food Processing and Preservation', as though to underline women's traditional role as nurturers and providers of food. During the launching of this jamboree, an award ceremony to install Mrs Babangida as 1989 'Woman of the Year', chosen by the Government's national newspaper, was held. In fact the New Nigerian Woman of the Year Award was initiated with Mrs Babangida, and became a much less prominent affair thereafter.

Impact on the Nation's Gender Politics

The endless parades of the overdressed wives of the military across the pages of the newspapers and the nations' television screens soon began to provoke criticism from several quarters. Since neither the First Lady nor any of the state BLP branches had any Federal or State budgetary allocation, no satisfactory answers were given when questions were raised about the sources of the monies being spent. Between 1989 and 1991, Gani Fawehinmi, the renowned lawyer, filed several lawsuits, protesting that since the First Lady had no constitutional position, she had no right of access to the nation's treasury. None of these suits were successful, but Chief-Dr-Mrs Maryam Babangida, as she was now known, declared that BLP hàd been 'self-financing', and continued to be unaccountable. The second BLP fair involved air travel and five-star hotel accommodation for governors wives, their advisory committees, their implementation subcommittees and the invited rural women — from all 21 states. In addition to all these expenses, all the governors' wives took out full-page newspaper advertisements to congratulate Mrs Babangida on being chosen as 'Woman of the Year', again at public expense. As if this were not enough, the same set of governors wives took turns congratulating her during the peak hour of national television news broadcasting throughout the week of the fair (Tongo 1990).

Still on the financial front, there were accusations (and there are witnesses to the fact) that public funds had been used to purchase items for display at the fair, where no such items had been produced by rural women. In some areas rural women complained that the BLP committees had seized their goods without paying for them, and did not return them after the fair. Others protested that the 'credit facilities' extended to them by BLP consisted of loans which charged exploitatively high interest rates (Tongo 1990). Yet other rural women complained that machinery had broken down and was not being maintained, or that it had been run by men rather than by the women themselves. In 1992, the Central Bank of Nigeria reported that BLP projects had cost 400 million naira over the first five years, a figure which did not include staff salaries, vehicles or other overheads (*African Guardian* 16/11/92:21).

The absence of systematic monitoring makes it hard to assess what the concrete achievements of the BLP have been. Because of the unaccountability of the First Lady, no annual reports were ever written. Nonetheless, many claims were made. Tongo (1990) reports the establishment of skills training in weaving and soap-making, pottery, palm fruit processing, yoghurt making, gari processing, the establishment of rural markets and small-scale industries in several states. Otu (1990) credits BLP with enabling women across the nation 'to go into lucrative businesses', and lists farming, animal husbandry, cottage industries and cooperative societies. It is worth pointing out that these are all activities which Nigerian rural women engaged in long before BLP came along.

The increased availability of loans and equipment, and the establishment of many cooperative societies since the advent of BLP, are also listed as major achievements.

After five years of BLP the claims were even grander: 10,000 cooperatives, 1,793 cottage industries, 2,397 farms, 470 multi purpose women's centres and 233 health centres were accredited to the First Lady's programme by the end of 1992 (*Newswatch* 2/11/92). A world press conference was called to laud the success of the BLP, commemorative stamps were issued and a specially commissioned film entitled 'Legacy' was screened to the same end. A medley of full page media advertisements once again congratulated the First Lady on her achievements.

In the absence of good empirical evidence, one can be forgiven for being sceptical. Rural women seem to be as industrious as they have always been, while poverty continues to be endemic. The dramatic decline in urban as well as rural living standards and the worsening security situation nationally has resulted in greater reliance on rural areas, and there is evidence to suggest that worsening conditions have encouraged people to return to their villages of origin.

Of more analytic interest is the management style of the BLP. This was run on military lines, with the First Lady issuing orders from State House. With no avenue for feedback, discussion or internal criticism, the programme was not set up in a way that allowed it to respond to any needs that rural women may themselves have identified (Tongo 1990). The low visibility of rural women further suggested that they were not involved in decision-making or direction of the programme, however much they may have embraced the BLP and thrown their enthusiasm behind it. Although governor's wives were ordered to travel to the rural areas and familiarise themselves with the plight of rural women, and some consultative workshops were staged, the real authority and direction of the BLP rested with the First Lady herself. It cannot therefore be described as democratic in any real sense of the term. 'Rural women' were the targets but not the decision-makers, and their interests had already been decided.

On closer examination of the pronouncements made in the course of the BLP, we can see that Mrs Babangida assumes the interests of rural women to coincide with national interests, as these have already been defined by a state that has consistently excluded women from decision-making. The fact that different social groups may have very different perspectives on just what the national interest might be, or that women's exploitation has never been addressed in national development planning is not recognised. Instead rural women are portrayed as a passive and under-utilised community who can be mobilised to do more productive work by elite women, for the betterment of their communities. The irony of this is that whereas elite women are almost by definition unproductive, even at the household level, it has long been established that rural women are already the most hard-working sector of the population: the problem is that their work is undervalued and under-remunerated (WIN 1985). Changing this fact is likely to require a great deal more than the authority and wealth of the First Lady.

There were also other events that need to be considered in appraising the democratic and feminist potentials of this style of gender politics. The BLP was not only high profile and expensive. It was also extremely conservative. On no occasion did Mrs Babangida give a public address without distancing herself from any kind of 'women's lib' or feminism, by stressing that the first duties of women are the traditional ones of wifehood and motherhood. Her conservatism is further attested to by the way in which traditional rulers across the land, better known for obstructing efforts to educate and uplift women, rewarded Mrs Babangida with titles. In December 1991, the University of Nsukka conferred an honorary doctorate on the President's wife, who rewarded the university administration by delivering a badly-needed donation of 7.5 million naira to this poverty-stricken and crumbling edifice of higher learning. Later that year she was also awarded doctorates by the equally impoverished universities of Ogun, Port Harcourt and Ogbomosho.

In September 1992, Mrs Babangida, perhaps stung by Gani Fawehinmi's law suits, attended a policy briefing of the elected Senators and called on them to make the post of the First Lady constitutional, stating that this would be 'One of the most functional symbolisms of the truly liberal political system in the Third Republic' (*The Guardian* 12/9/92). In other words, advancing her in this way would be a good way of appearing liberal. In the course of her address she emphasised her respect for women's traditional roles, pointing to her literary debut 'On the Home Front' as evidence. Her call was not supported by the only woman out of the 91 senator-select, Mrs Kofo Bucknor Akerele (*National Concord* 22/9/92). Perhaps this manoeuvre is best seen as one of several of Mrs Babangida's attempts to institutionalise and consolidate her position. The second involved the National Commission for Women, and here we shall see that she was a little more successful.

Institutionalising Femocracy

In 1990, the National Commission for Women, decreed into being by the Federal Government at the end of the 1989 BLP Fair in Lagos, was inaugurated. A nominally independent NCW Board was appointed and headed by Professor Awe, a widely respected women's rights campaigner and academic. One of the first matters the new structure sought to address was the BLP, which the board assumed would come under the auspices of the NCW, now the legitimate governmental body for all women's affairs. The NCW board conducted a tour of BLP programmes, concluding that:

> the programme did not have the sort of structure that would enable it to permeate down to the grassroots and to cover a wide area (*Newswatch* 2/11/92).

On the basis of their findings, plans were made to strengthen the administrative structure. These plans were never carried out, for reasons that become apparent below.

That there were likely to be stresses between the BLP and the NCW became evident when the state level NCW offices were set up. There were now parallel structures across the Federation: BLP offices answerable to the First Lady, and NCW offices answerable to the Chairperson, and both ultimately answerable to the Head of State. Relationships between the NCW leadership and State House appear to have reached a climax in July 1992 when the organisers of a seminar on women's development at which Professor Awe was to deliver the keynote address, were suddenly arrested. When Professor Awe went to request their release, she too was detained and subjected to humiliating interrogation by members of the state security services. A delegation of highly respected women in Abuja for the same seminar failed to persuade the First Lady to have them released. It was only when President Babangida sent his own personal assistant to the police station that Mrs Awe was freed· and allowed to be driven back to her hotel (*African Guardian* 16/11/92). Matters did not end there.

The following month, in August 1992, Decree 42 was issued by the President, repealing Decree 30 under which the NCW had been constituted. It was now to be restructured so that it would henceforth be headed by the wife of the President, with an appointed Director-General reporting directly to her. Professor Awe's resignation was tendered thereafter, the reason given being that she was 'unable to carry out the objectives for which the commission was set up', a statement which did little to quell widespread speculation that she was forced out by the First

Lady (*African Guardian* 19/11/92). In any case, the entire board of the NCW was dissolved by the Federal Government only a month later (*Democrat* 18/9/92). Only now that the whole NCW was controlled by the President's wife did the BLP offices move from State House to become a department within it.

In view of this history, it is not surprising that there were those who felt that the NCW was simply a front for Maryam Babangida's continued access to the treasury and the growing personality cult she had established for herself. In fact BLP was the only operational department, although a Child Welfare Department was also to be formed — or rather moved — from the Ministry of Social Welfare. In addition to these two operational departments there is a Research and Planning Department and two departments concerned with the bureaucratic servicing of the NCW itself — finance and personnel.

The NCW was not the only structure for women established during Mrs Babangida's tenure as First Lady, and dominated by her. In November 1989, the Federal Government laid the foundation stone for a multi-million naira Centre for Women and Development. At the launching, President Babangida commended the BLP and 30 million naira was collected on the spot. Donations came from the Ministry of External Affairs (US$50,000), the Nigerian National Petroleum Corporation (3 million naira), Ministry of Works and Housing (2 million naira) and the Chief of General Staff's Office (100,000 naira). The President then announced that the Federal Government would provide whatever else was necessary (*African Guardian* 16/11/92). State Governors' wives proceeded to hold similar high-profile fund-raising events for women's centres in their various states.

The Centre was completed in record time and must be the largest women's centre in Africa, if not the world, comprising a conference hall, a library, a shopping complex, a bukateria (restaurant), an exhibition hall, an administrative complex, accommodation and multi-storey car parks. The main exhibition running continuously is the 'Hall of Fame', dominated by portraits of the First Lady and glass cases filled with local and international awards won by her. It comes as no surprise that after a meeting between Mrs Babangida and selected 'women leaders', it was decided to name the centre after her, and so it became known as the Maryam Babangida Centre for Women and Development.

Prospects for Women and Democracy

From the above it is clear that Nigeria has seen the emergence of a femocracy, rather than the development of a women's movement, or the creation of a feminist space in Nigerian politics. Given this state of affairs, it is worth considering the impact of Mrs Babangida's femocracy on the position of women in Nigeria, and whether the BLP, the NCW and the Maryam Babangida Centre, all established during the Babangida regime, can be described as creating any democratic space for women. A further question which remains, now that the Babangidas have been obliged to leave the Presidency, is whether femocracy can be transformed into a viable machinery through which the aspirations of women from all the different sections of Nigerian society can be articulated and realised: can it be converted from a femocracy into a feminist movement? One way of assessing this is to consider whether the political status of women was improved by the high profile activities of the First Lady and the governors' wives who clearly gained some influence by being plunged into the media limelight. The establishment of the BLP, the NCW and the Maryam Babangida Centre for Women and Development, combined with the frequent appearance of the wives of the military in the mass media clearly planted women firmly in the eyes of the public.

There were also a series of women appointed to high offices for the first time by President Babangida. Professor Grace Alele Williams became the first ever woman to be appointed as a University Vice Chancellor, and two state governors were persuaded to have women as deputies: Mrs Celia Ekpenyong in Cross Rivers and Alhaja Sinatu Ojikutu in Lagos. Five women were appointed Director-General at Federal level (including Hajiya Aisha Ismail at the NCW). Several other women were appointed to high office in parastatals (PID, September 1992). In the structures purportedly designed to effect the transition to civilian rule, only one woman was appointed to the National Electoral Commission; and we have already noted that the Federal Government rejected the recommendations of its own Political Bureau regarding women. When it came to the political parties and the local and gubernatorial elections, not to mention the cancelled presidential primaries, we see that neither the electorate nor the political class has been significantly transformed. In descending order, only one woman was elected to the 91-member senate, none were elected as state governors, and only 13 women were elected to the National House of Assembly (eight for the Social Democratic party and five for the National Republican Convention). Women appear to have fared only slightly better in the state level assemblies: only 27 women were elected out of 1172 seats nation-wide, leaving 14 of the 30 states with no female representation in the legislature at all. Nor have women made significant inroads into local government councils.

Senator Kofo-Bucknor Akerele's motion for there to be a Women's Committee to liaise with the NCW and other women's organisations was thrown out by the Senate in June 1993. Interestingly enough, one of the reasons male senators gave for rejecting this proposal was that it would provide another conduit for the BLP and the First Lady (*The Guardian* 19/6/93). This suggests that women are being subjected to something of a backlash, with male reaction to the power wielded by the President's wife obstructing women's political participation. Even more disturbingly, women members in the House of Assembly are reported to have been harassed with insults and cat-calls whenever they tried to speak (The Guardian, op cit.). All of this suggests that women, rural or urban, were going to continue to be grossly marginalised in the Third Republic.

One thing that has changed is that wives of party leaders and Presidential candidates are now expected to be in the public eye, so that the non-appearance of Bashir Tofa's wife (or wives?) was criticised by a national media now accustomed to parades of first and aspirant first ladies. Abiola and Kingibe's wives were given prominent coverage whenever they appeared on the campaign trail. Since both the SDP leaders are polygamous, this meant that they were able to dispatch different wives to campaign in the different parts of the country from which they originated (*National Concord* 13/6/93). Another is that, in contrast to the Second Republic politicians, both parties found it incumbent upon them to issue statements about their plans for women, with Abiola promising at least four women ministers, and Tofa pledging 'appropriate' numbers of female appointments and pledging support for ending discriminatory laws.

We can conclude from this evidence that femocracy has affected the gender politics of the nation, but not in the way that one might have hoped. It cannot be said to have enhanced gender equality or to have in any way challenged conservative attitudes to women. Instead, eight years of femocracy has generated promises to appoint token women, and has made the parading of expensively attired wives into a political tradition. Absent from the political discourse is any discussion of more fundamental change. In the event of a transition to civilian rule, Nigerian women are therefore faced with the prospect of becoming media adjuncts to their spouses' political campaigns, rather than making a more successful entry into politics.

Women's commitment to democratisation has been much in evidence in the months following the return of the military under General Sani Abacha. When the Presidential election results were not released in June 1993, women joined men in taking to the streets and calling for the military to hand over power. Women were amongst those shot and harassed in the repression that followed. With the dissolution of all elected structures and the replacement of an all-male interim government by another all-male military regime, the prospects for democracy and for women's participation in future governments are bleak. Even the femocracy is no longer in evidence with the departure of Mrs Babangida, because the current first lady, Mrs Sani Abacha, has so far remained relatively inconspicuous. This cannot be deemed to be a great loss, because if women's voice in politics is to rely on the personality of the First Lady, the prospects for women having any democratic space are poor, regardless of whether we are under a civilian or military administration.

All this leads us to conclude that femocracy is not a viable political phenomenon, and that it does not lead to any sustainable change in women's political status, or to any enduring improvement in the lives of ordinary women. Nor can it be successfully transformed to create a democratic space for women, when the democratisation of the whole society has been set back by a further extension of military rule. The longer term achievements of Mrs Babangida's femocracy were limited to creating more media space for the wives of the ruling elite, and mobilising ruling class women's support for the most populist policies of the various totalitarian regimes that have ruled Nigeria. Almost as a side effect, we have also seen the Federal Government establish several state structures whose democratic potential cannot yet be ascertained. Whatever potential there is within them is unlikely to be realised under continued military rule. Nor is it likely to emerge as long as structures for women remain under control of the President's wife, or the wives of other soldiers and politicians; women who have no mandate in their own right, and who derive their influence solely from that of their spouses.

Note

1. See for example, Kramarse and Treichier, 1985; Mitchell and Oakley, 1986. In her classic text, *Feminism and Nationalism in the Third World*, Kamari Jayawardena defines feminism as going beyond agitation on women's issues, and beyond movements for equality and emancipation which seek to redress prevailing discrimination against women, to embrace 'movements for equality within the current system and significant struggles that have attempted to change the system' (1986:2).

Part Three

Civil Society and Democratisation

6

The Mass Media in the Struggle for Democracy: Constraints and Possibilities

Y. Z. Ya'u

Introduction

The current wave of struggles for democracy sweeping across the world has, in Nigeria, coincided with two other significant processes. The first is the growing discontent against the hardship provoked by the Structural Adjustment Programme (SAP), which was instituted in the country in 1986. The second is the continuing struggle to terminate military rule in the country. The tumultuous events of the late 1980s coming as they did in the wake of the collapse of the Stalinist structures in Eastern Europe and the subsequent collapse of the Soviet Union have sent social scientists back to the drawing board to re-assess the role of the various organs of civil society in the struggle for democracy. One of such organs is the mass media, the subject of this chapter.

The mass media in Nigeria has experienced phenomenal growth since 1859 when the first newspaper in the country, Iwe Irohin, started publishing. This growth has been most active after independence, and during the 1980s. Today, there are over 33 radio stations and 40 television stations, with the print media publishing more than 200 titles, ranging from dailies to weeklies, news magazines and special interest journals. In terms of ownership, the electronic media is wholly owned by government. Although some private broadcasting stations were registered late in 1992, none of them has yet started broadcasting. For the print media, three modes of ownership exist, private, public and joint (private and public).

In the electronic media, English language shares air time with indigenous languages. In the print media, English is dominant with very few papers publishing in Igbo, Hausa and Yoruba. Electronic media coverage is virtually nation-wide, though the high cost of receivers and the absence of electrical power supply in rural areas have limited the penetration of the medium. The print media are also predominantly urban-based. These short-comings notwithstanding, the mass media in Nigeria is a visible force in the dynamics of the political socialisation of the people of the country. What follows is an assessment of the extent to which the mass media has contributed to the struggles for the expansion of the democratic space in Nigeria, especially since the introduction of SAP. In carrying out this assessment, five specific questions are addressed:

1. SAP and the media: in what ways and to what extent has the economic crisis engendered by SAP affected the mass media?

2. The media and the crisis: how has the mass media responded and adjusted to the economic crisis?

3. Owners versus media workers: how did the media's response to the crisis reflect itself in the editorial practices of the media and what conflicts or tensions did it engender between media owners and journalists?

4. The media and popular struggles: how have the media reported popular struggles in the country?

5. Government versus the media: to what extent has government tolerated media criticism and what measures has it employed to tame the media?

The Structural Adjustment Programme and the Media

For the Nigerian Press, December 1986 was the time the Structural Adjustment Programme (SAP) started. In that month, the price of the Oku-Iboku newsprint rose from 965 naira per ton to 2,925 naira, an increase of more than 300 per cent. The Oku-Iboku plant, (owned by the government), was the only newsprint factory in the country, and its monopoly of the market was virtually complete. The reason given by the Nigerian Newsprint Manufacturing Company (NNMC) for the increase was that the second-tier foreign exchange market (SFEM), introduced by the government earlier in the year, as part of the adjustment mechanism had hiked NNMC's cost of production three to five times (*African Guardian* 15/1/87). But it was actually the drastic devaluation of the naira occasioned by SFEM, and the 50 per cent import duty placed on newsprint importation in the 1986 budget that forced media owners to patronise Oku-Iboku. This sudden increase threw the media owners into an immediate crisis. Production costs rose to about 78 kobo per copy while the cover price was still 20 kobo. The Newspaper Proprietors Association of Nigeria (NPAN) protested to NNMC and demanded a rethink of the increase but to no avail. This led the NPAN to sanction a new cover price of 30 kobo.

The crisis was not limited to the price increment only. Oku-Iboku was unable to meet the need of the papers even at this new price. For instance, the *Daily Times*, which at the time used 36 tons a day could only get 125 tons allocation a week (*Newswatch* 19/1/87). Many papers were forced to devise measures to keep afloat as cover price increase did not match production costs. The *Daily Times* cut its production to about 60 per cent and reduced pagination from 32 to 16, while *Punch* and *Vanguard* reacted by retrenching staff.

The SAP also affected the electronic media. Three factors, however, prevented the crisis from becoming a full blown one. First, the government was in need of more media coverage to propagate its unpopular economic policies and could not afford to see the electronic media grounded. Second, because existing media establishments already owned their basic equipment and needed little day-to-day production inputs, the impact of the crisis was less severe, manifesting itself in the inability to procure new equipment or service existing ones.

Third, since they were not established as commercial outfits, much of the additional expenditure caused by the SAP crisis was taken care of by government subvention.

After the initial shock, newspaper proprietors became reconciled to the fact that with SAP, the high cost of production would remain. Apart from newsprint, they also relied on the importation of other important production materials, whose prices were now subject to the ever-sliding value of the naira. Hence they kept pace with the NNMC newsprint price increase by increasing the cover price of newspapers and magazines each time there was a rise by NNMC. Thus, between 1986 to 1992, cover prices have seen no less than seven price reviews (see Table 1).

The problem, however, was that rising cover prices failed to match production costs. In addition, it led to a general fall in circulation due to the large number of unsold copies. By 1991, as the size of unsold copies increased with every fresh increment on cover price, the NPAN pushed the cost of unsold copies onto the distributors and vendors by not only refusing to take back any unsold copies but making them pay for unsold copies. The distributors/vendors were also required to pay in advance for all the copies they took. This caused vendors in Lagos to strike for six days in June, 1991 to protest against the May cover price increment (*Media Review*, July 1990).

Table 1: Cover Prices, 1985-1994 (naira)

Year	Price of Newsprint (m/ton)	Newspaper Cover Price	Magazine Cover Price
1985	685.00	.15	1.00
1986	965.00	.20	2.00
1987	2,925.00	.30	3.00
1989	5,800.00	1.00	3.00
1990	6,500.00	1.50	5.00
1991	7,200.00	2.00	10.00
1992	11,000.00	3.00 / 4.00	15.00
1994		20.00	50.00

Source: Compiled by author.

Although both the vendors and the distributors association were unable to get the NPAN to reverse its policy on unsold copies, they nevertheless forced individual media organisations to adjust their production figures to the market so distributors could now take only what they were certain to sell. Technically, therefore, the problem was pushed back to the media houses. The result has been persistent shrinkage of circulation figures (see Table 2).

Table 2: Newspaper Distribution, Kano Zone, 1989-1992

Paper	1989	1990	1991	1992
Guardian	329,400	378,000	320,000	201,300
Champion	-	475,800	438,880	403,900
Punch	526,000	506,000	486,000	432,000
Tribune	415,000	407,000	380,000	256,000

Source: Compiled by author.

One rather paradoxical development during the period was the springing up of new media organisations in the country. In the electronic media, this tendency was essentially government driven. In the print media, however, where some papers were already folding up and newspaper owners were declaring that their businesses had become 'economic disasters', an explanation is needed. Four observations can be made about this growth. First there appeared to be a distinct trend towards specialisation, most notably among the magazines, with each catering for specific audiences and markets.

Second, although soft-sell (tabloid type) magazines had existed prior to 1986, the late 1980s saw a rapid rise in this genre. Indeed, the growth in soft-sell magazines appears to have been more rapid than that of the more serious press. Third, a number of the newly established serious papers were political projects of aspiring Third Republic politicians, established to aid their political careers. Fourth, the relative ease of obtaining capital due to the boom in the banking sector made it easier for many journalists who disagreed with their employers to set up their own media. A number of newly established magazines were born out of this circumstance. Examples include *Tell* from *Newswatch*, *Classique* from *Quality*, *Vintage* from *Prime People*, which itself had been a splinter from *Vanguard*, The *News* from *African Concord*, *Top Magazine* from *Topnews*, *Citizen* from *New Nigerian*, etc.

The Media Response to the Crisis

It was clear to those media organisations which survived the initial shock of the crisis unleashed by the Structural Adjustment Programme that the situation called for new strategies to stay afloat. In the past, advertisements had not been a crucial aspect of newspaper publishing. But to continue operating within profit margins, the media organisations were forced to rely more and more on commercial advertising to recoup their expenses, as raising cover prices only resulted in a drop in sales. Many newspapers also ditched previous policies they had on the type of advertisements they would carry in their publications. Thus the Concord Group, which had a policy of not accepting advertisements for alcohol, did a U-turn. The *Guardian* started to feature obituaries, contrary to its earlier principle of refusing to publish them. All of these were, of course, cosmetic changes in the face of more serious concessions to the 'forces of the market'.

The prelude to the movement towards advertising as a survival strategy was the dispute between the Association of Advertising Practitioners of Nigeria (AAPN) and the Newspaper Proprietors

Association of Nigeria (NPAN) in 1986. The point of dispute which underscored the nature of the conflict was that the NPAN insisted that advertising agencies must individually register with it, a move which the AAPN saw as not only undermining its powers but an unethical attempt by NPAN to regulate the practice of advertising (*African Guardian* 20/2/86).

Advertisements come principally from three sources; government establishments, the private sector and 'personal' ads. The government not only supplies a large proportion of media ads (through its agencies), it also has a major influence in the choice of media placement by the other sources. For instance, congratulatory messages, appeals and pleas to government are usually placed in media which has a cordial relationship with the government. Ordinarily, advertisers would chose their media on conventionally accepted criteria of target audience, circulation, etc. The practice in this country since SAP has been that both media organisations and advertising agencies lobby for ads. In response to this lobby, advertising sources have, over the years, arrived at unwritten criteria for advert placement which demand that the media be favourably disposed to and less critical in reporting government. Here then lies the subtle way the vibrancy of the media has been checked. In an attempt to get more ads and hence make profit, they have acquiesced to these unwritten criteria of advertising sources. A few papers which dared to differ suffered the consequences. In 1986 and 1987, the *Punch* almost collapsed as advertisers avoided it. Similarly, *Tell Magazine*, which, since its inception in 1990 had maintained a relatively critical position towards the Babangida regime ceased to get government related advertising.

Many of the editorial conflicts in the private media in recent years have been largely due to the action of proprietors trying to stop their editorial staffers from becoming too critical of the government. This is partly due to government attempts to cajole media owners into falling into line. The control of scarce newsprint had been used by government in this connection. The failure of the NPAN to overrun the AAPN in 1986 was partly due to lack of unanimity of action by the NPAN members, some of whom had accused its leadership of receiving seized newsprint from the government that had belonged to the Concord Press (*African Guardian* 20/286).

While the banning of *Newswatch* appeared to have been an *ad hoc* measure, the government's resort to arm-twisting in dealing with media organisations became clearer in 1990 when media criticism against it intensified after the trial of attempted coup plotters. This resulted in a clamp down on media houses. The government secretly organised a meeting with media executives in July, during which they were both bribed and threatened (*African Concord* 26/11/90). The government had earlier created an important forum of rapport with the media executives through the Vice-President's quarterly press briefing, at which attendance was compulsory. Its attitude to any media was largely dependant on how the particular media respected the 'accords' reached at the briefings. The banning of *Newswatch* and Police raids on the Republic newspaper were partly as a result of a breach of these so called accords (*African Guardian* 3/7/89).

To ensure that they did not attract the government's wrath, and thereby scare off advertisers, media owners not only demanded from their editorial staff that the government be given 'fair' press, they also prevailed upon their staff to reject ads from organisations perceived by government as adversaries, such as the Academic Staff Union of Universities (ASUU), Campaign for Democracy (CD) etc. Interestingly, the same media accept ads from faceless organisations campaigning for the continuation of the Babangida regime. Nearly all major papers have published ads from the following anonymous people using pen names — Dr. Keith Atkins, Dr. Farouk Ahmed and Third Eye (for examples, see *African Concord* 30/3/92 and *African Guardian* 28/12/92).

The electronic media response to advertising is a similar commercialisation of their news programmes. Thus, in 1986 the National Television Authority (NTA) decided to commercialise its news slot and charge fees for business and industrial organisations willing to have their activities reported as news. This extremely unprofessional measure virtually collapsed the conventional difference between news and ads, and henceforth only those who could pay would be featured in the newscasts of the stations. By the close of 1992, NTA was charging between 36,000 to 100,000 naira for a two-minute slot in its newscast. This commercialisation drive did not stop at news only. Programmes were aired on the stations on the basis of sponsorship. No programme could be aired, no matter how popular unless some company was willing to sponsor its transmission.

The implications of these new practices are obvious. First, it is only the rich who can feature in the news. Thus, it is only the glorified ideas of the rich that are disseminated in the electronic media. Second, news that is of crucial importance to the public cannot be aired unless it is in one way or another related to some company or government. Third, the choice of what to show on television in particular is now entrusted in the hands of a few multinational corporations. With their concern for 'stability' and profit, such organisations only sponsor programmes which either reinforce or underplay the status-quo vis-à-vis their control of the country's economy.

Fourth, the logic of government patronage has engendered a growing tendency for media organisations to acquiesce to government positions, at the same time making their pages available for the publication of unpopular and anti-democratic campaigns as the cases of Drs. Atkins and Ahmed have shown. All these have come to mean a progressive shrinkage of the potential of the mass media in promoting the struggle for democracy.

The Media Owners Versus Journalists

Although, lobbying and 'connection' are the principal mechanisms through which ads are obtained, an unread paper is useless to advertisers. Few would be willing to advertise in such papers. Unsold papers are equally an economic loss to the publishers. For these reasons, papers struggle to build and maintain wide readership. To retain and expand this readership, papers have to appear 'objective', 'fair', interesting and often criticise government where due. This is what gives the papers the credibility without which they would be no more than tissue paper.

The tendency of papers to avoid being in the bad books of government (which would threaten their advertising revenue) and at the same time maintain credibility before their respective readers has resulted in a delicate balancing act by the media in terms of their reporting and interpreting of government activities and policies. This creates an unwritten tactical division of labour between the proprietors and their staff. In this division of labour, the journalists are responsible for maintaining the credibility of the paper while the board, representing the proprietors, acts as a counter-balance to put the journalists in line as soon as they start straying into dangerous grounds.

The tension engendered working in this situation has made the journalist, like the proprietors, evolve survival strategies. Unlike the media owners, however, journalists did not evolve a collective approach to the problem. One of the most obvious of these responses has been the increasing use of cartoons by editorial departments to make social commentaries. The flight to cartoons, which became noticeable during the Buhari regime, has since become a regular feature of virtually all papers and magazines. And increasingly, the cartoons are becoming more political and militant in their messages. Another measure that media workers have adapted is the development of a delicate balancing act between news reporting (reporting facts as they are) and editorials (trying to mediate and conciliate adversaries).

In general, editors have also become circumspect in news selection and casting. Stories that are likely to irritate the government are pushed to obscure corners and pages while leads and front pages are reserved, (though not exclusively), for government officials and media owners. Organisations that are regarded as hostile to the government hardly make lead or front page news in their own right, except when they are presented negatively. The newsrooms have also helped to reduce potential conflicts by 'news killing', either to avoid attracting the wrath of the authorities or to please them. The electronic media are worse than the press in this practice. In 1987, both the NTA and Radio Nigeria did not give air time to the launching of Joe Garba's book, an occasion in which Obasanjo made his first major public attack against SAP. The unexplained cutting off of Professor Soyinka in mid-interview at Radio Oyo in 1992 remains one of the most clumsy attempts at 'news killing'. In spite of these elements at self-censorship adopted by editorial staff, the tension between them and their employers has often snapped in a number of editorial conflicts. Some of the most serious of these conflicts in the eight years of the Babangida Administration include:

1. *Newswatch* Post-deproscription Crisis (1987): This was between external members of the board and their internal colleagues, who doubled as editors. The basis of the crisis lay in the negative image of government presented by the magazine which some board members believed was detrimental to their business interests.

2. *New Nigerian* Newspapers (1987): The arrival of Sidi A. Sirajo as Managing Director as replacement for Mohammed Haruna who had been eased out of his job for allowing a religious advert that was critical of the government to be carried in the paper. This was preceded by the removal of Innocent Oparadike, the paper's editor, by the board for what was termed 'editorial bias'. Sirajo was, however, to push the NNN into a bigger editorial crisis as he set out to transform the newspaper group into an unabashed defender of government action.

3. *Today* (1987): Following the illegal deportation of Dr. F. Wilmot and Mrs. F.M. Adelugba of Ahmadu Bello University by security operatives, the editor of the paper, (a privately owned one), not only allowed the paper to give the government action 'unsympathetic' coverage, he also wrote a series of articles on the government's handling of the issue. The publisher, acting on pressure from

government, 'promoted' the editor out of his job and gave him the options of either being the Deputy Managing Director of the paper or a safe 'exile' in Harare, Zimbabwe.

4. *The Guardian* Press (1988): Although the immediate cause of the crisis was an intra-board disagreement with the publisher accusing the Managing Director of divided loyalty, it soon became clear that the Managing Director's 'divided loyalty' was his refusal to stop some editors of the paper from publishing stories which were embarrassing to government.

5. *The Republic* (1990): Following two police raids on the paper, the publisher sought to tame the editorial staff of the paper through dismissals and re-organisation. This caused a counter reaction by the journalists, resulting in strikes, occupation and its eventual temporary closure.

6. *Newswatch* (1990): The birth of *Tell* magazine in May 1991 was the culmination of a second round of conflict at *Newswatch*, this time between the founding editors of the magazine and its staff. The basis of the conflict was the perception by many ex-staffers of the magazine that since the death of Dele Giwa, (one of the four founding editors), the magazine had lost its fire. One particular incident that eventually led to the final parting of ways by the group now behind *Tell* magazine was a 1991 story in *Newswatch* which proclaimed the President as man of the year. Sources in *Tell* revealed that although the suggestion to proclaim Babangida as man of the year was the work of the reporters, who had drafted material to use for the cover, (which was an unsympathetic assessment of the president's years), the editors unilaterally substituted the reporters' material with copy they had written painting a flattering image of the president.

7. Sunday New Nigeria *(1991): Following the removal of Sidi Sirajo as Managing Director of the NNN, an attempt was made to build the reputation of the Sunday New Nigerian,* which until then hardly had any identity of its own. In the re-organisation that followed a new editor, Aminu Ibrahim, was appointed. In his zeal to turn the SNN into a respectable Sunday paper, he allowed his staff a wide margin of liberty and the paper soon started publishing some anti-government stories. After repeated attempts to get the editor to fall in line had failed, the Sole Administrator of the paper was eventually pressured by government to promote the editor to a newly created redundant

position of Editor-in-Chief. Most of the team were redeployed to other papers in the Group.

8. *Nigerian Television Authority* (1991): Here the conflict that occurred was of a more professional character. The Press Secretary to the Vice-President, Nduka Irabor, on March 8, 1991, telephoned the newsroom of the NTA at about 8.40 p.m. and informed them that they should broadcast the suspension of the embattled Chairman of the National Drug Enforcement Agency, Fidelis Oyakhilome, during the 9 p.m. newscast (*Media Review*, May 1991). Although the NTA news staff got the message, they decided not to use it, since there was an unwritten house rule that unwritten and unsigned news items were not to be broadcast. Government was angered by the refusal of the NTA to announce the news and did not hide its annoyance from the management board of the NTA, which promptly ordered the suspension of two of the news staff of the station.

9. *The Observer* (1991): In its August 19, 1991 edition, the paper used a rather unflattering photograph of the wife of the President on its front page. The board of the paper was angry about the incident and issued a query to the editor, who was subsequently suspended and later demoted for insubordination to the Board.

10. The *Daily Times* (1991/92): The appointment of Yemi Ogunbiyi as Managing Director of this conservative newspaper Group led to the emergence of a new lease of liberalism. The new boss had earlier headed the liberal Guardian Group, and he came with some of his former staff. This liberalism soon led to a collision with the government as the paper became more critical of the state. The immediate news story that led to the removal of the Managing Director on December 31, 1992 was the publication in the paper of Wole Soyinka's views criticising the December 14 local government elections carried out on the basis of the open ballot or queuing system. The government, which was celebrating the success of the experiment, did not take kindly to such an affront from its 'own' paper.

11. The *African Concord* (1992): The conflict in the *African Concord* was a spill over from its closure. The publisher had been assured that the Concord Press which was closed in April would be re-opened if he and his staff apologised to the President. The proprietor pressed his editorial staff to apologise. The staff insisted that they had done nothing wrong and would apologise to no-one. Four of the editorial staff decided to resign, rather than apologise.

The Media and Popular Causes

It must be said that the combined weight of economic concerns of media owners and self-censorship by editorial staff did not completely stop the media from occasionally reporting and interpreting events with a critical perspective. We examine below how some of these issues were handled by the media.

The Campaign for Human Rights

The Babangida regime claimed to have taken over power on a supposedly human rights platform and one of its first actions was the abrogation of the notorious Decree No. 4 (1984) under which two journalists from the Guardian Press had been jailed. The journalists were released and the Guardian Press officially pardoned. The detention cells of the notorious National Security Organisation (NSO) were opened to the media, who reported about the houses of horror they saw. The government also lifted the ban on both the National Association of Nigerian Students (NANS) and the Association of Resident Doctors (ARD), organisations at the forefront of the struggle against the repression of the Buhari/Idiagbon regime.

This romance with the human rights agenda was soon to be tested. In June 1986, students of the Ahmadu Bello University (ABU) Zaria, went on a peaceful demonstration to back up their demand for the recall of their colleagues who had been victimised by the university authorities for their role in an anti-American demonstration in May that year. The Vice-Chancellor called in the police to force the students back to classes and at the end of the brutal police intervention, several students were killed. This provoked a nation-wide condemnation of the government by the public. The Nigerian Labour Congress (NLC), for its part, set aside June 4 to hold a solidarity rally. The government responded by banning NANS and rounding up the National Leadership of the NLC. The media coverage of the demonstrations and the public reactions to it were extensive. In terms of interpretation of the events and the sympathy provoked, the media split into two. The government-owned media accused students of violence, arson and wanton destruction of public and private property and accused other media organisations of over reporting the issue and thereby escalating it. They said nothing about the police, except the lame defence that they killed only four students and not several as reported by other media. On the other hand, most of the private media blamed the university administration and the police for their brutality.

The police brutality against students and the subsequent detention of labour leaders and academics were by and large not seen by the media as a systematic manifestation of the realities of the human rights agenda of the regime. Even the banning of *Newswatch* in 1987 was yet to sensitise the media to the fact that the regime no longer respected human rights. Human rights reportage continued to receive scanty attention from the media until the end of 1988. Two things had happened to help draw the attention of the media to human rights violations. One was the campaign by the new leadership of the Nigeria Bar Association (NBA) for the repeal of Decree No. 2, with which the government had been indiscriminately detaining critics and innocent people. The second was the launching of the Civil Liberties Organisation's first mid-year report on the human rights situation in the country. The two events played a major role in sensitising the public into joining the struggle for human rights protection.

Thus by early 1989, when the campaign for the abrogation of Decree No. 2 had become a national movement led by the NBA and the human rights movement, the media opened their pages to the campaign. From then on, the print media gave a fair coverage to the activities of human rights organisations. The CLO's index on press headlines on human rights recorded 18, zero and five entries for 1986, 1987 and 1988 respectively, while the figure jumped to 1.22 for 1989. For the first quarter of 1990, it was 50 (*Civil Liberties Organisation* 1990). During this period, the media, especially the private ones, changed their position about the human rights standing of the government. The *African Guardian*, which less than a year earlier wrote of a regime with 'clear credentials', adopted a new line. In its editorial of August 8, 1988, it criticised the government's human rights record and called on the government to repeal Decree No. 2.

While most government media had a lukewarm attitude to this campaign, the *Daily Times*, perhaps seeing the rising tide of opposition against Decree No. 2, came up with its solution in an editorial in August. Following the ultimatum the NBA gave the government to repeal the Decree, the paper's leader writers conceded that 'Decree No. 2 is a dangerous decree.... capable of being abused' and advised that it either be repealed or modified (*Daily Times*, 21/8/89). Eventually the campaign was successful and the government was forced to amend the Decree and rely less on it in dealing with its critics. Media attention and sympathy were also helpful in restraining the government from banning human rights organisations, although it did not stop sending its security agencies to harass them frequently. This support has enhanced the work of the human rights movement, which has succeeded at least in placing the human rights agenda at the centre of the struggle for democracy in the country.

The Anti-SAP Protests

Although the struggle for a democratic society in Nigeria has always been alive, the introduction of SAP in the country gave a new impetus and momentum to it. The disastrous socio-economic consequences of SAP have convinced broad sections of the population of the need to terminate and reverse its policies. Yet people were also aware that given the predisposition of the Babangida regime, only a democratic government could end SAP. Therefore, the struggle against SAP came to be a rallying point for popular opposition against the regime itself.

Opposition to SAP was passive in its early days and acquired militancy only from late 1987, when the government mounted a media campaign to explain its rationale for removing subsidies on petroleum products. The NLC was spurred into action to resist the removal of subsidy and in December that year scheduled nation-wide protests. The government backed momentarily but not without detaining the labour leaders. The rising militancy of the NLC was eventually checkmated in February 1988 when government used the excuse of an internal disagreement within the Congress to dissolve both its national and state executive councils and appoint a sole administrator to run it. In spite of this, however, the April 10 increase in the price of petroleum products was greeted by wildcat strikes by students and workers across the country. The protests, which were started by the students of the University of Jos, were quickly converted into industrial action by local Joint Action Committees of labour unions, while university students continued with public demonstrations in support of the striking workers. Although the strikes, which lasted for more than three weeks, did not succeed in reverting the prices to their pre-April 10 level, the workers were able to secure some concessions.

Meanwhile, the students had learnt a vital lesson in the process: henceforth a protest need not commence simultaneously in all campuses before it could be effective. With this lesson, and having emerged from the April protests as the only organised national body, (in spite of being banned), NANS became the rallying point in the campaign against SAP. In early May 1989, it gave the government an ultimatum to terminate SAP or face a crisis. On May 24, students took to the streets at the University of Benin. The impetus soon spread and engulfed the whole country within two days. The government responded immediately by closing the institutions and arresting student leaders. But the struggle had reached the streets already where, school or no school, there were enough people to continue the demonstrations. No doubt, the media coverage of the protests had helped to link up campuses, letting students know that they were not fighting isolated battles.

The concessions that were granted by the government were not without some elements of vindictiveness. The government decided not to reopen some institutions closed in the wake of the protests as a punishment. This decision was popularly condemned by the public and well reported in the media. Editorials were written condemning the government and calling on it to reopen the affected institutions. Even the *Daily Times* (3/7/89) was forthcoming this time, pleading that the schools be re-opened. The government had no option but to reopen the institutions.

The protests achieved one other thing. They succeeded in raising and sustaining a serious debate on SAP. The government, having been pushed on the defensive, challenged critics to come up with alternatives to SAP, adding at the same time, however, that there was no alternative to it. The challenge was soon taken up and the media facilitated this debate by allowing their papers to be used in this contest of ideas. It was the media that published the Economic Commission of Africa's African Alternative to SAP (AASAP) much to the government's annoyance.

While the government was restrained and allowed the media debate to continue, it did not extend the same restraint to other forms of debate. Thus, when a group of 'radicals' gathered in July 1989 to discuss 'Alternatives to SAP', it made sure that the discussions were never held. Security agents swamped the venue and arrested leading members of the organisers of the seminar. Thanks to media coverage, however, the essentials of the radical alternatives to SAP were able to get out to the public as the aborting of the seminar became a news subject for many magazines and papers. For instance, the *African Concord*'s cover of July 3, 1989 gave an extensive review of the papers that were to have been presented at the seminar.

Reporting the Transition

The haste with which the government proscribed *Newswatch* for publishing excerpts of the report of the Political Bureau on the government's political transition programme should have made it clear to political observers that the programme the government was about to foist on Nigerians would be essentially undemocratic. It would appear, however, that this observation either did not register in media circles or else they had an entirely different conception of democracy. In its reporting of the progress of the transition, the media did not see the undemocratic content of the programme as an issue deserving serious attention. Instead, they were more concerned with subsidiary issues: what progress has so far been made, who wins, who gets disqualified, etc. Thus when the government decided to sack elected local government councils in 1990, there were few protests from the media. Similarly, when at the eve of the governorship elections in 1991 the government gave the NEC wide powers to disqualify candidates as it pleased, no serious media campaign could be mounted against it. The media were more interested in counting the casualties.

The media's retrospective comments on the imposition of the two government parties were mild in relation to the political damage that measure did to the democratic process. The feeble opposition to the open ballot system adopted by the government was not enough to sensitise people to appreciate the dangers the system posed to democracy in the country. The result was that instead of people becoming active in opposing the system, they simply became apathetic and decided not to vote. In fairness to the media, it was not that they did not report these issues. They did, but the reporting was shallow. No attempt was made to interpret issues and show how they advanced or failed to advance the democratic aspirations of the people. Even within the media, there was a realisation that their role in the political transition programme was way below expectations. The *Daily Champion* (16/9/92), for instance, lamented that 'the blame for the empty campaigns is to be laid at the doorsteps of the media.'

One factor that constrained the performance of the media in reporting the transition, especially during the presidential primaries, was its outright partisanship. This was not unexpected, since many of the papers were established primarily to promote the political ambitions of their owners. Almost all the media reported that the primaries were rigged but when it came to the question of who was doing the rigging, each singled out the opponent of its patrons. The media also showed a tendency of siding with undemocratic positions or actions when these suited their patrons. For instance, the *Nigerian Tribune* (2/2/89), was pleased when the President declared his one-man dictatorship by dissolving the Armed Forces Ruling Council in February 1989. Similarly, the *Sunday Concord* (11/10/92), assumed that the banning of the candidates involved in the first presidential primaries might allow its proprietor to get the exalted office and declared that 'the cancellation of the primaries was perfectly in line with the transition to civil rule Decree 13.'

The struggle for the democratisation of the transition programme was one area where the human rights groups and other democratic organisations did not achieve much. Although it cannot be said that this was due to an unsupportive media, greater concern with the democratic content of the PTP by the media could have helped the cause.

The National Conference

By the middle of 1988, it was clear to most democrats that the government's 'transition to democracy' programme was bound to fail. To salvage the situation, they proposed a national conference to examine a number of vital questions on the survival of the nation and came up with an alternative to the government's PTP. The CDHR was the moving force behind it, but somehow the NLC and a group of some former technocrats were also interested in the conference. The initial response of the media to the call for a national conference was largely to see it as the work of rabble rousers. In response to the NLC's May Day call for the National Conference, the *National Concord* (14/5/90), in an editorial, chided the NLC and advised it 'to admonish its teaming membership to cooperate with the government, towards the successful implementation of the transition programme'. By and large, this was the attitude of the media to the national conference: allow the government's transition programme to be 'implemented successfully'. Thus even when the government aborted the September 1990 National Conference, the media did not see the event as a major political one.

The patrons of the media soon found out that there were many stumbling blocks in the PTP, deliberately placed by the government. In tune with their patrons, the attitude of the media with respect to the national conference changed from one of indifference to that of taking a firm position on it, largely along regional lines, with most of the 'southern' media supporting the call and their 'northern' counterparts opposing it. Hence each side reported and interpreted events in relation to its own position.

Two factors contributed to the promotion of the national conference to the editorial and front pages of the press as well as on prime air time of the electronic media. First, was the growing scepticism of the political class about the intentions of the military. With every 'adjustment' to the PTP, the fear that the military would perpetuate itself in power become more real, prompting politicians to call on the government to accede to the call for the conference so that some of their doubts about the PTP could be assuaged. Second, in their jostling for offices, the politicians started a debate as to where the next president should come from. This debate reached a rather frenzied level when the second botched presidential primaries 'returned' northerners in both parties. Thus the proponents of a southern president, in an apparent loss of confidence in the electoral process, became converts to the call for a national conference.

The debate about the presidency succeeded in shifting the focus of the national conference in the media from one that was concerned with the economy, politics, law, culture, etc. to one more or less exclusively devoted to discussing the 'national question'. It was not surprising therefore that the debate on the conference centred on two related issues: the presidency and the structure of the federation. Reporting the national conference/question has been more of a paradox. It has enjoyed a wide coverage, yet for the general public, the result has been largely one of confusion as it is difficult to differentiate between two trends, a call for a national conference on the 'national question' and a national conference on 'major national problems', which was the intention of the originators of the campaigners of the national conference. It is not surprising that the campaign has failed to take root among the people.

The 'Interim Government/IBB Must Go' Campaign

One of the points made by the original sponsors of the national conference was the demand for the formation of an interim government, to replace the Babangida government. The objective of the interim government was to facilitate the convening of the national conference and the evolution of an alternative transition programme. This demand was anchored on the fact that the Babangida regime was not willing to leave office, in spite of all its pronouncements to the contrary. The media again did not take this call for interim government seriously. The cold reception that the idea of an interim government received and the lack of progress with regard to the national conference led the CD to modify its position to a more modest campaign to ensure that the military left by January 3, 1993.

The media was largely not averse to the 'No Extension' campaign. Even the government media allowed space and air time for views calling on the government to honour its promise. Obasanjo's letter advising the President against any further extension of the PTP was widely reported and published by both the private and public owned media. Ironically, however, the signal of the November extension appeared as a subtle rationalisation in an editorial in the *Daily Times* (25/9/92), in which the paper argued that the fact that political aspirants were calling for a cancellation of the primaries was a way of asking the government to extend the PTP. Whether this was kite-flying, or a profound editorial prophesy, it was too accurate for comfort. The November 17 (1992) address of the President simply did what critics of the government had long predicted it would do by extending the PTP to August 1993.

Vindicated, the Campaign for Democracy rolled out its programme of opposing the latest extension. The response of the media to both the President's speech and the campaign against the extension was immediate. The reporting was more or less balanced, especially among the private media. Three positions emerged. First, there were those who openly supported the extension. This group, led by the *New Nigerian* and *Daily Times*, consisted mainly of government-owned media. The *Daily Times* (17/9/92), had indeed called for an extension even before the President's speech. Thus in its two-part editorial entitled 'The revitalised transition', shortly after the address, it not only welcomed the extension, but also attempted to defend it, insisting that it was necessary (*Daily Times* 25/11/92).

In the second group were those who accepted the extension as a fait-accompli. The *Guardian* (30/11/92), and the *Citizen* (23/11/92), belonged to this group. The group shared the same attitude with the *New Nigerian* group in their call for an interim government; it believed it was not relevant. Lastly, there were those who were not only opposed to the extension but had also opened their pages for the coverage and articulation of the interim government/IBB must go campaign. This group, led by *Tell* and Newbreed magazines, consisted mostly of the private weeklies.

As January 4 came and went, all the media sympathetic to the 'IBB must go' campaign became silent. They had been defeated. The failure of the campaign to achieve its objective of getting the military out of power by January 4 cannot be explained from the disposition of the media to the campaign, but from the inability of the campaign to develop into a mass movement capable of resisting the government on its own terms.

The June 12 Crisis

After the botched August Presidential primaries, the government banned all those who contested the primaries from further participation in the presidential elections and introduced a new system for the nomination of the presidential candidates. This new system, tagged 'Option A4', is a staggered system in which a successful candidate has to go through the ward, local government, state and finally the national primaries. At the end of their primaries, M.K.O. Abiola and Bashir Tofa were nominated to contest the Presidential election on the SDP and NRC ticket respectively.

While both candidates had a lot of money, they lacked a solid political base. In addition, there was general apathy towards the candidates which was caused by a combination of factors. The Presidential election held on June 12, 1993, recorded a low, though peaceful, voter turnout. After having formally announced the results of 20 out of the 31 electoral units of the Federation, the National Electoral Commission (NEC), was ordered by the government to suspend further announcements of the results. However, given that the results were already known in the states, the complete results of the election soon became public knowledge. Abiola of the SDP had won overwhelmingly. This opened the floodgates of chauvinism and opportunism. The *National Concord*, for example, had a week before the annulment of the elections rejected a press statement from the National Association of Nigeria Students (NANS) criticising Babangida's handling of the June 12 crisis. However, following the annulment of the elections, Concord lifted the statement from the Guardian and published it free.

As the position of the media was not based entirely on principles, their reporting of the June 12 protests contributed in no small measure to the regionalisation and ethnicisation of the June 12 mandate, thus turning a popular democratic mandate into a liability to the democratic struggle. In general, the media saw Abiola as either the 'Yoruba Candidate' or the 'Southern President'. Following this logic, they concentrated their reporting of the protests only in his 'base' while ignoring protests in other parts of the country.

The result was that the media helped in building the impression that only people from Abiola's base were protesting for the restoration of the mandate which simultaneously isolated those protesting in the north and reinforced negative regionalist attitudes in the south, both of which prevented an effective nation-wide approach to the struggle. The private media, on the other hand, were, on the whole, with the possible exception of those directly under NRC control, opposed to the annulment. Many of these papers came out boldly against the cancellation, as a result of which five media organisations were closed while a host of journalists were detained. This led to a new twist in the relationship between the press and the state.

Many of those who escaped arrest decided to continue publishing and distributing their papers illegally. For the first time in Nigerian press history, registered newspapers went underground and started publishing with 'unknown' printers. As they had virtually been turned into outlaws, they became much bolder because they no longer had anything to lose. The criticism of the government by papers such as *Tell, Tempo, Razor* etc. became extremely virulent and effective and the state machine became virtually powerless in containing them, except by harassing vendors and seizing whatever copies they could lay their hands on. Eventually, the state itself was dragged into 'illegality' as state security services were said to have started printing and circulating fake copies of anti-government newspapers and magazines with pro-government messages. The object was twofold, reach the wide audience that had been cut off from the pro-government press and discredit the anti-government press.

Some final points need to be made about the conduct of the private media in relation to the campaign for the restoration of the June 12 mandate. First, the degree to which these media were committed to the campaign for June 12 was dependent on their proximity to the 'direct' beneficiary of the 'mandate'. Thus while the *Concord* Press (owned by Abiola) and the Nigerian Tribune (controlled by a significant section of the SDP) were very vociferous, the *Guardian* and *Newswatch* were very cautious. Second, none of these media could be said to have supported the June 12 campaign from a purely liberal-democratic perspective. Their subsequent accommodation with the new military regime that replaced the Shonekan-led ING confirms this assertion. Evidence of this could also easily be seen from the general disposition of the media. Although many in the SDP saw the annulment as primarily directed against them, the majority of Nigerians saw in the cancellation an attempt by the Babangida regime to perpetuate itself in power.

The massive protests that greeted the annulment were thus directed at ensuring that the military left by August 27. The rider that the June 12 mandate be restored was only a logical extension of that since there was no alternative popular power base in the civil society. The media split immediately into two camps. The government-owned media hailed the cancellation as the best thing that had happened. The campaign was led by the FRCN, Kaduna and the *New Nigerian*. The government media launched a propaganda against both the pro-democracy movement and the June 12 mandate movement. They presented the protesters as mischief-makers who were bent on fomenting troubles among the peace loving citizens of the country. At one stage, the FRCN carried a fabricated story by Uche Chukwumerejie, then Minister of Information, about plots to bomb strategic places in Kaduna, Abuja and other cities by the pro-democracy movement.

The Government Versus The Media

The Babangida regime's romance with the media, epitomised by its abrogation of the notorious Decree 4, hardly lasted a year. In February 1986, barely six months after taking power, six journalists from the *Newswatch* magazine were arraigned before Justice Uwaifo's Panel on political detainees for contempt following the magazine's critical comments on the verdicts of the panel. From then on, *Newswatch* staffers became regular visitors to police and state security service offices until the magazine was proscribed by the government in April 1987. The proscription of the magazine had actually preceded the murder of founding member and Editor-in-Chief of the magazine, Dele Giwa, in October 1986, a parcel bomb, whose origin has yet to be determined. Is widely believed to be the handiwork of state security operatives.

A little earlier, another incident which was a foretaste of what the relationship between the government and the media would become had occurred in the Plateau State-owned paper, *Nigerian Standard*. The Managing Director of the paper and its editor were dismissed for what the government described as a 'persistent bad image of the paper', a euphemism for the paper's unsparing criticism of government policies. Although the editor was later reinstated, he was to be dismissed again in less than a year, this time for his criticism of the dismissal of two bank executives who had voiced their disagreement with the handling of the regime's monetary policies by the Central Bank of Nigeria (CBN). The editor of the Ibadan-based *Sunday Sketch* was lucky on this score as he survived the wrath of his governor, who ordered the seizure and burning of all copies of the edition of the paper in which the criticism against the bankers' dismissal featured (*Newswatch*, 4/9/89).

The banning of *Newswatch* was certainly the first major conflict between the media and the government. While the ban dented the image of so called government respect for press freedom, the action of the editors of the magazine, by publicly apologising to the government for a non-existing offence, set a not too courageous precedent which was to re-occur in the history of the regime. Apart from the closure of *Newswatch*, 1987 was a tortuous year for the media. The editor of Newswave magazine was detained over a cover story entitled 'How many Generals Now?' The government stopped the Guardian and *Vanguard* from the serialisation of the memoirs of Major Gen. Joe Garba and Nzeribe's book 'The Turning Point' respectively. The editor of the *New Nigerian* and his reporter were detained and subsequently dismissed over a story on the President's wife. The pattern of government response to news reports which it did not like had already been set in motion: it consisted of harassment, intimidation, arrest and detention, and in rare occasions, arraignment before a court. Indeed by the end of 1987, 20 such actions had been taken by the government on both private and public owned media (see Table 3).

Table 3: Punitive Government Actions Against Journalists and Media Organisations: Summary, 1986-1992

Year	Physical harrass- ment	Arrest detention	Closure occupation	Seizure of published materials	Discipli- nary action	Charged to court	Censored (not including electronic media censorship	Total
1986	3	1	1	0	2	6	0	13
1987	3	9	0	1	3	1	3	20
1988	3	6	1	1	7	8	1	27
1989	0	16	0	0	4	0	0	20
1990	4	34	5	1	0	3	0	47
1991	3	7	1	-	6	6	0	22
1992	6	2	1	1	7	0	1	18

Source: Compiled by author.

This trend progressively continued through 1988 (27 cases), 1989 (20 cases) and peaked in 1990 with about 47 reported cases (*The Guardian* 30/11/92). In that year, five newspaper organisations were closed for a total of nine months between them (see Table 4). More than 30 journalists were detained compared to 16 in 1989 and 6 in 1988, (the figure for 1987 was seven). Some of these journalists were detained for considerably long periods without any charges, (for example, both a reporter on the *Metropolitan Weekly* and F. Aborishade of the *Labour Militant* were detained for eight months each).

Although, the number of reported cases was less in 1991 and 1992, (22 and 18 respectively), what happened in those years was more outrageous. The Guardian Press was closed for 12 days on the orders of the Lagos State Governor for publishing a story in its *Guardian Express* on the death of two students of the Yaba College of Technology during a protest in the campus by the students. Six of its staff were detained and charged to court for publishing 'falsehood'. Although the story could not be refuted as it was true, a police spokesman later said that their action was to prevent, (read intimidate), the media from further giving publicity to the deaths, in an attempt to prevent possible sympathy protests by students in other campuses, as in 1986.[2] The Guardian Press was eventually reopened and its journalists released unconditionally in spite of its refusal to apologise as demanded by the governor.

Table 4: Media Closed or Proscribed Between 1986-1992

S/N	Media	Date	Duration
1.	Newswatch	April 1987	5 Months
2.	Observer	October 1988	-
3.	Punch	April 1990	21 Days
4.	John West	April 1990	39 Days
5.	Newbreed	April 1990	92 Days
6.	Vanguard	April 1990	61 Days
7.	Champion	April 1990	5 Days
8.	Guardian	July 1991	12 Days
9.	Concord	April 1992	-

Source: Compiled by author.

The bizarre cases at the *Observer* and at the *Nigerian Television Authority* have already been discussed. The other case of interest in 1991 was the expulsion of a foreign journalist, William Keeling of the London *Financial Times*, from the country. The paper had on 26 and 27, June 1991 published two articles by Keeling in which he gave an estimate of the oil windfall that accrued to Nigeria due to the Gulf War and indicated that about $3 billion was not reflected in the accounts of the Central Bank and might have been used in hosting the OAU's Heads of State summit in Abuja, maintaining ECOMOG forces in Liberia and building of the Abuja International Centre. The government, which did not refute the substance of his report, accused him of being unsympathetic to the government of Nigeria and gave him 24 hours to leave the country.

In 1992, it was the turn of the *Concord Press* to be closed. Its offence was the consistent criticism of the government's handling of the economy and of the transition programme by the *African Concord*. Although no legal charge was brought against the *Concord Press*, the government made it clear that it was displeased with the contents of the

April edition of the *African Concord* and demanded a public apology from both the publisher and the editors of the magazine as a condition for reopening the media house. Unlike the publisher of the Guardian Press, who stood by his staff, the *Concord Press* publisher insisted that the staff concerned apologise or resign from the magazine, an option which they found more honourable. Their departure settled the quarrel and Concord Press was allowed to resume publication. But 1992 did not close without journalists being reminded that the killing of Dele Giwa might not have been the final attempt on the lives of journalists. In May, the Kogi State Correspondent of *Concord* was bathed with acid as he was entering a restaurant in Lokoja. The culprits are yet to be found although an investigation by the Nigerian Union of Journalists (NUJ) believed that the reporter was attacked with acid because of his critical reports about the Kogi State government.[3]

As the August terminal date of the PTP approached, the Babangida government became even more intolerant of the media. In the first quarter of 1993, no fewer than three media organisations were occupied by security agents. *Tell* and *The News*, in addition to being occupied, suffered seizures of copies of their publications. Similarly no less than 30 journalists and editors suffered arrest and detention in the period. Following the annulment of the June 12 Presidential elections, five more newspapers were closed while more journalists and editors, and even members of their families,[4] were harassed. Seizures became more frequent. Eventually, the fleeing Babangida government sought solution to the media opposition by enacting a decree backing the closure of the five media houses. This decree remained in force until the demise of the Interim National Government following a palace coup by a faction of the military. It is an understatement to say that the media have received 'a real bashing from the government in the last eight years. Yet the government itself had recognised the ineffectiveness of this strong arm-twisting tactic in moulding the media into a docile one. Hence it, along with this, had employed other measures to come to terms with the 'media-boys' and their bosses.

Under the Babangida regime, bribing journalists both individually and collectively became widespread. The reluctance of the government to do anything about the newsprint situation was seen as another measure to contain the media.[5] The Nigerian Union of Journalists has, on its part, largely been unable to prevent the recurrence of attacks on its members by government. No doubt it did intervene on a number of occasions to seek the release of its members or demand the reopening of a closed media house but these were reactive actions which did not aim at preventing future occurrences. In 1987, it took the case for press freedom to the Constituent Assembly. They collaborated with the NPAN to demand the repeal of some of the old laws which tended to deny the media access to government information. The Assembly did not think the freedom needed by the press required them to 'separate the freedom of the press from the freedom of the individual' thereby sticking to the counsel earlier given by the President.[6]

Perhaps the only area where the NUJ was able to hold the government was on the media council decree. The government, having failed to muzzle the press through its rough tactics and bribery, sought a legal solution to the problem. As the country had no media control board, the government argued that there was a need for such a body, a point easily acceded to by bóth media practitioners and proprietors. The government-proposed media decree, (No. 59), was indeed not new, at least in content. It was similar to the 1978 Nigeria Press Council Decree No. 31, proposed by the Obasanjo regime but which could not be implemented due to opposition by the media organisations over the powers and composition of the council.

The same type of opposition met the 1987 draft. The Nigerian Press Organisation (NPO) — consisting of NUJ, NPAN and the Guild of Editors (GE) — responded to the draft decree on a point-to-point basis and when they met the Minister of Information, he assured them that their recommendations would be taken into account in the final version of the decree. But when it appeared that the version signed into law by the President in December 1988 still vested the power to register journalists in the council and pegged GE membership to one, the NPO announced that it was withdrawing its support for the Media Council and made it clear that its constituent bodies would not submit the names of their representatives to the Council unless the two major disagreements were sorted out. With this, the inauguration of the Council was stalled and continued to be so until in 1992 when the new Minister of Information acceded to the NPO demands and increased GE representation to two and reverted the power to register journalists to the NUJ. This paved the way for the eventual inauguration of the Council in late 1992.

Conclusion: Constraints and Possibilities

The Structural Adjustment Programme unleashed a crisis in the media sector. The response of the media to that crisis has engendered three notable trends which have serious implications for the democratic struggle. First, SAP has priced media products above the economic level of the average citizen. This trend appears to be growing with further commercialisation and the establishment of private broadcasting, new taxes and service charges for the electronic media and continuous increases of cover prices of print media. The ability of the media to influence the public is reduced with its reduced accessibility. Such a development has negative consequences for the use of the media as an effective instrument for reaching the public in the struggle for democracy.

Second, the response of the media to the crisis has significantly altered its own contents. This is particularly serious in the electronic media where commercialisation has meant that airtime can only be afforded by the rich. There is thus a concomitant shrinkage in the space available for the propagation of ideas other than those favoured by the rich and powerful.

Third, liberalisation, coupled with the economic crisis, has ensured that only the rich can own and sustain viable media organs. This has effectively strengthened the control of the media by the ruling class. Private broadcasting, when it finally takes off, will only accentuate the trend as only the rich can afford the large capital outlay required for the establishment of a radio/television station. This too would tend to undermine the struggle to unseat the status-quo.

Yet the possibilities for the media to advance the cause of democracy are real. Although the ownership structure is firmly in the hands of the ruling class, the plurality of ownership does ensure that the media does not present a monolithic interpretation of events and issues. This plurality of views was evident even within groups with the same type of ownership. Thus, we found in the private press the *National Concord* opposing discussions on the National Question while the *Guardian* was committed to such a discussion. In the same vein in the public domain, while the *Daily Times* was pleading for the opening of the universities closed as punishment for their role in the anti-SAP protests, the *New Nigerian* was busy attacking SAP critics.

On some occasions, the media have acted more or less independently of the ideas of their controllers. Even the *Daily Times* had to admit the obvious rising cases of human rights abuse by the government following the arrest and detention of many anti-SAP protesters under Decree No 2. This occasional daring response can be seen within the context of the Gramscian concept of hegemony in which the ideas of the oppressed suddenly found expression in the ruling class-controlled media. But the reality is slightly more complicated. Some of the issues that the media promoted were not fundamentally antagonistic to the interests of the ruling classes. It was indeed in some instances in their interests to oppose the government.

In all the cases reviewed, success or failure of the campaign to force concessions from government was not necessarily dependent on media support, although media coverage had a significant influence. The success of the campaigners was determined by their ability to turn their actions into a mass movement of the people, capable of engaging the government in serious confrontation. Thus when the movement against SAP and human rights abuse acquired momentum and became a popular struggle, the media abandoned their earlier position of cautious reminder to become a virulent attacker of the human rights abuse of government and to expose the evils of SAP. The end result was that the government conceded on both issues. On the other hand, the campaign for a national conference and interim government, both of which failed to become mass based, did not attract the media with the same force.

While SAP has the tendency to undermine the capacity of the media with respect to its utility in the struggle for democracy, this utility is not in doubt. It is, however, conditioned by the level and momentum of the struggle. At 'normal' times, the media, more often than not, maintains its support for the status-quo. However, as the struggle expands and involves more people, its momentum gives the media the confidence to dare the status quo, and take sides with the democratic forces and demands of the society. Thus, the utility of the media in the struggle is not given, but rather evolves and develops along with the sustained struggle for popular democracy.

Notes

1. I wish to thank A. O. Onoja of *The Sunday Magazine* and O. Uche of the Champion for their assistance in locating some of the materials I needed for this chapter.

2. For details see *Media Review*, July 1991. It is possible that the police, who were the major protagonists in the closure of the Guardian Press, had been offended by persistent 'bad press' from the paper, such as reports embarrassing to the force on the Ogunbuaja (the ex police officer) case and the killing of Dr Okeke of Klinsite by the police.

3. Interview with a member of the Nigerian Union of Journalist Committee set-up to investigate the incident, Lagos, December 1992.

4. For example, when the State Security Service operatives couldn't find the editor of *The News*, they arrested his wife and their three month old baby in proxy.

5. Interview with some media executives.

6. In his Inaugural address to the Constituent Assembly, President Babangida had declared that no institution should be guaranteed freedoms that are not guaranteed to the people and that press freedom cannot be above the freedom of the individual.

7

Student and Youth Vanguardism in the Struggle for Democracy

Kole Ahmed Shettima

Introduction

While youth and student activism has significantly diminished in Europe, North America and Latin America, (Altbach 1991; Levy 1991) the situation in Africa and other parts of the Third World is different (Nkinyangi 1991; Choi 1991). African students have been at the forefront of the struggles against autocratic regimes and the IMF's harsh structural adjustment programme imposed on the people.

In Mali, Niger, Senegal, Kenya and South Africa youths and students have been and still are pillars of opposition. The school has become a major space for social struggle. The contest between government and democratic movements for the control of the campuses is fierce.

Although students and youth have not single handedly led to the collapse of autocratic regimes, they have undermined the legitimacy of governments and precipitated their collapse. The general public has come to appreciate the critical voice of students and youth.

The focus of this chapter is on the National Association of Nigerian Students (NANS), the umbrella organisation of the student movement. The discussion is on the activities of the association at the national level. I have overlooked specific campus activities unless they are part of a national struggle. One of the important organisations overlooked is the National Youth Council of Nigeria, a government recognised umbrella organisation of youth that has played no significant role in political struggles.

Students have a radically different conception of democracy. For students, democracy is a new way of transforming different components of society. These include the educational, political and socio-economic sectors. By arguing for a new democratic society, students challenge conventional notions and experiences of democracy in Africa, which are usually limited to the elite selection or election process. The point should also be made that students' concern with democracy in Africa predates the collapse of the Berlin Wall. There is a long history that can be traced to the beginning of the anti-colonial struggles.

The chapter starts with an overview of the two major theoretical perspectives which dominated student movements since the 1960s. These are perspectives which place emphasis on individual consciousness while others focus on the structure of society. A discussion of the activities of the student movement in the politics of decolonisation as well as that of the postcolony until the 1970s then follows. This is intended to give a historical perspective on the role of the student movement in the struggle for national liberation.

The fourth section is on the struggle for a democratic education. The democratisation of education is one of the key issues which has occupied the attention of students since the 1980s. The next section analysis the struggle by students against Structural Adjustment Programme (SAP). Students view adjustment as a recolonisation package imposed on Africa by Western creditors. The impact of SAP in the view of students, will not only worsen the conditions of learning but also make education inaccessible to a majority of citizens. Thus, the struggle against adjustment is part and parcel of the struggle to make society democratic.

The next section focuses on the struggle for a democratic political system. Students have reinforced the case for a liberal democratic society in Nigeria since 1982. In conjunction with other democratic organisations, they formed various alliances including the Alliance for Democratic Rights (ADR) and the Campaign for Democracy (CD). The discussion on the struggle for a democratic political system is followed by tentative statements on students and the New Left in Nigeria — similar to the situation in the colonial struggles, students and former student activists are in the forefront and constitute the cadres of several social movements. Finally, the potentials and limitations of student movements are discussed.

Theoretical Perspectives on Student Activism

Literature on student movements has stagnated since the 1960s with the decline of student activism in Europe and North America. It is as if student movements ceased to exist in other parts of the world as no major theoretical breakthroughs have been made since then. Two major perspectives have dominated the literature on student activism. There are scholars who dwell on consciousness while others focus on structuralism, the former are labelled negativists and the latter positivists. Among the scholars who champion the consciousness perspective are Bakke (1966), Bereday (1958), and Mannheim (1972). These scholars characterise student activism as vague, emotional, aggressive, depicting it as puberty rites, youthful exuberance, fear of the adult world, and generational disequilibrium. Student activism is analysed as an individual's behaviour. According to Lewis Feuer, one of the leading exponents of this perspective:

> The student movement have thus far been too largely an example of projective politics, (Feuer's emphasis), in the sense that they have been largely dominated by unconscious drives; the will to revolt against the de-authorised father... A politics of the unconscious carries with it untold dangers for the future of civilisation (Feuer, cited in Munoz, 1989:12).

A number of criticisms have been made against the individualistic explanation of student activism: too much emphasis on psychological factors, inability to explain a very large amount of student activist phenomena, status quo oriented, bias towards Western society and racism (Munoz 1989; Yusuf 1991).

The structuralists on the other hand, stress factors like authoritarianism in the educational sector and the wider society, the critical role of intellectuals, inequality in society, adverse economic conditions and the nature and character of third world societies (Munoz 1989; Choi 1991; Nkinyangi 1991). These scholars dwell on political, economic and social aspects of society. Among the structuralist are activists of the student movement, the New Left and their sympathisers.

Academic writings on Nigerian student movements have been dominated by structuralists. Among these are Yusuf (1991), Ayu (1986) and Madunagu (1980). Both Madunagu and Yusuf argue that conflict is inherent in all capitalist systems because of the irreconcilable contradiction between labour and capital. What they overlook is that students as a group are not directly involved in social production, they are not owners of capital or waged workers. They are petty-bourgeois. Students as a social group have different and sometimes contradictory interests. Some are part-time workers or workers on in-service training, others are parents and wards. The contradictory nature of students means that it is difficult for them to articulate a definite class position. In addition, the general crisis of capitalism and the autocratic nature of the political system impinges greatly on the student body. The educational sector, which is mostly publicly funded, comes under pressure over the removal of subsidy, curtailment of allowances, increase in tuition fees etc. Students and parents bear the enormous cost of education. The government also tries to control the academic environment through authoritarian structures. These contradictory situations have implications for student activism.

Student Vanguardism: A Legacy of Struggle

Youth and student involvement in the struggle for a democratic society is intrinsically linked to the struggle for national liberation. The West African Students Union (WASU), formed in 1925, was the forerunner of the Nigerian Union of Students of Great Britain and Ireland, and the National Union of Nigerian Students (NUNS), later the National Association of Nigerian Students (NANS). The WASU was a major force in the decolonisation process in West Africa. Some prominent members of the organisation played a critical role in the nationalist struggle. Similarly, some of them played important roles in the post-colonial period. Among these politicians were the late Kwame Nkrumah and Milton Margai (Olusanya 1982). WASU had close relationships with the Fabian Society, the League Against Imperialism and supported the British Labour Party in the 1945 election. It was as a result of disappointment with the performance of the Labour Party in power that WASU openly campaigned for positive action and turned to Marxist theories for inspiration (Olusanya 1982).

The Nigerian Union of Students of Great Britain and Ireland (later the Nigerian Union of Students) was formed as the momentum of the national independence struggle intensified. In 1943, the Union held an important rally which, according to Coleman (1963), was a critical moment in the political mobilisation of the youth. The rally eventually led to the formation of the Nigerian National Council, which later became the National Council for Nigeria and Cameroons (NCNC). The NCNC was the dominant oppositional nationalist movement until the 1950s. Activists of the NCNC were the core members of the Zikist Movement, a youth organisation committed to radical change in Nigeria.

The National Union of Nigerian Students (NUNS), founded in 1956, had a history of militant student unionism. In 1961, the NUNS led students to demonstrate against the murder of Patrice Lumumba, condemned the Balewa regime for supporting the Monrovia group in the process of the formation of the Organisation for African Unity, and successfully campaigned against the signing of the Anglo/Nigeria Defence Pact. Other activities of the Union included the campaign against the corrupt Gowon military regime and resistance to the regime's decision not to hand over power to civilians in 1974; it denounced the

American Peace Corps Programme; and supported radical organisations such as the Nigerian Youth Congress and the Pan African Youth Movement (Aminu 1986; Yusuf 1991). No doubt, foreign policy issues dominated the activities of NUNS for a long time. The 'Ali Must Go' 1978 revolt was the most dramatic national issue in the history of the Union. The revolt developed in reaction to a new policy leading to an increase in the cost of education. The proposed increase in meal and lodging fees would have been 400 per cent and 50 per cent respectively (Aminu 1986). After nation-wide demonstrations, nine students were killed, seven academic staff, two university administrators and a journalist lost their jobs (ASUU 1986a). Hundreds of students were suspended or rusticated and the union was banned.

The ban on NUNS was disregarded by students and they eventually formed the National Association of Nigerian Students (NANS). The formation of NANS coincided with the beginning of the Second Republic in 1979. The government of Shehu Shagari (1979-1983), introduced austerity measures which, coupled with mismanagement and corruption, did not escape the attention of students. To control the student movement, the government devised a divide and rule strategy. It sponsored the formation of rival student groups aligned with the ruling political party, the National Party of Nigeria, but none of them were able to develop a substantial following. NANS waged serious campaigns against the government. The Buhari regime (1984-1985) was also at loggerheads with the students and ultimately banned NANS. In 1984, students protested against the withdrawal of centralised catering services and the removal of other support facilities to the educational sector. In 1985, students were the only organised group that actively supported the Nigeria Medical Association and the National Association of Resident Doctors in their fight over the collapse of the health sector. The popular campaigns by students along with other democratic groups against the Buhari regime on issues relating to civil and human rights as well as economic policies was capitalised on by General Babangida when he carried out his coup d'etat of August 1985.

The Struggle for the Democratisation of the Educational Sector

If for spouses democracy starts from the home, for students, it starts from the school. The struggle for democratisation of the educational system has been one of the major demands of NANS. The Charter of Demands, the main document which contains the guiding principles of the Association, enunciates the need for a democratic educational system.

Among the issues raised in the document are student's democratic representation and participation in faculty and departmental decision making bodies, the election and representation of students in the senate(s), council(s) and governing bodies of universities, the existence of independent student unions, the right to form associations, the establishment of a new educational policy written by representatives of students and workers in the educational sector and the funding of Primary and Secondary education by the Federal Government (NANS 1982:8-9).

Student's demands for democratisation of the educational sector is informed by their experience of the problems associated with the authoritarian governance of schools. Military regimes, which have ruled for more than two-thirds of the post-independence period, relate to students in a military 'zombie' style. Orders from the top are given on opening, closure and suspension of students and schools. School authorities have virtually lost their autonomy in deciding basic issues like their academic calendars. It is not surprising, therefore, that students are concerned about the democratisation of the educational system. For example, in 1986, there were nation-wide demonstrations to protest the killing of students in Ahmadu Bello University, Zaria. After that crisis, the government directed that membership of student unions should henceforth be voluntary and no fees should be collected by any authority on behalf of any union except for sport activities (Maianguwa 1987). The objective of the order was to curtail and render ineffective student unionism. At the same time, the close relationship between the central labour organisation, the Nigerian Labour Congress (NLC) and NANS was severed by the government. The NLC called its members out on nation-wide sympathy demonstrations with students. The government warned that 'a student union is not a trade union and therefore should not get involved in trade unionism' (FGN 1986:16). Trade unions were also warned not to interfere in student unionism.

Furthermore, in order to break the democratic spirit of the student movement, the government directed that there should no longer be general congress meetings attended by all students and that all decisions should be made by student parliaments and student executive councils. All student unions and NANS were banned, the latter being banned only five months after the ban imposed since 1984 was lifted. In announcing the ban on NANS, the Minister of Education said NANS:

... is still intransigent. We regrettably have to ban such organisations because they have no rightful place in our system. The organisation is well and truly banned for reasons of national interest and cannot continue as a lawless body (ASUU 1986b).

However, NANS has consistently argued that it cannot be banned by any government as the reality of its legitimacy does not lie in the recognition of an oppressive regime. Its legitimacy is derived from the recognition of the Nigerian students and the Nigerian people who recognise the successful articulation of their interests in the organisation's activities (Lukman 1989:9).

In 1987, the government took a decisive step to control student unionism by promulgating the Students Union Activities (Control and Regulation) Decree 47. The decree made student union membership voluntary, and more importantly, confined unions to individual institutions. This made national student unionism illegal. Any student union was to be proscribed if it was 'not in the interest of national security, public safety, public order, public morality or public health' all euphemisms for state control of student unions. The Minister of Education was empowered to expel, suspend or withdraw any student from any institution of learning and the President of the Federation had the right to proscribe any union. Persons who failed to comply with the decree would be tried by a tribunal and be 'liable on conviction to a fine not exceeding 50,000 naira or imprisonment for a term not exceeding five years or both' (FGN 1989:A711-13).

Despite the attempts by the state to intimidate, harass and break student unions, it has not succeeded. Whenever student unions are banned, professional and departmental associations provide platforms for popular mobilisation and protection of the democratic rights of students. It was only in 1993 that the government lifted the ban on NANS following its inability to intimidate and harass the central student body. However, NANS, to the government's embarrassment, rejected the 'magnanimous' offer to lift the ban and declared that the only legitimacy and recognition it is interested in is that of its constituency, the students and the Nigerian people.

The Struggle Against Economic Adjustment

Since the official announcement of the Structural Adjustment Programme (SAP) in 1986, students have been its most consistent critics. In April 1988 and April 1989 students led nation-wide demonstrations against SAP. Similarly in March 1990, students were on the streets to protest against the World Bank loan to Nigerian universities. The protests by students against the implementation of SAP is informed by their view that SAP is a recolonisation mission sponsored by the International Monetary Fund and the World Bank. The deregulation of the economy has hit the poorest sections of the society the hardest. Students as intellectuals consider it an obligation to lead the struggle against massive impoverishment. The Principal Officer of the association has argued that:

> NANS views with serious concern the total failure of the SAP imposed on the nation by the IMF and the World Bank. Delegates hold that SAP and its components — Foreign Exchange Market (FEM), privatisation, and the so called debt-equity swap — are designed by Western countries as part of the conspiracy to sabotage the destiny of our country and subject our people to perpetual penury and slavery (Amidu and Ekeocha 1988:1).

Similarly, NANS viewed the policy of a removal of subsidy on education as a strategy to make education accessible only to the rich minority. In August 1988, the association reminded its members that:

> The consistent resistance of NANS has halted the total commercialisation of education, introduction of school fees, rationalisation and increase in the fees of accommodation... all part of the IMF package (NANS Publicity Bureau 1988:4).

In 1988 and 1989, students initiated demonstrations which assumed a national character. Marketwomen's associations, professional bodies, workers and pupils joined the demonstrations. As usual, the government took panicky measures to close down educational institutions, some for as long as nine months, banned student unions, detained student leaders and harassed and intimidated activists. However, in tacit recognition of the hardship people were experiencing due to SAP, the government introduced a SAP relief package.

The Struggle for a Democratic Political System

Nigerian students have recognised their role as a vanguard in the struggle for a socially and politically just society. This is reflected in the NANS Charter of Demands which calls for a society in which individuals have the right to form associations, express themselves freely without any hindrance, and participate in partisan politics. Other democratic demands of NANS include the rights of individuals to privacy and free movement and a free press as well as the abrogation of the Public Order Act, under which individuals are arrested on superficial grounds (NANS 1982:13-15).

NANS has closely monitored the political transition programme initiated by the Babangida regime. In 1986, NANS's submission to the

Political Bureau, which was charged with the responsibility of collating the views of Nigerians on the country's political future, advocated socialism as the guiding philosophy for the country. It called for a broad based National Conference to debate social and national questions confronting the country.

Subsequently, NANS expressed its concerns about the genuineness of the political transition programme because of the government's unilateral rejection of the will of the people by rejecting the fundamental recommendations of the Political Bureau, in particular, the Bureau's recommendation that most Nigerians had asked for a socialist society. The composition of the Constituent Assembly, which had a very significant number of government nominees, and the imposition of an agenda on the body were also criticised by NANS.

Other concerns of NANS were the doctoring of the Constituent Assembly report by the military government, the registration of political parties by the Armed Forces Ruling Council instead of the National Electoral Commission, the guidelines on party formation, (the parties must endorse SAP, pay a registration fee of 50,000 naira and submit detailed files on all party members) and later the imposition of two political parties. Furthermore, the Association expressed concerns on the unilateral dissolution of elected local government councils, the unwarranted revision of the transition programme and electoral laws, the dismissal of elected local government officials because of disagreements with military officers, the clampdown on workers unions and the gagging of the press (*Solidarity*, (Lagos) 1990, Vol.1, No.1:1-6; Amidu and Ekeocha 1988; Lukman 1989). These measures, according to NANS, indicated that the regime intended to perpetuate itself and SAP directly or through its stooges:

> It is our position that the content and spirit of any genuine transition must
> be democratic and its implementation must also take place in a
> democratic environment (NANS Publicity Bureau 1990).

NANS expressed its lack of faith in the military government because it has so far proved not only incapable of finding solutions to the fundamental problems of the society but has accentuated and deepened these problems. Moreover, according to NANS, the military has created a political atmosphere within which these problems may be very difficult to resolve. Among the problems listed were the debt burden, violation of human rights, corruption and the imperialist control of the economy (NANS Publicity Bureau 1990; NANS 1990b).

When the government created the political stalemate in July 1993, NANS posited that it was a sad vindication of its position since 1987: the military government was not sincere about the transition programme. Being a member of the Campaign for Democracy, NANS participated actively in the campaign to oppose the entrenching of undemocratic structures in Nigeria. Its position on the June 1993 elections echoed the concerns of many other mass organisations (see Shettima 1993). NANS called for:

> The immediate release of the results of the June 12 election, termination of military rule on or before August 27, 1993 and the convening of a sovereign national conference comprising legitimate representatives of mass democratic and populist organisation (Jaafar and Onoja, *The Guardian*, July 16, 1993).

It cautioned that its support for the release of the results of the June 12, 1993 election was not an indication of its acceptance of the transition programme, from which it has disassociated itself, but 'a credible way forward as far as a complete exit of Babangida military junta from power is concerned' (Guardian, July 16, 1993). NANS condemned the idea of an interim government as proposed by the two political parties and the government. Many NANS activists were arrested and detained during its 30th Senate meeting in Enugu for their role in the pro-democracy demonstrations in July/August 1993. Indeed, it is widely speculated that the government timed the presidential elections at about the time of the closure of the universities and polytechnics to keep the students off campus. If students were on campus in June 1993, the government would have found it difficult to create the political stalemate it had planned.

The Student Movement and Popular Organisations

The struggles waged by students since colonial times have been conducted in conjunction with other popular and democratic organisations. This is based on the realisation that students as a group have limited potential to overthrow a current system and construct another. In 1982, the Alliance for Democratic Rights (ADR) was formed as a result of the violation of people's economic, political and social rights by the Shagari regime. The ADR was launched by various mass associations including NANS, Women in Nigeria (WIN), socialist parties and study groups. Among the objectives of the ADR were the establishment and consolidation of democratic rights and social justice, the right to form political associations, resistance to re-colonialisation of Nigeria via the IMF and the World Bank etc., and support for other struggling peoples all over the world (Mohammed 1986:54).

To establish better relations with the labour movement, NANS signed an accord with the Nigeria Labour Congress (NLC) in 1983 to protect their common interests. It was in the spirit of the agreement that the NLC called for nation-wide sympathy demonstrations to protest against the government's handling of the May 1986 student crisis. The government mobilised all its resources to crush the planned demonstrations. Similarly, at the end of the 23rd Senate meeting of NANS in 1990, it was agreed that the association should consolidate its alliance with human rights organisations to better protest against the abuse of the rights of the people, champion the cause of a national conference and campaign for democracy (NANS, 1990a). It is not surprising that NANS was one of the most active initiators of the botched National Conference in 1990. NANS's submission to the Conference argued for an immediate end to military rule, the setting-up of a constituent Assembly, an interim government with a 12-month transition period, a unilateral moratorium on the nation's debt, abrogation of all dictatorial decrees, respect for the rule of law, increased spending on education, health and transportation and multiparty democracy (NANS Publicity Bureau 1990:2. See also Labour Militant, July-August 1990).

It argued that the Constituent Assembly should be composed of representatives of mass organisations and professional associations. The Assembly should be mandated to design a new constitution and constitute itself as an interim government to organise a 12-month transition programme to a multi-party democracy that would reflect the socially differentiated nature of Nigerian society. A Campaign for Democracy (CD) was launched by the following organisations — NANS, Movement Against Second Slavery, Civil Liberty Organisation, Committee for the Defence of Human Rights, National Association · of Democratic Lawyers, Gani Fawehinmi Solidarity Organisation, Committee for Unity and Progress and Women-in-Nigeria. The CD was to ensure, among other things:

1. A democratic transition to civil rule which includes the urgent formation of a democratically elected national constituent assembly whose function is to conduct a free transition to democratic civilian rule.

2. The abrogation of all draconian and undemocratic decrees.

3. Immediate restoration of the right of all citizens to finance associations.

4. The establishment of a national emergency programme NOW (emphasis original) to provide adequate and free education and medical care for all.

5. The establishment of a National Emergency Housing Programme to provide cheap, affordable housing and transportation for every citizen.

6. The establishment of a new national minimum wage (Solidarity, Vol.1, No.1:7).

The Campaign for Democracy is currently the largest pro-democracy movement and students are the largest constituents of it.

Conclusion

The student movement has been pro-active in the struggle for democracy in Nigeria. Since the adoption of the Charter of Demands in 1982, it entered into various alliances with democratic and mass organisations to campaign for social justice and democratic norms. The vision of the student movement is essentially that of creating the conditions for the emergence of a socialist democratic state. In the alliances formed both in the ADR, CD and with the NLC, the students' views were consistent with the objectives stated in the Charter of Demands. Thus, the struggle for a democratic society by students is not a fallout from the collapse of the Berlin Wall. Nor does their vision of a democratic society stop at the superficial level of what is normally considered as the basic principles of a democratic society, such as plurality of associations, respect for the rule of law and freedom of the press. Students have consistently added social and economic demands, such as good and affordable transportation, basic general healthcare, decent housing and good education in their struggles.

The aim of NANS is to struggle for a national socialist democratic society in alliance with other forces and associations because it realises its limitations as a student movement that is located outside the direct production process. It accepts it is a middle class group with limited membership and limited capacity to confront the state. Alliances with different associations like the NLC are formed to remedy some of these limitations. NANS as a New Left project is seen clearly from its involvement with popular organisations in general and women's groups in particular. During demonstrations, market women have been close allies of students. Similarly, the Women in Nigeria organisation and the Nigeria Labour Congress Women's Wing have attended NANS activities and vice versa. Students have also been active in the struggle against racial discrimination. The Youth Solidarity on Southern Africa was one of the major fronts in institutions of learning that campaigned for racial justice in Southern African.

At another level, NANS has provided the cadres for most of the mass organisations in the country. Many of the cadres of mass and human rights organisations were 'baptised' in the student movement. These organisations include Women in Nigeria, Nigerian Labour Congress, Campaign for Democracy, Committee for the Defence of Human Rights, Civil Liberties Organisation, Nigeria-ANC Friendship and Cultural Association and Community Awareness for Popular Participation. The student movement is the largest constituency of the CD which is why the government found it expedient to keep the doors of the universities closed during the period of the presidential elections in 1993.

While the student movement has been in the vanguard against structural adjustment and autocratic structures, its weaknesses should not be overlooked. First, the closure of universities at the period of the political stalemate exposed the limitations of student vanguardism. Students can only be effective if they are found in large numbers on the campuses. Moreover, the fact that NANS was not able to mobilise its other members whose institutions were not closed indicates organisational weakness.

Second, since the mid-1980s, there has been organisational weaknesses linked primarily to its inability to recruit and sustain cadres. The sources of its cadres, which are the various radical movements of the campuses, have not been effective. Such campus movements include the New Age Youth Movement, Movement for Progressive Nigeria, League of Patriotic Students and Youth Solidarity On Southern Africa of Nigeria. Similarly, the Patriotic Youth Movement of Nigeria, which is the coordinating unit of these organisations has been weak. Finally, NANS has also suffered from the increased fragmentation of the student movement brought about by economic pressures, the proliferation of institutions of learning and increased sectarianism.

8

Intellectuals and Academics in the Struggle for Democracy

Attahiru Jega

Introduction

The authoritarian disposition acquired by the Nigerian state under prolonged military rule has resulted in constrained, curbed and curtailed popular political participation. The state has consistently acted in ways which have tended to shrink the political arena. Yet, under crisis and adjustment, the Nigerian state has propelled complex patterns and dynamics of political struggles aimed at expanding the Nigerian democratic space. The IMF and World Bank-inspired Structural Adjustment Programme (SAP), combined with the highly restrictive Transition Programme of the Babangida regime, have demarcated the parameters of the democratic space allowed by the state. At the same time, these programmes set the agenda for the struggles which surfaced, aimed at widening the scope of democracy in Nigeria both under authoritarian military regimes as well as for the post-military Third Republic.

Active and vibrant groups have emerged and have been actively involved in the struggle for democracy. Other traditionally conservative groups have become reinvigorated, if not rejuvenated by the dynamics of SAP and the politics of transition such that they have also come to play crucial roles in the democratisation process. Economic deprivations occasioned by SAP have taken away many of the opportunities hitherto taken for granted by these traditionally conservative groups such that many individuals have had to come to grips with matters of basic survival. Thus, the struggle for democracy has become inextricably intertwined with the struggle for protecting or guaranteeing basic rights and privileges.

The case of intellectuals and academics provides an interesting and highly illuminating illustration of the contradictory ways in which this segment of the so-called middle class has played crucial roles in the democratisation process, as well as in the general struggles for the expansion of the Nigerian democratic space. This chapter attempts to demonstrate that Nigerian intellectuals and academics, being part and parcel of the larger society characterised by ideological and political divisions, have played vital and decisive roles in the struggle for democracy. The specific nature and character of these roles are discussed in the context of the historical evolution of the group as well as that of the political and economic restructuring pursued by the Babangida regime. The second section defines the intellectual and the third reviews and assesses the origin, growth and development of Nigerian intellectuals and academics. The fourth section analyses and critiques the roles they have played in democratic struggles especially in the 1980s and beyond. The conclusion sets out the tasks and the requirements for effective struggles to expand Nigerian democratic space.

Defining the Intellectual

At a general level, intellectuals can be broadly defined as people who have a specially developed capacity 'for thinking, reasoning, relating, judging, conceptualising, etc.' (IESS). This capacity is mainly developed through acquired skills and training, and through a programme of studies mostly, but not exclusively, at the University level (Perry 1984). Gouldner sees intellectuals as people 'whose interests are primarily critical, emancipatory hermeneutic and hence often political' (1979:48). Their special skills and training enables them to assess and appreciate society and its problems better than others who are less endowed. They also have a better capacity and ability to postulate how problems can be solved, at least theoretically. In countries like Nigeria, intellectuals belong to, and are an essential component of, the middle class. Thus, they reflect as well as internalise many of the general political, economic and ideological characteristics of the middle class. They are differentiated along the major political and ideological lines in society. Many are opportunistic. They serve different class interests. They are affected and conditioned by the socio-economic dynamics and inter-relationships of the society. Hence, as Bangura noted:

> Intellectuals are pulled between several contradictory forces: tradition and modernity; sectionalism and universalism; and conservatism and radicalism (1993:4).

Depending on their social relevance and the class interests that they project or serve, intellectuals have been broadly categorised into two groups, revolutionary intellectuals and 'accommodative' intellectuals (Gouldner 1979). The latter seeks to either defend and preserve the status quo or at least accepts it; while the former challenges the status quo and strives to transform society to dislodge prevailing conservative and exploitative values, beliefs and practices. 'Accommodative' intellectuals, in the context of Nigeria, referred to by Tukur (1990) as 'neo-colonial Philistines', basically serve to 'accommodate the future to the past and to reproduce the past in the future' (Gouldner 1979:48). On the other hand, revolutionary intellectuals are perceived as being socially relevant given their role in challenging dominant and prevalent power relations in society. As a consequence of the role they perform, Gramsci refers to this category as 'Organic intellectuals'.

Some theorists see intellectuals as an emergent new class, especially in the developing societies. For example, Gouldner (1979:7) has argued that intellectuals in the Third World represent a '(relatively) autonomous social stratum...' which is not only cohesive, but also elitist and self-seeking and uses its special knowledge to advance its own interests and power, and to control its own work situation. This implies independence of action and unity of purpose in the role of intellectuals in society. This conceptualisation, however, is not correct. On the contrary, as Tukur (1990) observed:

> Intellectuals are neither independent of the process of production and appropriation of society's means of sustenance nor are they an independent class within society.

Indeed, it may be better to perceive them as '... isolated actors who cannot operate as a social force in the way organised groups tend to be' (Bangura 1993).

The terms academic and intellectual are often used interchangeably. Conceptually, however, an intellectual is not necessarily a member of the Academy, although academics may be broadly seen as intellectuals, given their specialised training and vocation. In the 1890s in America when the concept was first used, it was in reference to an 'alumnus or alumna of a University', who were not necessarily working in the university (Perry). It can, therefore, be said that academics are only a component, or a sub-set, of intellectuals, although a very important one. Indeed, academics may be the largest segment of intellectuals in any society. This is certainly the case in Nigeria, and the reason why they are accorded primary treatment in this study.

Nigerian Intellectuals: Origins, Growth and Development

Colonialism, colonial processes and colonial education in particular, have played a critical role in the emergence and conditioning of Nigerian intellectuals. The first generation of Nigerian intellectuals received their training and skills from British institutions. The majority of them can be categorised as 'accommodative' intellectuals who served the colonial masters as experts/intelligentsia in government and in the private sector. The academic component came into being when the University College, Ibadan, opened in 1948. Those who exhibited a radical or 'revolutionary' tendency under colonial rule ended up being self-employed, as lawyers, newspaper publishers/proprietors (the only exception was perhaps Herbert Macaulay) and they later came to play prominent roles in the nationalist and independent struggles.

The emergence of four additional universities in 1962 marked another phase in the growth and development of Nigerian intellectuals. Not only did these universities, together with Ibadan, produce graduates to swell the ranks of intellectuals, many Nigerians increasingly joined them as academics after receiving specialised training and skills.

The neo-colonial process, however, ensured that a preponderant part of the intellectual community served accommodative roles, and collaborated with the dominant classes in maintaining the status quo; a situation which not only favoured the imperialists but which also perpetuated prevailing power relations. Intellectuals served the state as technocrats, or as consultants and 'experts'. Those in the universities and other institutions of higher learning, busied themselves with drilling the 'pedagogy of the oppressed' into their students, when they were not consulting for the state or private firms. Only a tiny minority could be said to be critical and opposed to the status quo in any socially relevant way. Many Nigerian intellectuals during this period fall within Ayandele's concept of 'deluded hybrids', with a lot of idealism and illusory conceptions of their role in society, but basically socially irrelevant. Few attempted to be visible in politics or to in any way demonstrate relevance and activism, such as Soyinka's alleged commandeering of a radio station to articulate anti-state, populist ideas during the western region crisis of the 1960s.

The oil boom of the 1970s marked another phase in the development of Nigerian intellectuals. The educational system expanded rapidly and quite remarkably. The number of universities increased from 5 in 1962 to 13 in 1973 and to 21 in 1980. Student enrolment increased phenomenally from 3,681 in 1962 to 40,914 in 1976-1977 and to 92,116 in 1982-1983

(NUC). The number of academic staff increased from 1,000 in 1962 to 1,831 in 1970-1971 and to 7,545 in 1991-1982. In 1985-1986 it reached 11,016 (MOE 1990; NUC 1977 and 1983). Consequently, this led to the expansion of the middle class (Diamond 1988).

Political involvement and activism of the intellectuals during this period only showed or confirmed the differentiated ideological leanings or roles played by the intellectuals in the democratic process. For example, in the politics of the Second Republic, some liberal intellectuals joined the NPN government at both the federal and state levels while some left-leaning radicals were actively involved in UPN and PRP. Prior to this period (1979-1983), many intellectuals served the successive military regimes, while a few stayed away from government jobs and played the role of 'critical thinkers' not trapped by the prejudices and conventions of society at large' (Perry). Generally, Nigerian intellectuals remained socially irrelevant without any direct impact on the democratisation process. This is to the extent that the struggles of intellectuals can only make meaning and be socially relevant in the context of broad working class struggles, with the essential objective of advancing popular mass participation in politics and people-oriented policies and programmes.

Intellectuals and Struggles for Democracy Since 1980

The Nigerian economic crisis, which became entrenched in the early 1980s, has pushed the Nigerian intellectual to the cross-roads between social relevance and irrelevance. The heightened and intensified crisis, accompanied by prolonged authoritarian military rule, has in a number of fundamental respects, conditioned the role that intellectuals came to play in the democratisation process as well as in the struggle for democracy. The apparently bleak future has generated opportunism and crude collaborative tendencies on the part of some intellectuals while, at the same time, giving rise to deep concerns and propelling some of the intellectuals, who ordinarily only care for a liberal atmosphere for their intellectual pursuits, to actively be involved in struggles for popular democracy in organised fora. This has been largely facilitated by what Diamond (1988:33) identified as the 'steady growth of the social infrastructure of democracy — a free press, a rapidly expanding educational system, a sophisticated legal system, and a diverse array of autonomous social cultural, and economic organisations'.

The transition programme initiated by the Babangida regime in the middle of the 1980s, which was conditioned and tempered by the biting effects of the Structural Adjustment Programme that he also introduced, brought into focus the dynamics of the differentiated and contradictory roles of the Nigerian intellectuals in the struggles for democracy. At one level, prominent and otherwise respected intellectuals collaborated with the regime in its ill-fated experimentation with democratic processes and so-called social engineering. Some, notably political scientists, proffered the theoretical postulations and the methodologies for the regime's political transition programme. They also became 'transition handlers' and managers. Others served the regime in the mobilisation campaigns perceived as essential in fostering the 'new' political and democratic dispensation. Others served in the National Electoral Commission (NEC); the Centre for Democratic Studies (CDS); the Presidential Advisory Commission (PAC); the National Council on Inter-Governmental Relations (NCIR); and in the Directorate of Food, Roads and Rural Infrastructure (DFFRI), an agency meant to provide the socio-economic infrastructure for instituting lasting 'grassroots' democracy. Many others served as the Presidential speech writers who articulated and/or manufactured some of the most profoundly undemocratic aspects of the transition politics, such as the dissolution of the 13 political associations; the decreeing of the two government created political parties; the open ballot electoral system; Option A4; and so on.

Babangida's regime proved to be one of those typical 'cohesive and self-confident authoritarianisms' described by Stephan which, as he shows: 'Can enlist numerous middle class intellectuals, clergymen, journalists and other professionals on its side (1990:431)'.

Those intellectuals the regime successfully drew to its side served it very well, in various capacities, including that of playing the role of combatants deployed to counter other segments of the intellectual community who have opted to participate in struggles to expand the democratic arena. In this capacity, for example, Jibril Aminu, one-time professor and vice-chancellor of a university, 'combated' the Academic Staff Union of Universities (ASUU), describing its leadership as irresponsible, facilitating its incarceration and finally banning it in 1988.

Also, Ikenna Nzimiro, one-time professor, in his capacity as a member of the Presidential Advisory Council (PAC), attempted to 'combat', intellectually, the perceived excesses and unco-operative disposition of ASUU leaders by resorting to 'Marxist' polemics in lengthy letters to

ASUU presidents between 1987 and 1992, apparently aimed at instructing them on the benefits of collaborating with the Babangida regime, with illustrations from the Nigerian Labour Congress (NLC) methods and tactics. In a somewhat different context of intellectual polemics and 'combat', a triumvirate of political scientists who worked very closely with President Babangida, wrote or edited at least six books glorifying the Babangida era and defending their roles in the regime.

The Babangida regime exhibited an incredible capacity to co-opt and absorb any intellectual willing to serve it, regardless of previous ideological posturing. The Soyinkas, the Solarins, the Aboyades, the Jerry Ganas, and the Rimis of the Nigerian intellectual community all got sucked into the Babangida regime's drag-net. The devastating impact of the economic crisis on the living conditions of the intellectuals in general, and the academics in particular, led many to opportunistically collaborate with, as well as accommodate, the undemocratic excesses of the regime.

At another level however, some intellectuals participated in the democratic struggles against the regime's authoritarian and undemocratic disposition, reflected not only in its method of governance based on harassment, intimidation and use of coercion against perceived opponents, but also in its political transition programme, as it unfolded. The role of this category of intellectuals was conditioned by their principled, radical, if not revolutionary, ideological orientation, as well as by the objective conditions of survival under crisis and Structural Adjustment. SAP eroded the purchasing power of the middle class and unleashed a process of 'proletarianisation' onto a sizeable number of the lower middle class. Fresh graduates with good professional degrees in either law or engineering found themselves under-employed or unemployed, having to rely on multiple livelihood coping strategies (Mustapha 1992). This objective condition has had a somewhat radicalising effect on this segment of the Nigerian community of intellectuals and professionals, pushing many of them into organised popular struggles, linking matters of basic survival with the broad concerns of democratisation (Jega 1993).

Trade unions and organised professional groups provided the organisational platform for the struggles of this category of intellectual. The effectiveness of the struggles was enhanced by the forging of broad democratic alliances cutting across several civil society groupings. The resilience of this group, despite all sorts of tactics of co-optation, led the state to develop strategies of containment. One such method contemplated by the state early in the 1980s and implemented by the

Babangida regime, was that of preventing academics, technocrats and other public servants from active participation in partisan politics. In 1982, for example, about the same time that ASUU embarked upon a successful strike and became nationally prominent, and academics started demanding an expanded role in partisan politics, the then Secretary to the Federal Government articulated a position to the effect that it was unhealthy for academics to be involved in politics. He argued that rather than become fully involved, 'the universities could help accelerate the pace of the development of the democratic process in other ways', namely as recruiting grounds for consultants and advisers 'to help facilitate the task of governing', academic staff and the universities he argued, should remain 'conscientious watch-dogs of the democratic process' rather than become actively involved (Musa 1982). The Babangida regime moved from persuasion to compulsion when it decreed that no public officer could belong to a party or contest elections.

The method of containment described above was accompanied by another method of berating and harassing those intellectuals who refused to compromise their activist opposition role in the democratic struggles. They were branded all sorts of names, and harangued by top government functionaries at the slightest opportunity. The following quotation, from a speech by General Babangida, captioned 'IBB raps "frustrated critics"' illustrates this tendency:

> Your nation and mine cannot do with citizens, young and old, who, with antecedents littered with the debris of unutilised and mismanaged opportunities, have recourse to the desperate measures of wanton criticisms or who having had a myriad of economic and political opportunities and failed, would turn round and visit the current generation, the frustrations of unfulfilled dreams emanating from their own ineptitude of yesteryears' (*National Concord* 19/3/92:24).

When these methods proved ineffective in checking the critics and in moderating the increased role of the 'proletarianised' mass-oriented intellectuals, suppression and detention without trial was resorted to. By the dying hours of the Babangida regime, several academics, professionals and human rights activists had been jailed and many newspapers and unions had been banned.

With respect to the academic staff of Nigerian universities, their union, the ASUU, provided the platform for struggles which combined welfare and basic survival issues with broad democratic struggles. The union's ability to gain the confidence of its members, due to sustained struggles and a number of achievements on welfare matters, allowed its leaders the lee-way to put broad democratic concerns onto the agenda of

ASUU struggles. The objective needs and requirements of the struggle for survival and professional integrity have conditioned a generally petty bourgeois middle class group of intellectuals to recognise and accommodate the need for broad democratic struggles as an integral part of its general objective interests. Hence, although, as Bangura (1993) noted, the ASUU was not able 'to regulate individual coping strategies and responses', it was, nonetheless, able to get involved in broad democratic struggles and in alliances with other pro-democracy forces, a situation which culminated in General Babangida's 'stepping aside' on August 26, 1993.

It is significant to note that the struggles of some segments of the intellectuals to expand the horizon of democracy through the ASUU, has its own contradictory dynamics. These contradictions, largely arising from the conflicting ideological perspectives of union members, sometimes exhibit themselves so dangerously as to threaten the cohesion, if not the corporate existence, of the union. The position taken by the union relating to the June 12 crisis, for example, as articulated in the Nsukka National Executive Committee (NEC) Communique, coming in the context of a prolonged strike combined with the uncertainties surrounding Babangida's departure from power, at that point in time, almost created undesirable strike-breaking reaction in some branches. These contradictions have, however, been largely tempered and contained by the incredible confidence that the Union has gained from virtually all the members, regardless of their ideological orientation or inclination.

Conclusion

The experience of Nigerian intellectuals in the struggle for democracy suggests that efforts to concretely expand democratic space based on an organised platform can succeed only if 'the task of democratic opposition under authoritarian regimes' has been carefully assessed, prioritised and actualised. This task, according to Stephan (1990:431), involves the following:

1. Resisting co-optation and integration into the regime;

2. Demarcating and safe-guarding zones of autonomy;

3. Disputing and challenging the legitimacy of the regime;

4. Raising the costs of authoritarian rule; and

5. Creating, nurturing and sustaining a credible democratic alternative.

Essential requirements in defining and actualising this task consist of discipline, perceptiveness, a high-level of probity and accountability, selflessness, organisational versatility, organisational cohesion, a sound democratic tradition in organisation, and a people-oriented guiding principle. Many unions and professional organisations in Nigeria used by intellectuals as platforms for democratic struggles are yet to acquire, in a concrete way, these essential requirements. To this extent, the struggles for the expansion of democratic space in Nigeria have a major handicap requiring an urgent surgical operation.

9

The Left and the Struggle for Democracy

Adebayo O. Olukoshi

Introduction

A major debate is raging in Africa on various aspects of democracy. At the heart of the debate are issues related to the political changes which have taken place or which are still unfolding, most of them focusing on the collapse of single party (and to a lesser extent military) rule and the introduction or reintroduction of multiparty politics. The continent is at a cross-road that represents a clear break with the authoritarian political forms and practices that pervaded the African continent after independence (Anyang' Nyong'o 1987; Legum 1990).

Several questions have been posed. How genuinely representative of the democratic aspirations of the people are the political changes which have been witnessed in Africa since the late 1980s? Is a country democratic merely because it adopts multiparty political forms and holds elections according to a predetermined cycle agreed to by the main political actors? How relevant are the notions of democracy which have been promoted on the continent to the African reality? Should the transition to democracy be anchored on domestic social forces or are these forces so weakened by Africa's long-drawn economic crises and the elaborate machineries of authoritarianism put in place by the continent's rulers as to make inevitable the anchoring of the African democratic project on external forces and Western political conditionality? What place is there for the notions of human and peoples' rights, derived from Western political traditions, and now seemingly acquiring a universal controversial appeal, if not applicability, to Africa's own democratic quest? These and many other questions have been debated in activist and left intellectual circles in Africa since the second half of the 1980s when Mikhail Gorbachev launched his twin programmes of *perestroika* and *glasnost* in the now defunct Soviet Union.[1]

In many respects, the debate since the second half of the 1980s on the African democratic project echoes earlier discourses on the issue at the dawn of African independence from colonialism in the late 1950s and early 1960s. The irony of the early post-independence years in Africa is that both on the right and the left, their eventual disenchantment notwithstanding, many African intellectuals were to justify the widespread adoption of single party rule on the continent for different reasons. For the intellectuals on the left, a major 'developmentalist' objective underlay support for single party rule especially where it masqueraded under the label of 'socialism', be it 'African', 'humanistic', 'authentic' or 'scientific'. This attachment to single party rule found easy justification in the experiences of the Soviet Union, Eastern Europe, China and Cuba where full blown experiments were already well-established in the 'dictatorship' of the proletariat and the vanguardism of communist parties which enjoyed a monopoly on power.

There was also a concern in certain left circles to uphold and extend the fragile nationhood of many African countries and in so doing overcome the difficulties for nation-building and development created by the forces of colonialism. There were strong hopes that a single party framework guided by a socialist ideology of one kind or another provided the best chance not only for emancipation from the shackles of neo-colonialism but also for the social advancement of the majority of the people. Of course there were left intellectuals who actively rejected some of the single party experiences, whether they had a socialist tag or not, but the opposition came not so much over the imposition of a single party framework, as over sectarian ideological differences and clashing perceptions regarding the rigorousness or otherwise of the people charged with the task of building the socialist society and democracy.

What is interesting about the ongoing debate in Africa on the political changes since the late 1980s are the responses which they have elicited from the left. In many respects, African left responses have been partly conditioned by attitudes to Gorbachev's earlier programmes of *perestroika* and *glasnost* although the point should be stressed that the centrality of social and economic factors in the definition of the democratic project also played a major role. What seems clear, as evidenced first by the Anyang Nyong'o/Mkandawire/Gutto debate and then by the Ibrahim/Mafeje/Amin exchanges and the commentaries of such scholars as Mamdani and Shivji, among others, is that the African left is seriously polarised on the value which should be placed on the ongoing quest for political reform on the continent and the direction of the democratic project.

On the one hand, there are those left academics and activists who, contemptuous of bourgeois political forms, are suspicious of a continental democratic quest which draws inspiration from liberal Western political traditions and seeks to reform the African political landscape through the promotion of multiparty politics, human rights, nationality rights, the rule of law, the right to self determination, and other such notions. They reject the equation of political pluralism with multipartyism, and point to the inapplicability, irrelevance or limited relevance of concepts such as the rule of law in a continent where the rural majority not only confront unjust laws but also traditional authority structures in which the ruler is the embodiment of all powers of prosecution, trial, appeal and punishment. They also caution against an uncritical celebration and embrace of bourgeois values, an option which they believe has become appealing because of the collapse of the Soviet Union and the socialist states of Eastern Europe. They insist that in a continent ravaged by widespread poverty, disease and illiteracy, democracy ought to mean much more than the freedom of speech or the freedom of association or the right to vote and should encompass the pressing social and economic concerns of the people as well as concrete political reforms which have a direct bearing on the day to day lives of the majority of the rural and urban poor. Moreover, the transplantation to Africa of notions of individual and group rights developed in other historically different environments cannot serve as the basis for the construction of a democratic and just social order tailored to the needs of Africans (see Shivji 1989; Mafeje 1993; Amin 1993).

On the other hand, there are scholars and activists who take the view that the democracy project in Africa cannot be advanced fully if its political dimensions are ignored or downplayed for whatever reason. They argue that the bane of the African left is its refusal to take liberal democratic issues seriously, dismissing these out of hand as bourgeois or merely paying lip service to them but never operationalising them when in fact the achievement of the respect for human rights and the rule of law was as much the result of working class struggles as of anything else. The construction of a democratic society in the framework of a socialist project cannot be complete if it does not take cognisance of individual liberties and human rights. The tendency of many left activists to see the expansion of democratic space merely as an instrument to be used for achieving other supposedly loftier goals is rejected by these analysts who insist on the recognition of civil, political and individual liberties as building blocks that are integral to the construction of a pluralistic socialist order.

Individual political liberties and human rights should not merely be seen as the means to an end but as values that must be at the heart of a new socialist order. It is inconceivable that the people could ever overturn the domination of their lives by a backward bourgeoisie or even realise their social and economic aspirations if they have not, in the first place, secured the right to freely organise and associate. And were a socialist society to be built without those rights being widely recognised and defended, there is nothing to stop their denial even under a government purporting or genuinely seeking to rule in the name of the oppressed majority (see for example Ibrahim 1992).

The two schools that have emerged to dominate the ongoing debate on democracy in Africa have valid points which ought to be taken full cognisance of in the quest for the fundamental restructuring of African societies. While a wholesale embrace of Western notions of rights is clearly not desirable, it is certainly true that historically, the left in Africa has been more interested in economic and social rights and less with political rights, including individual and group liberties. In a continent where widespread economic and social privations go hand in hand with the denial of the most elementary political rights (individual and group) and a gross disregard for human dignity, particularly the dignity of women, no social transformation can be complete which does not embrace political reforms that aim to unshackle the populace and guarantee the space within which they can freely organise in defence of their interests.

If the insistence on the central place of political rights in the struggle for a more just social order is dismissed as merely bourgeois, it should not be forgotten that all over Africa, the bourgeoisie has failed to promote even liberal political forms/reforms, erecting instead different kinds of extremely repressive political systems that are aimed to stifle the popular aspirations of the people. This is a reality which the African left cannot ignore and in our view, it is one which the Nigerian left is gradually addressing even though more emphasis is still placed on the economic and social dimensions of democracy than on the power relations within which a project of social transformation might be realised.

Left Perspectives on Democracy:
The First and Second Republics

The Nigerian left has, since its emergence at the end of the Second World War as a political force of some sort, presented itself as the authentic bearer of the struggle for national liberation, social justice, and democracy. It has sought over the years, either on its own and/or under the auspices of other groups, to push to the fore of the national political discourse issues of democratic accountability, popular power, and social equality both in the workplace and the wider society. Between 1945 and 1960, it acted both through its own independent organisations and under the auspices of the Zikist Movement that was associated with the National Council of Nigerian Citizens (NCNC), the Northern Elements Progressive Union (NEPU) and, to a much lesser extent, the Action Group (AG). The left was also very active in the trade union/labour movement, the student and the youth movements. This pattern of simultaneously acting through its own organisations and under the auspices of broadly left of centre political parties as well as organisations of the working class and the youth was carried over into the post-colonial period. We have elsewhere described the methods by which the left has sought to achieve its vision of a more just and democratic society and the gains as well as setbacks which it has suffered over the years. The independent organisations which the left has set up over the years have varied in scope and objective. Some were established explicitly as political parties, others as organisations aimed at mobilising the left itself (Abdulraheem and Olukoshi 1986).

The Nigerian left's perception of its role at different points in the country's post-colonial history has been central to its definition of its attitude to the 'democracy question'. For a political orientation which is heterogeneous and marked as much by internal sectarian strife as the international working class movement, there have been sharp disagreements on strategy and tactics as regards the way in which progressive political forces should relate to state-organised or state-initiated political processes.

Two broad positions have dominated left responses to post-colonial politics in Nigeria. On the one hand, there are those left intellectuals and activists who take the position that within the limits of bourgeois politics, it should be possible for revolutionaries to join forces with broadly 'progressive' left of centre parties with a following among the workers, peasants, urban poor, youth and women in order to advance positions which are beneficial to oppressed people. In the thinking of these left activists, what is important is the need to recognise the limits of this entryism in order not to have exaggerated expectations or suffer disappointments arising from a failure to understand the limits of entryism. They argue that once it is understood that participation at various levels in national political processes sanctioned by the state has its limits, it should be possible for the left to push the welfare and nationalist positions which, left to the bourgeoisie, would be left undefended. Among this category of activists are to be found a majority of those who considered political liberties in instrumentalist terms.

On the other hand, there are left groups which insist, against the views of the entryists, that there is little to be gained from direct participation in a formal political process that is not only sanctioned by the state but directed from above. According to this position, bourgeois politics in Nigeria is both backward and alienating, providing little scope for the left or other progressive political forces to be a positive force for change. Rather than responding to state-dominated or state-sanctioned structures of politics, the left should attempt to develop a strong independent political line and structure which will enable it to work directly with the oppressed majority and their organisations like the trade and students unions, peasants and workers cooperatives, women's associations, and other popular groups.

Besides, given the relative weakness of the left in organisational and political terms, entry into the arena or the structures of bourgeois politics is fraught with the danger that the left will either be so overwhelmed as to be ineffective or be tainted by the opportunism of Nigerian bourgeois politics. There can be no short cut in the struggle for the transformation of Nigeria into a more just and democratic society. The left's democratic project is not compatible with bourgeois democracy; indeed, the objective of the Nigerian left is to replace bourgeois democracy with socialist democracy.

The two broad left responses to bourgeois politics which we have described above are far more complex when we consider in detail the positions of individual organisations and groups, but for the purpose of understanding the general attitudes that informed participation in or abstention from the formal political structures and processes of the Nigerian First Republic (1960-1966) and the Second Republic (1979-1983), they will suffice.

During the First Republic, those left activists who felt that they could not stay aloof of the political process that was unfolding (and many felt so for a variety of reasons) sought a role for themselves in NEPU, the AG and, to a lesser extent the United Middle Belt Congress (UMBC) and the NCNC. Others formed their own organisations/parties through which they attempted to campaign for change. Left activists were prominent in the trade union movement as well as in a variety of youth and professional associations. Some combined membership of and activism in or through independent left organisations with participation in the formal political structures and processes recognised by the state.

The general pattern of left responses to politics during the First Republic was carried over into the Second Republic. While some activists and intellectuals sought to chart an independent course of action, many joined political parties such as the People's Redemption Party (PRP), the Unity Party of Nigeria (UPN), and, to a lesser extent, the Nigerian Peoples' Party (NPP) and the National Advance Party (NAP) which, in their estimation, offered opportunities for them to push reforms which were in the interest of the working people. There were spirited debates in the early 1980s on the kind and level of participation in such parties as the PRP, widely seen by left activists as the successor to the radical populist heritage of the NEPU.

While some took the view that a limited, issue-by-issue approach to relating with the PRP was the most desirable path that should be followed because it would neither endanger the autonomy of the left nor taint it in any way whilst simultaneously permitting the left to grow, others opted to go full scale into the party in the belief that this way, they could strengthen the hands of the progressives within it and build an organisation that could be in the vanguard of the struggle for change in northern Nigeria particularly and the rest of Nigeria in general (see for example Toyo 1985; Essien-Ibok 1982; Traore 1982; Abdulraheem and Olukoshi 1986; Mustapha 1985). Extreme and widespread disappointment with the politicians who were at the centre of the Second Republic was to push many on the left to discard this type of entryism and seek ways of popularising an alternative national discourse that entailed a widening of the notion of democracy.

It is necessary at this stage to note that whether entryist or not, the majority of the left groups and activists in Nigeria held on to a position which saw liberal democracy or aspects of it in instrumentalist terms. Working from the, in our view very valid, premise that liberal democracy cannot by itself be a sufficient basis for building a society in which the majority of the people, namely the workers, peasants, youths and women, can realise their class/social aspirations, many on the left proceeded to relate to issues of liberal democracy in terms of instruments that could be used to achieve other, more lofty or socially relevant ideals. Indeed, there was something of a contempt that was prevalent on the left for issues like the freedom of speech, association and thought, human rights, press freedom and other such liberties for these were seen basically as bourgeois values that, on their own, meant little or nothing to the majority of the people. To the extent that the left related to these values, it was in order to exploit them for other purposes that were considered to be more important. The consensus was that the freedom of speech, of association, of the press and other such liberties meant nothing to the majority of the people who had no means of exercising them. They were minority freedoms; the struggle of the left was for majority freedoms and these could only be achieved through far-reaching social and economic changes. There were, of course, differences on how these goals could be achieved and whether short-term alliances with 'progressive' bourgeois or petit bourgeois factions were helpful or whether only a long-term approach was desirable. As we noted earlier, it was only at the beginning of the 1980s that left attitudes to liberties that were hitherto derided as 'bourgeois' began to change as the Nigerian political system entered a decisively authoritarian phase.

The Left and Military Rule

Post-colonial governance in Nigeria has been dominated more by the military than by elected civilian politicians. With the military ruling Nigeria for 24 out of 34 years of independence, it would seem appropriate to argue that civilian rule has been more of an aberration than military rule although the latter is supposed to be the real abnormality. Of the eight post-independence governments which Nigerian has had, six have been military, a fact which is indicative of the high level of militarisation of politics and the politicisation of the military. The dominant left explanation of this centres on the perception of civilian politics as being driven by factionalisation corresponding to the same trends within the Nigerian bourgeoisie. This factionalisation, along economic, political, regional, religious and ethnic lines, has meant that bourgeois civilian politics has been extremely unstable, paving the way for military intervention in the governance of the country, purportedly to prevent a slide into anarchy and the dismemberment of the country. For much of the period from 1966 to the late 1970s, the dominant view on the left, of military intervention in politics, was of a force which seized the centre stage of national governance in order to prevent civilian politicians from endangering the entire system of bourgeois rule in Nigeria. Military rule was therefore seen from the outset as being essentially in the service of the bourgeoisie and thus not in the interest of the exploited and oppressed groups in the country. Attacks on military rule by the left derived mostly from this perspective.

Left commentators on military rule and most activists in Nigeria saw very little qualitative difference between military and civilian governance; the two forms of administration were lumped together as being basically the same in orientation and objective. Neither military nor civilian rule offered a greater prospect of democratic participation in the affairs of the country to the majority of Nigerians nor was there much to choose from between military and civilian rule. As with the issue of civil liberties, it was only in the late 1980s and early 1990s that some left intellectuals began seriously distinguishing between military and civilian rule and insisting that the latter, based on the popular vote, ought to be supported over and above the former which is always unelected. The view began to be popular in left circles that military rule, characterised by extreme arbitrariness, corruption, and ineptitude, should be resisted in favour of elected civilian governmental authority on which left demands for democratisation can be made. We shall return to this later.

Before the swing of the late 1980s against military rule in whatever form or guise, there emerged in the second half of the 1970s an influential view on the role which progressive sections of the military could play as a revolutionary vanguard. Military vanguardism in left circles in Nigeria drew its inspiration from the emergence in 1979 of Flight Lieutenant Jerry Rawlings onto the Ghanaian political scene at the head of youthful officers claiming revolutionary credentials (see Beckman 1986). Military vanguardism in Nigeria was boosted by the coup of youthful officers in Burkina Faso led by Thomas Sankara, which also made revolutionary claims. Some left activists and intellectuals began actively to canvass support for a possible progressive junior officers coup as a tactic for moving Nigeria towards a more just social order built on the principles of socialism. References were made in some cases to the 1966 coup attempt led by Major Chukwuma Nzeogwu Kaduna to argue the case for the existence of a progressive, if not potentially revolutionary group in the Nigerian Army which the left ought to support in order to achieve its goal of a socialist democracy. However, the disillusionment which soon followed the inauguration in Ghana and Burkina Faso of governments led by Rawlings and Sankara was soon to dampen the enthusiasm for military vanguardism in Nigeria. Taken together with a growing national resentment against military rule as a whole, a resentment which the Babangida years did a lot to strengthen, the notion of military vanguardism vanished, to be replaced by an active campaign against military rule and, in many cases, even a vulgar anti-militarist 'ideology'.

The Left and the Struggle for Civil Liberties: 1980-1994

The beginning of the 1980s witnessed the start of a gradual shift in mainstream left opinion in Nigeria in favour of civil liberties and rights, which had previously been dismissed contemptuously as bourgeois. This period coincided with the emergence of a deep-seated national economic crisis which had adverse consequences for the wage-earning classes, the rural poor, salaried professionals, and the youth. This served as the context for the sharp increase in state authoritarianism that resulted in growing attacks on the most elementary rights of various categories of Nigerians, including professionals.

As the economic crisis deepened and state authoritarianism grew, so human rights came under severe attack. The adoption in 1986 of an IMF/World Bank-sanctioned Structural Adjustment Programme (SAP), the severe hardship which it caused to many Nigerians and the restrictive political regime that accompanied it, only further strengthened interest in left circles in the political liberties of Nigerians and the place of civil liberties in the struggle for democracy in the country. The events in the former USSR, centring around Mikhail Gorbachev's twin projects of *perestroika* and *glasnost*, had reverberations in Nigeria, as elsewhere, as left activists were drawn into a self-introspection and critical re-examination of the concept of the vanguard party and the place of political pluralism and civil liberties in the quest for a socialist order.

The embrace by a significant section of the Nigerian left of issues of civil liberties and human rights was by no means an easy or straightforward matter, even though as far back as the early 1980s, a national alliance of left groups for the defence of those rights had been established. There were still some activists who treated issues of civil liberties as inconsequential, not worthy of attention or as being essentially bourgeois. References were made by some of these activists to the dangers of revisionism and the need for the left to stick to its own principles. However, for a growing number of activists and left intellectuals, increasing state repression and the absence of real commitment in bourgeois political circles to resist authoritarianism meant that they had to address the issues of civil liberties and human rights themselves.

Of course, the reasons that informed this interest in the defence of liberties and rights varied from left group to group. There was no relationship between the view of *glasnost* and *perestroika* which the groups held and their stand on the place of rights in the democratic struggle. There were, for example, groups which, while being active in the emerging national human rights/civil liberties movements, bitterly denounced Mikhail Gorbachev and his *glasnost* and *perestroika* as betraying the international working class movement. There were also left activists who not only welcomed Gorbachev's reformist policies but, additionally, attached much value to the work of the civil liberties groups in Nigeria, seeing the groups as essential to the construction of a just social order that could avoid the errors made by the Soviet Communists.

Whatever the factor(s) that influenced the embrace of civil liberties/human rights by various left groups, many organisations that were established from the mid-1980s onwards had the explicit purpose of defending the rights of Nigerians and extending the frontiers of civil liberties in the country. For many activists, the struggle for human rights and civil liberties became part and parcel of the struggle against social and political injustice in a context whose defining feature was essentially repressive and authoritarian. Indeed, for some left activists, the vigorous campaign for human rights and civil liberties became one of the most potent forms of struggle against the authoritarian, militarised state.

In this struggle issues of the rule of law, involving attempts to compel state officials to stick to established rules and curtail their appetite for arbitrariness, became important. Specific references were made to the domination of national politics by the military and the ways in which this could be overturned. Many on the left were convinced that the Nigerian military had become the single most important obstacle to democratisation and that no democratic project would be complete which did not ensure that the military submit themselves to the authority of elected civilian officials.[2]

Perhaps no experience better exemplifies the new role which the left came to play in Nigerian politics than the elaborate and fraudulent programme of 'transition to civilian rule' which the military government of General Ibrahim Babangida introduced in 1986. While condemning the rejection by the regime of the recommendation by the Political Bureau that Nigeria should adopt a socialist ideology, many on the left were extremely sceptical about the desirability of the two-party system on the basis of which General Babangida and his confederates hoped to inaugurate the Third Republic.

Left opposition to the two party framework imposed by the state was strengthened by the decision of the government to write the constitutions and manifestos of the parties, give them their names, build their offices and then invite politicians to join. So deep-seated was opposition on the left to this queer political engineering that, in time, its voice became the most vociferous and consistent against the Babangida political programme and in support of unrestrained multi-partyism.[3] With politicians repeatedly humiliated by the military but still prepared to play along with them in spite of the fact that many of them were unhappy with the transition programme, left groups and coalitions became the main, visible source of opposition to the ruling military oligarchy. It is little wonder that when the transition programme came unstuck and General Babangida's cynical manipulation of the Nigerian political process reached its limits, the left was placed in a position where it became, through the Campaign for Democracy (CD) and other organisations, at the vanguard of national sentiment against continued military rule and for democracy. The prestige of the CD before it went into crisis was, without doubt, reflective of the prestige of the Nigerian left at that stage of the national struggle for democracy. The CD succeeded several times in bringing much of the country to a standstill and it made Nigeria increasingly difficult for the military and its civilian lackeys to govern.

The crisis which afflicted the CD in the period from the second half of 1993 and which resulted in an open split in the organisation opened a new dimension in the Nigerian left's struggle for democracy. Prompted as much by problems of internal democracy in the management of the CD's affairs as by differences over tactics and strategy and bitter personality clashes, the CD crisis led to new debates on what the left should do and how it should deploy its national influence. The view which appeared to predominate was the one which insisted that the left must move beyond pressure group politics and actively make a bid for power on the basis of a solid programme and an equally formidable national presence. The experience, according to this view, which the left had of pressure group politics was simply to create the space for one bourgeois/military faction to dislodge the other. If this was not to continue in perpetuity, the left must build itself up in order to make a direct claim for power with a view to building a democratic society that accommodates the principles of pluralism, human rights, social justice and equality.

Concluding Remarks

There is no doubt that in the period since the mid-1980s, Nigerian left perspectives have shifted in favour of issues of human rights and civil liberties. As noted, the context of this shift is the deepening national economic crisis that started in the early 1980s and the political authoritarianism that accompanied attempts to manage the national economic decline. For many on the left, this context necessitated a more serious embrace of issues of human rights and civil liberties even if only side by side with other forms of struggle against bourgeois rule in Nigeria.

The extreme backwardness and opportunism of the Nigerian ruling class, including the successive military oligarchies that have dominated the centre-stage of national politics, has meant that with the worsening economic situation in the country, the most elementary rights of the people can no longer be taken for granted. The entry of left activists into the front line of the struggle for the defence and advancement of human rights, civil liberties and democratic accountability opened a new, important phase in the campaign for a more just social order in the country. The violence and vehemence with which the state has attempted to suppress this struggle is evidence of its potency in the political mobilisation of the Nigerian people. The challenge the left now faces is how this form of struggle can be made an integral part of efforts at constructing a more just society when eventually bourgeois rule is toppled.

Notes

1. For a Nigerian response to the consequences of *perestroika* and *glasnost* for global democratic struggles, see Yahaya *et al.*, 1991.

2. Interviews conducted in Lagos with five activists heading different organisations were held on September 18 and 19 and on October 3, 4 and 6, 1992.

3. See Bangura 1987 and Ibrahim 1986 and 1993. It is interesting to note that the Nigerian Labour Congress, the central umbrella organisation of trade unions, floated a Nigerian Labour Party as another dimension of the response of the left to the Babangida transition programme. For details, see Olukoshi 1991.

10

Trade Unions and Democracy

Issa Aremu

Introduction

Democracy and social justice are the two cardinal objectives of the trade union movement in Nigeria. The right to strike and engage in independent solidarity action and the right to freedom of association are essential for unions to operate. Indeed, trade union rights are part of universally acclaimed fundamental human rights. Some of these rights, namely the right to free speech, movement and worship, have already been sanctioned by the various constitutions that the Federal Republic of Nigeria has had, although they have virtually never been in force due to persistent military rule. Nigeria has also ratified the International Labour Organisation (ILO) conventions 87 and 98 dealing with freedom of association and the right to organise and collectively bargain respectively.

Nigerian workers have actively taken advantage of these rights to organise and bargain for welfare improvement. However, there is a widening gap between the constitutionally guaranteed rights of trade unions and the worsening anti-democratic practices of intolerance by the state and employers alike. The task for the unions is to overcome the obstacle placed in the way of realising the constitutionally guaranteed rights as well as expanding the space for more rights. This chapter explores the possibilities for the trade union movement to realise constitutionally guaranteed rights and expand the scope for democratic space in general. In examining the potential for trade union involvement in the struggle for democracy, a critical evaluation of the performance and structure of trade union organisation becomes necessary. To what extent, for instance, do the emerging bureaucratic or oligarchic tendencies in trade union organisation limit their capacity to defend the rights of members and assert themselves in society? As organisations, what are the democratic limitations of trade unions?

In addition, the ultimate goal of the labour movement is to transform economic progress and growth of the enterprises and the country as a whole into individual prosperity for their members. Thus beyond civil and political rights, the right to economic welfare and security of tenure and employment is an important trade union right. The challenge for the unions is to see how economic and social rights concerning work and a reasonable standard of living and education, are not only protected but enforced in Nigeria. To what extent have trade unions ensured the protection of these rights?

This study is also aimed at examining how a democratic dispensation can translate into workers' welfare. The question is whether democratic values are 'consummatory' or 'instrumentalist' for the trade union movement? Will democracy become another formal or utopian expression of civic values devoid of social and economic goals geared towards improving the living conditions of workers — the primary objective of trade unions? These are some of the fundamental issues that form the basis of our inquiry into the complex relationship between democracy and the trade union movement. This study aims to contribute to the search for ways and means of improving the democratic practices of the trade union movement with a view to promoting members' welfare.

Theoretical Issues

Different perspectives of trade union relevance offer varying possibilities for their role in the democratic struggle. The classic view of the trade union as an agency that is meant to 'mitigate' the evils of industrial competition confines the exercise of workers' rights to the workplace (Sidney and Beatrice Webb 1897). Both the unitarist and institutionalist pluralist also share the view that workers' organisations are to engage in collective bargaining, rule-making and job regulation in the workplace. Within this limited preoccupation, the options left for the workers are not open-ended. The right to strike is not shared by the unitarists. For the institutionalists, however, as long as the conflict is not 'dysfunctional', workers could withhold services to press for improved conditions. To the extent that the institutionalists recognise government as a third factor (after workers and employers) in industrial relations, the tripartite pluralist ideology of the International Labour Organisation (ILO) tends to have its origin in this school of thought. Most ILO conventions deal with the ways and methods of democratising the workplace alone.

Marxist theorists stress a 'political agenda' for trade unions. They are seen as 'instruments' for achieving a new social order. It is in this instrumentalist sense that one can then assess the role of trade unions in the struggle for democracy. This perspective assigns a 'cause' as distinct from a 'service' role. The 'cause' of trade union is decidedly political as distinct from 'economism' in service pursuits. Unions are expected to engage in political struggle aimed at transforming social and economic relations. In this struggle, the leading role is assigned to the proletariat. But the performance of trade unions under the 'popular democracy' of the former Eastern European countries in which the unions became an appendage of the ruling party calls for a critical assessment of the political agenda of Marxism.

In contrast to the system-changing assumptions of Marxism, there are those who throw up extremely pessimistic views about the relevance of trade unions. Olson (1982), for instance, sets out to question the assumptions of solidarity and collective action as the universal strong points of the workers' movement. It is argued that without selective negative and positive sanctions such as due-picketing, closed shop arrangements, compulsory check-off of dues and prompt legal services to protect activists, no worker would want to be part of the union. Relying on behavioural analysis, Olson argues that an enthusiastic union member may not be willing to expend time or energy to achieve the group's collective good, which in any case as a public good would still be achieved without an additional member. Thus according to him, a rational worker is a potential 'free rider', which makes the relevance of a trade union as an organiser of a collective doubtful.

Sociologists of organisations also address different issues in union relevance. Dating back to Weber, the preoccupation is with the extent to which the unions, as large scale organisations, have assumed an autonomous life of their own as distinct from the expectations of their founders, the workers. Do the unions fit into the Weberian notion of 'routinised, impersonal, hierarchically structured relations'? To what extent has the union become an inflexible or a bureaucratic machine unresponsive to the aspirations of workers. Are specific empirical questions begging for answers? Are trade unions sufficiently representative of members' interests such that they can rightly champion the course of democratisation in the larger society?

There has been an attempt to broadly divide these different, perspectives into two: 'economic' and 'political'. There are those who have, however, argued that the division of trade unions' role into the 'political' and 'economic' represents a 'false dichotomy' (Cohen 1974; Otobo 1978). The argument is that ideal-type unionism is non-analytical and doctrinaire. We are therefore asked to have a dynamic view of the changing role of trade unions based on the socio-political setting of any country and the strategic positions trade unions occupy at any specific historic situation. The fact is that trade unions do engage in both economic and political struggles. The trade unions of Western European Countries are often seen as models of business — or — economic concerns. Yet in these countries, unions perform some political functions in an attempt to improve members' welfare. In the USA, for instance, trade unions do engage in political lobby to push for pro-labour legislation while they also raise money and materials to campaign for pro-labour candidates during elections. In Britain also, notwithstanding the preference for collective bargaining, the relationship between the TUC and the Labour Party has been more than casual as the former constitute a large part of the support base for the latter. This is partly due to the fact that the party was born when the unions, and others, decided to campaign for parliamentary representation.

Conceptualising Democracy

Conceptualising 'democracy' is as problematic as conceptualising the social purpose of trade unions. Simplistic assumptions tend to inform public discourse about democracy in Nigeria. Yet we need to come to terms with the concept of democracy before we can assess the performance of trade unions in the struggle for democracy in Nigeria.

Democracy is said to be an ideology of 'majoritarian decision making'. Dated to 19th century radicalism, it claimed to put an end to the absolutism of the 'ancien regime' in Europe. It is governance 'achieved' as distinct from governance 'ascribed' by status. 'Political democracy' wrote Hirst (1990), 'challenged the restriction of political decision making to privileged position and a society in which fixed orders of rank stood in the way of the final legal and political equality of all citizens'. The classical version of democracy as demonstrated during the French revolution underscores the question of 'popular power'. Thomas Paine's Rights of Man advocates and celebrates the slogan 'put the issue to the people'. Democracy as 'popular power' emphasises the participation of ordinary people or the rank and file in the decision making process. One could ask: what makes 'popular power' really popular? Is it the quality of the decisions arising from 'popular power' or the active involvement of the mass of people in the process of the exercise of power? According to Hirst, a democratic decision is an open either/or. The 'people' can choose Christ, or Barnabas, to ban fur hunting or to outlaw homosexuality. Democracy can no more guarantee 'good' decisions than unregulated markets can guarantee full employment or balanced growth. In multi-ethnic and religious societies such as Nigeria, how will 'popular power' be exercised without polarisation and civil war? In any case, the Athenian 'small, poor and virtuous republics', were closed shops to the extent that democracy was restricted only to the tiny minority who were 'citizens'.

In liberal democracy, participation assumes that periodic elections give elected officials the power to take decisions. We thus have institutions (such as parliament) with procedures and formal rights, namely the right to associate, assemble and form parties as is the norm in the developed countries of Europe and America. This 20th century 'representative democracy' had come under criticism from radical authors and political activists (Hyman 1975). Marxists alluded to the class character of liberal democracy and preferred to replace 'bourgeois rule' with 'proletarian rule', a new variant of 'popular power'. But the controversial performance of what Lenin had characterised as 'democracy of the oppressed classes' in a number of countries of Eastern Europe further problematises the issue of democracy. In Africa in recent times, all variants of democracy have been put to the test with controversial outcomes; Kenya's 'guided democracy', the 'indemnity clause' for democracy of Rawlings' Ghana, and the 'national conference' of the Benin Republic to mention a few. One fundamental question, however, is whether democratic values are 'consummatory' or 'instrumentalist'?

To what extent is democracy compatible with growth and development in an increasingly impoverished continent? If military dictatorship has proved imprudent, will democracy make a difference? Why are the country's creditors pushing for democracy, openness and transparency? Is democracy not another international orchestrated managerial prerogative which normally offend national dignity and undermine national developmental efforts? (Beckman 1990). The point here is that discussing democracy raises a number of ideological questions. In the world of work where the trade union is an active actor, democracy takes the form of 'industrial democracy' although ambiguity characterises the meaning of the concept. In the United States and Britain for instance, 'industrial democracy' takes the form of collective bargaining and shop steward representation in which government is held suspect. It is an adversary labour regime in which labour is in permanent opposition to check employers' domination. In such countries as Belgium, Netherlands, France and Spain, 'industrial democracy' assumes the forms of workers' representation in 'works councils' as part of a broader, socialist inspired challenge to capitalism. In Germany, workplace democracy is expressed in terms of 'co-determination' in which 'real parity of board representation' is maintained between workers and management. Thus, different countries with different histories and economic development paths have thrown up different forms of 'industrial democracy' (Kassalow 1982). Democracy is therefore a broad and dynamic concept. But common to all perspectives of democracy are the concepts of fundamental human rights and social justice. Yet these concepts are no less problematic. The culturalists insist, for instance, that 'human rights' is a Western concept whose universal applicability should be questioned. In Africa references are made to values of 'communalism and brotherhood' as distinct from the oppositional and individualistic values of the West. Political economists hold that the arguments of the culturalists are romantic, defensive and even racist. They contend that it is uncritical to trace rights of men and women to certain roots. Natural rights defined as legitimate claims made by human beings have universal applicability. They emphasise that we should expand rather than restrict the scope of rights to cover social and economic well-being in addition to the original preoccupation with civil and political liberties (Hendrickson 1985). Others have pointed to the inadequacy of the two approaches, stressing the necessity for a deeper understanding of 'civil society', particularly the complex relationship between class, region, ethnicity and religion and variations in human rights performance in different countries. The interesting study by Howard (1991) has applied four categories of key rights to critically assess the prospect for democracy in both Nigeria and Indonesia.

At the level of trade unions and democracy, the interest of the employers is to get the best from the workers in the process of making profits for the enterprise. Most employers would naturally pursue their goal with the cheapest means available, including cheaper labour. Many, if not all, employers would even employ inhuman methods such as child labour, corporal punishment and even imprisonment to ensure labour compliance with set objectives of production. Without constant checks, employers may not even promote workers, for as long as the work lasts. Employers would prefer summary dismissal, fines and wage deductions. On the other hand, workers are interested in decent wages and benefits for the labour and services rendered.

Precisely because of this basic opposition or conflict in interests, workers have seen the need to come together to present a common front against the employers. The natural front is the trade union. It has been observed that trade union organisation 'is the most obvious foundation for workers' action'. Individual workers may very well act alone in resistance against the employers' domination. Indeed individually, workers may engage in industrial sabotage, goods' theft, malingering and absenteeism as plausible ways to check the indifference of management. But these are short-lived methods of resistance. For one, individual workers are haunted almost permanently by the prospect of termination when caught in the act of 'sabotage'. Only through collective actions represented by a trade union will workers transform their state of powerlessness. With trade unions, workers can become an equal partner to employers. They recover their dignity and above all they may exchange their labour for a 'fair wage'.

The Nigerian Experience

The existence of wage labour in Nigeria dates back to colonial times. Before the advent of European rule, the traditional economy relied on either family or communal labour. Since there were no distinct employers with distinct interests in this subsistence economy, 'workers' in the modern sense and trade unions were non-existent. Colonialists assaulted and dismantled this old order and erected an economic system which 'became synonymous with collision, conflict and class struggle'. Colonialism required wage labour in public works, infrastructure construction such as ports and railways and the administration. Early trade unions thus emerged mainly in the colonial service sector. The first generation of trade unions included the Nigeria Civil Service Union (1912), the Nigerian Union of Teachers (1931) and the Nigerian Union of Railwaymen (1932). The unions came into existence with the main objectives of ameliorating the deplorable working conditions that existed during colonial rule. Since the emergence of the first generation trade unions, thousands of trade unions have been formed in Nigeria. Today, Nigeria has a vast system of industrial unionism. This system means that trade unions are established along industrial lines: that is every 'junior' grade of workers in an industry belongs to the same trade union. There are 41 industrial unions and all of them are affiliated to a single centre — the Nigerian Labour Congress (NLC), which came into being in 1978.

The history of trade unions in Nigeria does not support the thesis of political exclusion of the working class. In his work, Crisp (1984) has correctly emphasised the central themes of 'labour control' and 'labour resistance'. According to him, methods of labour control employed by employers often elicit resistance on the part of the workers. Forms of labour resistance that have been identified include strikes, sabotage and political direct action. Cohen and Hughes (1971) have argued that the 'short-lived and limited success' of 'economism', i.e. wage and benefit demands, made 'wage earners to seek a more specifically political solution to their occupational grievances'. Nigeria is one country where direct involvement of labour in political and democratic struggles has been very pronounced. From colonial times, the relatively underdeveloped state of the economy characterised by stagnant wage-rates and the arbitrariness of colonial managers as well as the vintage position of organised labour, conferred on the unions a significant role in the struggle for independence and national development. The unions' actions in the form of demonstrations, rallies and strike actions made them exhibit more political tendencies.

The experience of Nigeria shows that the economic struggles of the workers are inseparable from political issues. Workers' protests against the low wage policy of the colonial administration, obnoxious policies of inequalities in compensation and forced tax served as an impetus to demand for an end to colonial rule as a whole.

Politics is about agenda setting. Politics for trade unions is therefore perceived as another means to pursue workers' interests. It is in this 'instrumentalist' sense, that labour's involvement in political and democratic struggle can be appreciated. Cohen and Hughes (1971) identified three interrelated methods that were used as part of the strategy to expand the democratic space during the colonial times. The first was through direct party formation. As far back as 1930, a partisan political movement named the Nigerian Labour Corporation (NLC) had been formed to 'defend the cause of labour'. The second method took the form of the popular front approach. The obvious shortcoming of independent political action compelled labour to ally with the progressive 'national bourgeoisie' in an attempt to improve workers' conditions. The popular front approach involved campaigns for progressive increases in African representation. To some extent, enfranchised labour found a worthy ally in the party of notable nationalists such as Herbert Macaulay's Nigerian National Democratic Party (NNDP) and the subsequent militant National Council of Nigeria and the Cameroons (NCNC). The third approach was more inspirational than real. It involved contacts with the international communist movement which favoured the abolition of exploitation and the enthronement of a new social order.

Trade Unions and Democracy

In our attempt to examine the role of trade unions in the struggle for democracy, we will rely on Howard's (1991) four categories of key rights:

1. Survival Rights: life, food and health.

2. Membership Rights: family, non-discrimination.

3. Protection Rights: habeas corpus, independence of the judiciary.

4. Empowerment Rights: education, freedom of the press and of association.

The 'heuristic devices' in Howard's categories also contain civil, political, social and economic rights as contained in the International Bill of Rights and Universal Declaration of Rights. They are fundamental to the effective performance of labour in areas of democratic struggle.

Rights to Free Association

The right to form or belong to a trade union, like the right to free speech, movement and worship, is one fundamental right sanctioned by the Constitutions of the Federal Republic. Nigeria has also ratified ILO conventions 87 and 98 dealing with freedom of association and the right to organise and bargain collectively. A widening gap, however, exists between constitutionally guaranteed rights of unions and the anti-democratic practices of intolerance by both the state and employers in Nigeria. Government labour policies date to colonial times and are characterised by violations in the form of proscriptions, arrests, and murder (Zasha 1985; Otobo 1987). Indeed, the exercise of the right to free association by workers had been asserted well before constitutionally guaranteed rights. The task of trade unions has centred around overcoming obstacles placed in the way of free assembly. The Nigerian state has actively intervened in the administration of the trade union movement in ways that tend to limit democratic space in line with the principles enunciated in the Universal Declaration of Human Rights.

The existing Nigeria Labour Congress (NLC) was decreed into existence in 1978, after the then military authority banned independent efforts of unionists to form a common centre. At inception, 42 industrial unions were registered as affiliates of the NLC but today 41 affiliates are functional because the Custom and Excise and Immigration Staff Union was deregistered by the military regime. Also the Trade Unions (Miscellaneous Provisions) Decree terminated the independent efforts of the Academic Staff Union of Universities (ASUU) to join the NLC in 1986. In March 1988, the government dissolved the NLC, in what was clearly a violation of the independent process of conflict resolution between rival factions of the labour movement as laid down by Trade Disputes Act of 1976. The dissolution was also seen as an attempt to impose the unpopular Structural Adjustment measures by the government (ACAS BULLETIN, 1989).

At the enterprise level, freedom of association has also been impaired as police, on the orders of government and employers, often halt peaceful workers' protests and strikes (Bangura and Beckman 1989). The reaction of labour to some interventionist measures of the state has raised some critical questions about the universal application of conventions. Hashim (1986) showed that the state intervention of the 1970s actually strengthened the unions' financial base through the automatic check-off of dues and enhanced the status of trade unions in the labour market. The existing industrial unions are products of that 1978 industrial restructuring.

The single trade union centre represented by the NLC is a product of the state's restrictive policy of 'guided democracy'. But the policy of a single labour centre remains popular among Nigerian trade unionists. Out of ten unionists drawn from private and public sectors who were asked their opinions on the creation of more labour centres, none answered in the affirmative. Their preferences were for consensus-building, unity and national solidarity that promotes bargaining power. However, the International Labour Office committee of experts repeatedly frowns on the enforced and legislated trade union unity in Nigeria. The ILO points to the adverse consequences of non-competitive union structures which includes the fact that imposed unity only conceals internal conflicts rather than eliminates them. It argues that one single labour centre can deny other organisations, such as the Senior Staff Consultative Association (SESCAN), the right to be consulted on labour matters as the labour laws do not provide for another labour centre (see Panford 1988).

The strategy of the state in legislating for a single labour centre is to ensure it has easy control over it. The capacity of the NLC to resist the obnoxious policies of government and employers must show the vulnerability of the state strategy. The discredited Interim National Government (ING) actually employed the ILO's argument of the right to association to threaten the NLC with rival centres in the wake of the national strike against increases in fuel prices. During the Second Republic, some sections of the ruling party evoked the principles of ILO to present a bill for the formation of another labour centre. But the real reason behind the move of the politicians was to 'tame' the rather 'recalcitrant' NLC with more controllable 'labour centres'.

The dilemma of a single labour centre underscores the instrumentalist value of industrial democracy either for the employers or labour. The recent restructuring of industrial unions from 41 to 29 currently being initiated by the trade union movement shows that it is not necessarily when democratic space is expanded that people and mass organisations assert their rights. The expectations of unions by voluntarily accepting to merge include strengthening the financial and membership base of the unions. Labour also strives to remove the divide between 'junior' and 'senior' staff as members of industrial unions. It should be noted that Nigerian labour law disallows senior staff from belonging to trade unions. The right of unions to international affiliation was only restored in 1993 following labour's insistence after a decade-long ban. Many unions have actively taken advantage of affiliation to empower themselves through education and international solidarity.

The Right to Strike
The right to strike is essential for the effective functioning of the trade union movement. Nigerian labour laws prohibit strikes and lock-outs although national strikes are not uncommon. The right to strike is sanctioned by Article 3 of Convention 87 of the ILO which provides that trade unions should be able to organise their activities and formulate their programmes in full freedom. The Committee on Freedom of Association of the ILO also stated that:

> The right to strike is one of the essential means through which workers and their organisations may promote and defend their occupational interest.

Essential services have also been defined by the ILO in the strict sense of the term as services on which life, personal safety and health depend. The contrast with the industrial relations regime in Nigeria, in which the definition of 'essential services' is made so open-ended so as to disallow a considerable number of workers not only from unionisation, but from going on strike, is remarkable. In spite of restrictive laws, workers have withheld their services to demand their rights.

The scale of strikes varies between enterprises. The so-called essential sectors such as energy, petroleum and electric power, have witnessed total withdrawal of services. The responses of the state to union activists has varied from life imprisonment to the termination of employment contracts. The challenge for trade unions is to overcome the obstacles placed in the way of the right to strike. One positive step is for trade unions to fight for the abrogation of the Essential Services Clause in labour legislation.

Protection Rights

Howard (1991) indicated that military rule has denied protection rights in Nigeria. This he attributed to the 'national security ideology' favoured by single-leader monocratic military regimes. Most unionists interviewed by this author reported frequent 'security harassment'. Labour has been groaning under the regime of 'industrial relations by decrees'. Decree 17 of 1984, for instance, does not allow workers whose services were terminated to seek legal redress. The industrial relations machinery was perverted through numerous restrictive decrees. Part of the legal framework involves 'arbitration panels' that are empowered to stop all strikes for 'arbitration' and to convict union leaders who are 'contemptuous' of the orders. Many trade unionists have been detained under obnoxious detention laws. In 1988, NLC leaders were arrested for protesting against the removal of the petroleum subsidy. In 1984, National Electric Power Authority (NEPA) unionists were tried before the 'Anti-Sabotage' Special Military Tribunal and sentenced to life imprisonment for organising a strike in a so-called essential service. The pressure from NLC and civil society led to their eventual release.

Direct Political Action

In general, protection rights have been violated more under the prolonged military rule than during political civil arrangement. Protection rights are central to political involvement. The Federal Constitutions (1979 and 1989) have been repeatedly suspended by the military. These constitutions guarantee fundamental human rights. The involvement of labour in the 'democratisation process' is one attempt to protect workers' rights. No organised group has been more constructively involved in the political programme of a return to civil rule than the labour movement (Beckman 1991; Oramulu 1993). It articulated workers' views before the Political Bureau in 1986 on such issues as human rights, the role of the military in governance and rural development (NLC 1986). Some trade unionists also participated in writing the 1989 Constitution. Following the inauguration of the Nigeria Labour Congress political commission, labour formed the unregistered Labour Party in May 1989. With the official formations of the National Republican Convention (NRC), 'a bit to the right' and the SDP 'a bit to the left' the labour movement naturally declared its support for the SDP. Labour's partisan involvement has provoked controversies, but there is no doubt that it has contributed in the expansion of democratic space in the country. From the rather dubious perspective that labour is a 'liability', the politicians and even the civil society as a whole have come to see the organisation as a worthy 'asset'.

The NLC rightly supported the graduated electoral process known as Option A4, which produced the most participatory process of party selection of presidential candidates in Nigeria. It mobilised its members to exercise the democratic right to vote in the presidential election, believed to be the country's freest and fairest in conduct and outcome.

Following the annulment of the June 12 1993 presidential election by the military, the NLC, through its political commission, made a strong protest. It called on the National Electoral Commission to release the remaining results and declare the winner. Subsequent meetings of the NLC unambiguously objected to the annulment of the votes of 14 million Nigerians. While the NLC could not succeed in making the Babangida regime retract its annulment of the elections, the labour movement joined forces with other popular forces to terminate the life of the regime on August 27 1993. At the end of its National Executive Council meeting in Port Harcourt, the NLC announced the resolve of Nigerian workers and the trade unions to 'challenge the legitimacy of military rule if its tenure extends beyond August 1993'. Labour gave effect to its threat on August 28 when it declared a week long strike to press home its political demands. The strike put to the test the legitimacy of the Interim National Government (ING), the ad-hoc political arrangement installed by the military. The ING, led by Chief Ernest Shonekan, entered into dialogue with labour representatives, an opportunity for labour to register once again its opposition to the annulment of a free and fair election.

The ING accepted labour demands that all detained human rights activists would be released and that henceforth, rule by decree would be stopped and that the National Assembly would henceforth take on its law making functions. The affirmative commitment of the government to the preservation of the democratic structures in place following the NLC strike was a significant step forward in the struggle for democracy.

The achievement of the NLC was short-lived, however, as the ING reneged on its earlier promise not to increase the prices of petroleum products 'until necessary dialogue had been held with all interest groups including the NLC'. In November 1994, amidst popular agitation by pro-democracy forces, the ING increased the price of petroleum products by 400 per cent. In reaction, the NLC called a general strike and the ING was forced to re-enter dialogue with labour. The negotiations became dead-locked leading to a resumption of the strike. The ING was overthrown at the height of the November NLC strike. The new military regime led by General Abacha, while agreeing to a cut-back of prices of petroleum products, took a series of authoritarian measures that constrained the democratic process. These measures included the dissolution of political parties, a new wave of arrests of political activists and the closure of opposition media houses.

Under the Abacha regime, Labour has again been making political demands. The goal of the NLC has been to:

> Evolve new initiatives aimed at creating a platform for dialogue in order to find a solution to the political crisis in the interest of the poor and suffering masses of our people in order to ensure peace and a smooth transition to democracy (NLC, NEC Communique of July 1994).

After a series of political representations and conference resolutions, it became clear that the military regime would not abandon its dictatorial policies for the democratic options favoured by labour. That led to the use of the strike option by the NLC. Labour's momentum was, however, derailed when the military junta dissolved the NLC Executive Council and appointed an administrator to run the affairs of the Congress. The governing councils of the two oil sector unions were also dissolved. The two unions had been engaged in nation-wide indefinite strike actions for an unconditional return to democratic rule. Be that as it may, the efforts of the labour movement have raised awareness about democracy among members and the wider society (see NLC Political Commission 1993).

Membership Rights

The exercise of membership rights is also at the core of the pursuit of the struggle for democracy. Membership rights have to do with the issue of non-discrimination in mass organisations and civil society as a whole. The current (December 1993) restructuring of the industrial unions within the tripartite framework of the National Advisory Labour Council (NALC) has reopened the issue of trade union membership. The state's strategy is to reduce the number of workers that can join trade unions through an open-ended definition of 'managerial' or 'senior staff', in the case of the public sector and exclusive job classification in the private sector (NLC 1993). The ability of the labour movement to press for the removal of these restrictions will increase the scope for unionisation. In Nigeria there are no legal restrictions to free movement of people on account of sex, religion and tribe. But the devolution of power to the local and state levels has given vent to the divisive ideology of 'statism'. Also unions will have to check the 'divide-and-manage' policies of employers through solidarity actions, currently lacking in the war of attrition over fairness in remuneration between the Academic Staff Union of Universities and the Non-Academic Staff Union.

Survival Rights

Survival rights cover the right to life, to food, rights to housing and health care. Well over 80 per cent of unionists interviewed ranked the right to life and rights to food and good health first and second respectively in preference to rights to free assembly, free association and fair hearing. This again points to the fact that democracy has only 'instrumentalist' value to the trade union movement. The pursuit of welfare is mainly within the context of collective bargaining, which covers wages and benefits. The labour movement has fought to sustain the principle of a minimum wage. Quantitative benefits have been on the increase though not in keeping with the pace of price increases (Aremu 1988).

The policies of the removal of subsidy and currency devaluation undermines the struggles of trade unions for the improvement of welfare. The implication is that in real terms, a trade union member's personal income has not improved. The challenge for the trade union movement is to work out new strategies to protect the real welfare of members. The movement must see beyond collective bargaining because of its obvious limitation as a distribution mechanism.

Concluding Observations

By way of conclusion, we wish to make the following observations on union participation, women's participation, organising the unorganised, poverty alleviation, empowerment and the definition of social purpose.

Organisationally, trade unions will have to develop flexible organisational structures and processes that will ensure workers' participation at union meetings and elections and make leadership accountable to members. Industrial unions tend to concentrate a lot of power at the union centre and headquarters. Many interviewed unionists agreed that their organisations are stronger at the national level than at the local level. This explains the visibility of the General Secretaries and Presidents over and above shop-stewards or organising secretaries. Union administration requires decentralisation of authority and responsibility.

One democratic limitation of trade unions is that they are male-dominated. There is an urgent need for positive action to increase women's participation if trade union rights are to be exercised by women. All-male national officers do not reflect the fact that there are women branch officers who can be encouraged to become full-time officers. Pittin (1984) has pointed out the significant underestimation of women's labour in official statistics in Nigeria as evidence of an ideological orientation that is sexist. In the specific case of the textile industry, Beckman and Andre (1988:16) argue that 'male homogeneity goes with higher levels of organisation and unity' while gender differences 'have been exploited for the purpose of divide and rule'. They also argue that there is evidence of job and wage discrimination within the industry (1984:9). I find the observation by Watson (1988) that trade unions in Britain can only enter the twentieth century if they abandon Victorian and patriarchal practices and deliberately encourage women's participation in unionism useful for the Nigerian situation. Membership rights must cover women's rights. One necessary step is for the movement to campaign for female employment.

Organised and protected labour represents a rather small but strategic section of the workforce. Informal sector labour is large but not protected, paid low wages and exposed to more hazards. The challenge for trade unions is to see that these unprotected workers, mostly women, are unionised. Union density is still very low in Nigeria.

Against the background of the collapse of wages, the trade union movement will have to overcome the limitations of collective bargaining, which are often conducted under the searchlight of the media. Quantitative benefits in the forms of wages must be complemented by qualitative gains in areas of health and safety, productivity bonus, promotion and enhanced status of labour. Collective agreements must expand in scope and content. Collective bargaining is characterised more by bluffing and haggling than by informed and factual bargaining and it is not surprising that their tenure and outcomes produce acrimony and strikes rather than real benefits for the workers. But bargaining skills are lacking among many unionists. The policy implication is that trade unions must creatively look for other means to improve members' benefits. This may include worker participation. The worthy efforts of the Labour Transport Services (LTS) was a rather timely appreciation of the transportation problems facing workers (Oshiomhle 1993). Poverty alleviation calls for cooperative but critical industrial relations as distinct from the present adversary industrial relations regime.

In order to improve on trade union consciousness, unions will have to educate their members. Few trade unions maintain a functional educational department. Thus sustainable and regular educational activities are lacking. Unions have to develop educational policy orientations that promote problem solving and skill development. Subjects may cover trade union administration, collective bargaining, health and safety, workplace and societal democracy and other trade union issues.

The ability of the labour movement to overcome its limitations will depend on the social purpose it defines for itself. Is labour a party in the market preoccupied with collective accumulation of wages and benefits for members? Will a trade union be a campaigning agent serving in the 'vanguard' of 'the revolution', a model whose abysmal performance in the areas of production and distribution in other countries has now made the struggle for egalitarianism suspect? The choice of social purpose will determine labour's strategy of resistance to the policies of employers and government. Where there is a fixation about the 'class enemy', the policy of 'total and indefinite strike' may be understandable as the case of the ASUU's long strike demonstrated. But to what extent does the strategy which leads to 'strike fatigue' promote members' welfare and democracy in the country? If the academic staff did not join the 1993 'pro-democracy' strike and the fuel price strike, it was because, willy-nilly, they had blunted the edge of the strike weapon in the first instance. Must we carry the zero-sum game nature of Nigerian politics into the field of industrial relations?

Diamond (1988, cited in Buijtenhuijs 1990) noted that democracy requires moderation and constraint. It demands not only that people care about political competition but also that they do not care too much. The issue is that the world of work and the state are complex. In particular, trade unions must recognise the development potential as well as retarding tendencies of the state (Doornbos 1989; Kiloh 1985; Ake 1990; Beckman 1990). It is doubtful if this point can be overemphasised in Nigeria where the relations between the state and labour has been characterised by contestation and cooperation. Yet the relations of unions with the state will come under the spotlight in the age of acute economic crisis when indebtedness and international managerial policies aimed at eroding the power of the state in the third world are rife. Will the unions join the state to call for debt relief, fair trade or debt cancellation or simply assert 'rights' that leave little scope for collective national survival? Can there be rights without responsibilities in the areas of competence, punctuality and productivity at the workplace?

Answers to these questions are difficult even for trade unions that operate within the context of single-leader military dictatorship, as we have witnessed in Nigeria. What is clear, however, is that a democratic dispensation offers trade unions a greater opportunity to face up to some of the challenges we have identified.

Part Four

Liberties, Rights and Citizenship

11

Civil Liberties, Human Rights Organisations and the Rule of Law

Femi Falana

Introduction

Since the emergence of Nigeria as a colonial entity at the turn of the century, its people, at a general level, have lived their lives without the enjoyment of civil liberties and the observance of basic human rights. They have also been denied the rule of law, which is anyway made without their contribution and often conflicts with their collective interests. In the post-colonial period, the lean democratic chapters of Nigerian political history have continued. The focus of this chapter is on the concepts of civil liberties, human rights organisation and the rule of law in Nigeria. Although some references are made to the operation of these concepts in other parts of the world, we situate these concepts within the Nigerian context to appreciate their unspeakable denial and the ways in which the masses of our people have suffered over the years.

Hopefully, such an appreciation will prick our conscience, strengthen our determination and propel us to redouble our efforts to stop these denials and restrictions. In conducting this examination, however, we shall attempt a brief definition of these concepts, enumerating some juridical documents in which their time-honoured principles and features are embodied. We shall not, however, expound on the philosophical foundations, the sociological fulcrum and the theoretical analysis of these concepts. Our task is to briefly state what they mean and to mirror Nigeria in relation to them.

Civil Liberties

The term civil liberties has been defined as 'personal, natural rights guaranteed and protected by the constitution; e.g. freedom of speech and of the press, freedom from discrimination etc. A body of laws dealing with natural liberties, shorn of excesses which invade equal rights of others. Constitutionally, they are restraints on government...' (Black's Law Dictionary, sixth edition, p. 246). It has also been said to be 'the liberty of an individual to freely exercise those rights guaranteed by the laws of a country' (Websters Encyclopaedic Dictionary 1989:271). What is clear from both definitions is that despite the universal acknowledgement of civil liberties, their content and form as well as the extent of their enjoyment are prescribed by the law or a set of laws governing each society. Relying on Chapter Four of the 1979 Constitution of the Federal Republic of Nigeria, the civil liberties that should be enjoyed by Nigerians include the:

Right to life,

Right to dignity of the human person,

Right to personal liberty,

Right to fair hearing,

Right to private and family life,

Right to freedom of thought, conscience and religion,

Right to freedom of expression and the press,

Right to peaceful assembly and association,

Right to freedom of movement,

Right to freedom from discrimination, and the,

Right of protection from compulsory acquisition of property.

These enumerated civil liberties styled by the 1979 Constitution as 'fundamental rights' are otherwise known as 'civil and political' rights which also include:

The right to marry and found a family,

The right to participate in one's government either directly or through freely elected representatives, and,

The right to nationality and equality before the law.

May we say at this juncture that these rights whose enjoyment and enforcement are guaranteed by the Constitution of the Federal Republic of Nigeria, are essentially hollow and do not meet the aspirations of the Nigerian people when critically examined in their observance, or rather, lack of observance by the state. There is no doubt that the circumscription of the exercise of these rights by the martial order of the military dictatorship that has bedevilled the Nigerian polity for over 23 years has exposed the inadequacy of the said fundamental rights in meeting the socio-economic needs of the people. We shall be returning to this in greater detail later.

Human Rights

According to Eze (1984:5):

> Human rights represent demands or claims which individuals or groups make on society, some of which are protected by law and have become part of *ex lata* while others remain aspirations to be attained in the future.

By this definition, with which we are in full agreement, it is evident that the scope of human rights is wider than that of civil liberties. These rights which encompass civil liberties which have been grouped above as 'civil and political' rights include the categories of 'economic, social and cultural' rights. The latter categories of human rights are the:

Right to work under just conditions,

Right to adequate standard of living,

Right to social security and welfare services,

Right to medical assistance,

Right to vocational training and guidance,

Right of the family to social, legal and economic protection,

Right to participate in cultural life and enjoy the benefit of scientific progress etc.

The bitter truth is that despite the plenitude of international charters, conventions, agreements and protocols to which Nigeria is a signatory, and despite the abundance of human and material resources which can easily sustain the enjoyment of the above listed socio-economic and cultural rights in Nigeria, the ruling class has made it impossible for the generality of our people to enjoy these rights. Relying on the enacted human rights bills, principles and declarations over the centuries in the West, the United Nations Organisation came out in 1948 with a document of immense importance and utility: The UN Universal Declaration of Human Rights (UNUDHR 1948). Some of the historical declarations, bills and principles which constituted the bedrock from which they were derived are:

Magna Carta (England, 1215 AD)

Habeas Corpus (England, 1679)

Bill of Rights (England, 1689)

Virginia Bill of Rights (USA, June 1776)

American Declaration of Independence (USA, July 1776)

French Declaration of the Rights of Man and the Citizen (France, 1789)

French Constitution,(1791).

The UNUDHR Declaration of 1948 led to a meteoric enrichment of the quality of international law which occasioned the 'mushrooming' of international and municipal human rights organisations and civil rights movements. The following international instruments have equally been made to complement the 1948 Declaration:

The UN International Covenant on Civil and Political Rights (1966 which came into operation on March 23, 1976);

The UN International Covenant on Economic, Social and Cultural Rights (1966 but came into effect on January 3, 1976).

The European Convention for the Protection of Human Rights and Fundamental Freedoms (1950 which came into force on 21 September 1970 and 20 December 1971).

The European Social Charter of 1961.

The UN International Covenant on Economic, Social and Cultural Rights (1966 but came into effect on January 3, 1976).

The Inter-American Convention on Human Rights (1969).

The African Charter on Human and People's Rights (1980).

It is necessary to set out these international instruments as we want to demonstrate that the human rights abuses in Nigeria are not due to a dearth of instruments which have either binding or persuasive force on the country. The closest Nigeria has got to recognising the social, economic and cultural rights which properly construed are the 'pre-requisites for the optimal enjoyment of other rights by most citizens' (Alemika 1992), is Chapter 2 of the 1979 Constitution. The breach of these provisions cannot be enforced in court. A close examination of Chapter 2 is needed to facilitate our appreciation of governmental pretension on the status of these provisions.

The chapter headed 'Fundamental objectives and directive principles of state policies' sets out the fundamental obligations of government, some of which are:

Section 14(1): The Federal Republic of Nigeria shall be a state based on the principles of democracy and social justice.

It is hereby, accordingly, declared that:

a. Sovereignty belongs to the people of Nigeria from whom government through this constitution derives all its powers and authority.

b. The security and welfare of the people shall be the primary purpose of government;

c. The participation by the people in their government shall be ensured in accordance with the provisions of this constitution.

Section 16(1): The state shall within the context of the ideals and objectives for which provisions are made in this constitution:

a. Control the national economy in such manner as to secure the maximum welfare, freedom and happiness of every citizen on the basis of social justice and equality of status and opportunity;

Section 16(2): The state shall direct its policy towards ensuring:

b. That the material resources of the community are harnessed and distributed as best as possible to serve the common good;

c. That the economic system is not operated in such a manner as to permit the concentration of wealth or the means of production and exchange in the hands of few individuals or of a group; and

d. That suitable and adequate shelter, suitable and adequate food, reasonable natural minimum living wage, old age care and pension, and unemployment and sick benefits are provided for all citizens'.

Other sections of the Chapter set out the other socio-cultural rights earlier enumerated. What is worthy of note is that the entire provisions of Chapter 2 of the 1979 Constitution even when the Constitution was fully operational could not be legally enforced. Their objective, it seems, is to mock and taunt the masses of our people.

Rule of Law

The cardinal notion of the concept of Rule of Law as it was developed in the era of dying absolute monarchism and the ascendancy of republicanism in Europe of the Middle Ages was that:

> Whosoever is called upon to rule a people must accept the fact that he himself is subject to the law even to the law he has made for the governance of the people (Aguda 1986:16).

However, time has augmented the implication of the concept of the rule of law and it now includes the independence of the judiciary, equality before the law, and that 'the executive has no inherent discretionary power to act against the interest of the citizen' (Nwabueze 1973:34). In a nutshell, the concept of the rule of law is supposed to be a guarantee against arbitrary rule.

Civil Liberties, Human Rights and Rule of Law in Nigeria

The colonisation of Nigeria by Britain at the turn of the 19th century brought about the exploitation of the human and natural resources of the country for the overall development of Britain. This exploitation could not but run into conflict with the above concepts. British colonialism at its most brazen, with all its denigrating postures, regarded the 'natives' as savages or a sub-human species who should not be accorded human rights.

The right which in our view is pivotal to the understanding of the denial of human rights suffered by Nigerians in the hey-day of colonialism is the right to self determination. This right, we dare say, is the most important one for a colonised people, contrary to the pride of place accorded the basic right to life by many scholars and human right commentators. It is the 'chief right' without which the enjoyment of other rights would amount to nothing. The essential issue is that the right to human dignity and the practice of colonialism cannot possibly have any meaningful co-existence.

Nigeria gained independence in 1960 with a Constitution that guaranteed some fundamental human rights. The Nigerian people witnessed significant progress in the protection of the said Constitutionally guaranteed rights during brief periods of democratic rule (1960-1966 and 1979-1983). But under successive military dictatorships, the protection of these rights has suffered a severe set-back. Not too much can be expected from post-colonial Nigeria, because when it is stripped of the camouflage offered by the national bourgeoisie and the deceptive embroidery woven by neocolonial scholars, the legacy left behind by the British colonialists is not a truly nationally independent entity but a vast, resourceful apparatus dedicated to the continued service of the engine of growth of western imperialism. Isolating the short duration of 'democratic governance' or civilian rule in Nigeria since 1960 and discussing the concepts of civil liberties, human rights and rule of law in that context, the low level of operation of these concepts is clear.

The right to life, the most basic of all human rights for instance, is not enjoyed by many Nigerians who die of hunger, starvation and widespread but preventable diseases like cholera, yellow fever, guinea worm etc. In fact, the life expectancy of an average Nigerian, using the WHO Report on Africa as an indication, is as low as 45 years. Similarly, virtually all the other civil liberties are only enjoyable by the few rich and powerful members of the society who have the wherewithal to challenge the violation of them. For example, the freedom of expression means nothing to millions of illiterate and dehumanised Nigerians in rural areas, or on the whole, to a people whose literacy percentage is below 45 per cent. In the same vein, the right to personal liberty is a shibboleth for thousands of citizens languishing in prison custody without trial.

In the absence of social economic and cultural rights the generality of our people cannot enjoy the political-civil rights or liberties enshrined in the constitution even where it is fully operational. The Nigerian legal system expects the person whose rights are being infracted to seek remedies and enforce these rights using their personal resources. Thus an impoverished Nigerian is effectively embargoed by the Constitutional provisions from enforcing his civil liberties since the cost of such enforcement in the law courts is outrageously prohibitive. As stated by Krishina Iyer:

> The scales of justice are inevitably weighted in favour of the richest people, who can afford the best lawyers and advice, whereas the person of average income may be excluded from his rights unless he is so irresponsible as to gamble — since there is always a risk that even a small claim might escalate to the House of Lords, wafted on legal nicety which may be interesting but could result in bankruptcy for him and his family (1980:81).

This brings us to the age-old ruse concerning the concept of the rule of law. Law, we insist, is not a neutral phenomenon and its rule cannot be neutral. The relevant question to which we will provide an answer below is — the rule of what law? The law of the ruled or the rulers? The Marxist theory of law to which we subscribe considers law as an intricate instrument of the ruling class backed by the coercive apparatus of the state, having as its objective the safeguarding, security and development of social relationships and arrangements advantageous and agreeable to the ruling class. It may not be absurd for a ruler to submit to the supremacy of his self-created law in consonance with the concept of the rule of law but an unquestioning submission by the ruled to the rule of the law meant to subvert his interest is inconceivable. Equality before the law is nothing but a myth. As pointed out by the eminent jurist Akinola Aguda:

> The notion that everyone is equal before the law branded about by lawyers is a myth, it has no basis in reality. Lawyers, and in this I include the judges, would like to force us to swallow this notion as an immutable concept, I refuse to swallow it.... It is nothing but a myth created by our political rulers and the lawyers to give cold comfort to the 'common man', so that they, that is our political rulers and the lawyers, can have a peace of mind. But the earlier we disturb that piece of mind the better (1986:25).

Citing an authority, he continued:

> A just legal order (which ours is not) is a hollow shell if a minority or an individual is denied access to that just legal order, access in the sense of understanding the law and its procedures, access in the sense of being capable of effectively utilising the law, access in the sense of participating in the rule — making process and access in the sense of experiencing positively the benefits of his society (1986:30).

Why then do human rights organisations, lawyers, judges etc. assert the concept of the rule of law and clamour for governmental adherence to it? Why the vigorous proclamation of the inviolability of the civil liberties guaranteed by the Constitution? The simple answer, in our view, is to expose the hypocrisy of the ruling class, strain the restricted scope of these liberties, expose their inadequacies with a view to having their frontiers expanded and thereby extract more concessions from the legal system. In doing this we do not lose sight of the fact that our law is in league with capital against the interests of labour. In a similar adoption of this attitude, the Nigerian Supreme Court — even when it appreciated that military rule was incompatible with the rule of law, had this to say in The Governor of Lagos State v Emeka Ojukwu Case:

> The Nigerian Constitution is founded on the rule of law, the primary meaning of which is that everything must be done according to law. It means also that government should be conducted within the framework of recognised rules and principles which restrict discretionary power which Coke colourfully spoke of as 'golden and straight wand of law as opposed to the uncertain and crooked cord of discretion'... More relevant

to the case in hand, the rule of law means that disputes as to the legality of acts of government are to be decided by judges who are wholly independent of the executive... That is the position in this country where the judiciary has been made independent of the executive by the Constitution of the Federal Republic of Nigeria 1979 as amended by Decree No. 1 of 1984 and No. 17 of 1985. The judiciary cannot shirk its sacred responsibility to the nation to maintain the rule of law. It is both in the interest of the government and all persons in Nigeria. The law should be even handed between the government and citizens (Justice Obaseki, NWLR, 1986:621-7).

Nigeria Under Military Dictatorship

A military dictatorship is by definition a regime sustained by force and violence and it does not derive its powers from the Constitution it has had to subvert in coming to power. It therefore establishes a new political order that is either an outright martial or a civil-martial order depending on the degree of resistance of the civil society to its hegemony. According to Osoba:

> Military rule does not mean rule by the military to the exclusion of the civilian population. On the contrary, our historical experience in Nigeria, like that of other people in Africa, Asia and Latin America, reveals military rule to be a kind of emergency system of governance adopted by the ruling class of a particular country for the management of a crisis situation that, in its judgement, is not amenable to resolution by Constitutional means or the rule of law. Under military rule, the military dictator or junta occupies the highest decision making and executive position but the vast majority of high-ranking state officials are recruited from the civilian arm of the ruling class and do not suffer the inconvenience of having to canvass for the support or approval of the public (1983:10).

Nigeria, as we all know, got her flag independence from Britain on October 1, 1960. After six years of somnambulist democracy which could not have been otherwise given the transfer of the reins of government by the British to the compradorial servitor of neocolonial interests, the military struck on January 15, 1966. With this military intervention began a 13 year misrule, during which Nigeria was dragged into a fratricidal 30-month civil war. Thus between 1966 and 1993, the military has ruled Nigeria for 23 years and has progressively eroded the fundamental human rights of the Nigerian people, contriving innumerable decrees and edicts ousting the jurisdiction of the law courts to entertain complaints of abuses. Military rule has therefore substantially abridged and sometimes obliterated some of the civil liberties guaranteed by the Constitution, the provisions of which in any case have been shown earlier to be inadequate in meeting the aspirations of our people.

Some of the infringements of the fundamental human rights of the people recorded by successive military regimes in Nigeria are: genocide and political killings; arbitrary arrests, detention and imprisonment of critics of government policies or officials; prolonged detention without charge or trial; severe and inhuman conditions of imprisonment and detention; torture; the death penalty; unfair political trials, detention of protesting students, striking workers and political opposition elements; extra judicial killings of protesters; trials of civilians before military and quasi-military tribunals; state-organised abduction and assassination of detainees and major opposition figures; public execution of persons convicted through unfair trials which fall short of humane and international standards; brutal and potentially fatal systems of interrogation; outright bans or legal curtailment of the exercise of civil, political and social-legal rights; civil punishments such as amputations and execution by firing squad without blindfold; terrorism of the civil populace by the security outfit of the regimes; passport seizure; censorship and closure of media houses etc.

Many decrees and edicts sanctioning some of the fore-going enumerated infringements enacted by the successive military regimes contain ouster clauses which have crippled the judiciary, strengthening the domination of the Armed Forces over the civil society and causing disrespect for the rule of law at all levels. As excesses of government cannot be challenged in court, a culture of violence has been institutionalised. Worse still, court orders are flouted with impunity while conditions of service of judges remains poor. This situation has made it difficult for the masses of our people to enjoy those conceded rights which they struggle to enjoy under a democratic governance.

The Role of Human Rights Organisations

With the return of the military to power on December 31, 1983 an unprecedented era of suffocating human rights abuses coupled with pro-imperialist economic policies began. The immediate response of Nigerian civil society was the springing up of human rights organisations and their engagement in taking up cases of human rights abuses and violations. Giving a chronological account of the human rights abuses over the last decade is not necessary given the scandalous number of these abuses and the wide coverage they have received in the popular press and specialised publications. It is worthwhile pointing out some of the most scandalous cases — the political murder of General Vatsa and others for alleged coup plotting, the massacre of students at Ahmadu Bello University, the assassination of Dele Giwa, the editor of *Newswatch*, the introduction of the Structural Adjustment Programme, all in 1986; the destruction of Maroko and the rendering of hundreds of thousands of people homeless in 1990; the Umuechem massacre of the same year; the massacre of the Garubas at Oko-Oba in 1991; and the killings that followed the Anti-SAP demonstrations of 1989, 1991 and 1992.

These are high points in Babangida's black calendar of human rights violations. His imposition of the IMF/World Bank dictated Structural Adjustment Programme and the fraudulent Political Transition Programme stand out as a reference point in the history of crimes against humanity. These two programmes are in violent conflict with the UNUDHR 1948 and the African Charter of Human and Peoples Rights whose relevant provisions are provided below.

Article 21 of the UNUDHR states that:

1. Everyone has the right to take part in the government of his country, directly or through freely chosen representatives.

2. Everyone has the right of equal access to public service in his country.

3. The will of the people shall be the basis of the authority of government, and this will shall be expressed in periodic and genuine elections which shall be by universal and equal suffrage and shall be held by secret vote or by equivalent free voting procedures.

Articles 20 and 22 of the African Charter state respectively:

Article 20:

1. All peoples shall have the right to existence. They shall have the unquestionable and inalienable right to self determination. They shall freely determine their political status and shall pursue their economic and social development according to the policies they have freely chosen.

2. Colonised or oppressed peoples shall have the right to free themselves from the bonds of domination by resorting to any means recognised by the international community.

Article 22:

1. All peoples shall have the right to their economic, social and cultural development with due regard to their freedom and identity and in the equal enjoyment of the common heritage of mankind.

2. States shall have the duty, individually or collectively to ensure the exercise of the right to development'.

That the right of equal access to public service in one's country provided by Article 21(2) of the UNUDHR is akin to the myth of equality before the law should not bother us here; what is noteworthy on a perusal of the above is that although Nigeria is a signatory to the two charters, it has not fulfilled its obligations under them. In recognition of this, the Civil Liberties Organisation (CLO), the Committee for the Defence of Human Rights (CDHR), the National Association of Democratic Lawyers (NADL), the Constitutional Rights Project (CRP), the Gani Fawehinmi Solidarity ·Organisation (GFSA), and Universal Defenders of Democracy among others have promoted human rights consciousness in Nigeria. While employing a combination of legal and political strategies which have resulted in the release of several persons detained without trial, they have ceaselessly drawn the attention of the masses of our people to the urgent task of terminating military dictatorship in all its ramifications.

More recently, following the unwillingness of the ousted military dictator, Ibrahim Babangida, to conduct an election and relinquish power in tandem with his transition programme, the human rights community, under the banner of the Campaign for Democracy (CD) was compelled to enter the political terrain, playing a decisive role in the ousting of Babangida from power after the criminal annulment of the June 12 election.

The State of the Nation

On November 17, 1993, a coterie of army generals led by General Sani Abacha took over the reins of government and re-imposed military dictatorship on the country. Since a change of government via a coup d'etat has since become anathema in the country, the latest military intervention was fraudulently disguised as a Constitutional change of government occasioned by the purported resignation of Chief Ernest Shonekan from his seat at the head of the defunct Interim National Government. Relying on Section 42 of the Interim National Government (Basic Constitutional Provisions) Decree No. 61 of 1993, which empowers the most senior minister to take over as the Head of State if the Head of the Interim National Government dies or resigns his appointment, the military high command coerced Chief Shonekan to step down and hand over power to General Abacha.

At the time that drama was going on at Abuja, a court of competent jurisdiction had declared the Interim National Government unconstitutional and the appointment of all secretaries (ministers) illegal. Since General Abacha was the Defence Secretary of the illegal ING, he could not have lawfully stepped into Shonekan's shoes. To that extent, the purported resignation of Chief Shonekan as Head of State and his replacement by General Abacha is illegal. However, most Nigerians were not prepared to address the legality or constitutionality of the Abacha regime having become totally disenchanted with a political class that had decided to toy with the destiny of the nation. Quite ironically, Nigerians felt relieved to learn that the political class that colluded with General Ibrahim Babangida and Chief Ernest Shonekan to scuttle the democratisation process had lost out.

Despite this, the demolition of the entire democratic structure which had been erected at an astronomical cost of over 40 billion naira was seen as a huge drain on the nation's resources. Equally worrisome was the popular belief that General Abacha lacked the moral rights to preside over the affairs of the country, having been part and parcel of the profligacy of the previous regime's eight years.

The Abacha junta's political propositions are unacceptable to advocates of human and civic rights. To start with, the proposed Constitutional Conference must be rejected. In its place, we demand the convocation of a Sovereign National Conference (SNC) to discuss the following items:

1. Equal and just relations among the various ethnic groups; structure of the federation; the preservation of minority rights; equitable revenue allocation and other aspects of the nationality question.

2. The termination of SAP and its replacement with a people oriented alternative that will revalue the naira, provide full employment and make food, clothing, shelter, education, transport and health affordable to all.

3. Genuine multi-party democracy that would enhance national cohesion, social development and democratic practices.

4. Preservation of the secularity of the Nigerian State and its harmonious co-existence of various religious and non-religious groups.

5. Safeguards against military intervention, dictatorship and abuse of power. This should include the restructure and reform of the armed forces, the police and other security agencies to make them amenable and accountable to civil authority.

6. Public Accountability including elimination of corruption and the recovery of public property.

7. The protection and promotion of human rights and the rule of law.

8. Freedom of speech and of the press.

9. The formulation of a popular Nigerian Constitution, guaranteeing its supremacy and the repeal of all unjust degrees (Campaign for Democracy, *The Guardian*, 11/12/1993).

For the resolutions of the Conference to be acceptable to the majority of our people, the SNC must be independent of government control and influence. There should not be any 'no go areas' in the deliberations while its decisions must not be subjected to any vetting or amendment by government. The composition should be based on ELECTION and not SELECTION. In this regard we suggest the election of two delegates per senatorial district while social and professional groups should elect or nominate their own delegates. The armed forces, the police and other security agencies should be represented in the SNC.

The June 12 Election Revisited

The military ruler, General Abacha, has recently urged Nigerians to regard the June 12 election as a watershed in our struggle for democracy. Yet his regime has come to scuttle the struggle for democracy. Since no rational explanation has been proffered for the criminal annulment of the June 12 mandate, it is the view of the CD, which I share, that:

> The struggle to enforce the outcome of the Presidential Elections of June 12, 1993 during which hundreds of Nigerians laid down their lives, limbs and liberty has been cardinal in the activities of the CD since the annulment of that election. From the onset, the CD has consistently emphasised that June 12 went beyond the symbols of that mandate, the Babangida parties, the entire Transition Programme or any ethnic group or groups... June 12 cannot be wished away despite the present ambivalence of its winners. It is a historic expression of popular will transcending ethnic, religious and other primordial barriers. It is a categorical and crisis free rejection of all forms of hegemony by a minority over the rest of the nation. CD therefore still stands for the democratic resolution of June 12 as a basis for the democratic advancement of the country (*The Guardian* 11/12/1993).

Broadly speaking, no country under a military dictatorship can lay any claim to the observance of human rights. For the Abacha regime to be taken seriously and accorded some credibility, it must do certain things. Since both the World Bank and International Monetary Fund which imposed the Structural Adjustment Programme (SAP) on Nigeria have admitted the failure of the programme to provide lasting solutions to the economic crisis plaguing our country, the time has therefore come for government to terminate SAP forthwith and replace it with a people-oriented programme as provided for under the Directive Principles of State Policy contained in Chapter 2 of the 1979 Constitution. As government is bound to control the commanding heights of the Nigerian economy, we condemn the on-going moves to privatise the Nigerian National Petroleum Corporation (NNPC) and sell our abundant mineral resources to foreigners and their Nigerian collaborators.

Having realised that corruption has eaten deep into the fabric of the Nigerian society, we reject the policy of the Abacha regime of covering up the stinkingly corrupt past of certain government officials. In fact, it is hypocritical to harass legislators over car loans while General Ibrahim Babangida and his 90 ex-military governors are allowed to go scot free with their criminal loot of the Public Treasury. The major issue should be that Babangida be tried for economic crimes. Equally, if the Abacha regime is serious about eliminating the corruption which was institutionalised under the Babangida-Shonekan regime, we call on members of the Provisional Ruling Council, Federal Executive Council and State Executives to declare their assets without any delay. Since declaration means to make known publicly, it is unacceptable for public officers to hide facts about their assets and liabilities.

Conclusion

The ineluctable agenda before the human rights community today is the consolidation of its pro-democracy role and the termination of the present incipient military dictatorship of the Abacha regime. Unless economic, social and cultural rights are made justiciable, our citizens cannot escape from the web of misery, decadence and poverty in which they are caught. Moreover, apart from addressing the social and economic inhibitions which militate against the enjoyment of human rights guaranteed in the Constitution, violations of the underprivileged members of the society by security agents and powerful individuals can be seriously checked by the adoption of the following measures:

1. Establishment of a National Human Rights Commission to investigate allegations of human right violations, recommend appropriate redress and undertake the education and promotion of human rights standards. The Commission should absorb and reorganise the Legal Aid Council, Prison Decongestion Committees and Public Complaints Commission.

2. Government should accord human rights organisations an untrammelled recognition and encourage them to operate without restrictions and persecution.

3. Special administrative machinery should be initiated in collaboration with human rights organisations to protect the right to liberty, press freedom, academic freedom and right of association in view of the regular violations of these rights.

4. Government should provide facilities to take care of the rights of the more disadvantaged and vulnerable segments of the society, for example children, women, workers, the disabled and peasant farmers.

5. As a matter of urgency, Government should ratify all yet to be ratified human rights conventions and other instruments.

6. Apart from compensating victims of human rights violations, Government must discipline security agents, authorities or persons who violate the rights of citizens.

7. Immediate repeal of all laws which derogate from fundamental rights, provisions, for example Decree 2 and similar decrees which oust courts jurisdiction.

The above recommendations are not all-encompassing, for it remains to be said that the formation of Regional Human Rights Monitoring Groups, proliferation of national human rights organisations and enactment of more charters, protocols and agreements can increase awareness which may influence dictatorial regimes the world over to observe these rights. To compel dictatorial regimes to observe human rights needs a lot of concrete work. It took the African Americans several years to realise that the sacred provisions of the Bill of Rights alone could not guarantee the preservation of their inherent rights as human beings; street protest and marches did. The South Africans are on the verge of reaping the fruits of almost a century of persistent national liberation struggle.

In the unfolding struggle for the convocation of the Sovereign National Conference, the strategic objective is to avoid the enactment of yet another hollow document in the name of a Constitution. The people must be mobilised to participate in the Conference and their input must be the basis of the determination of all questions thereat. In the words of Tolstoy:

> The abolition of slavery has gone on for a long time, Rome abolished slavery, America abolished it and 'we did, but only the words were abolished, not the thing.

We have an opportunity to abolish 'the thing' of socio-economic serfdom and set our society and its people on the path of peace, social progress and a harmonious existence. Let us seize this opportunity and utilise it.

12

Ethnicity and Democratisation in Nigeria: A Case Study of Zangon Kataf

Abdul Raufu Mustapha

Introduction: Democratisation or Re-tribalisation?

The 'wind of change' that swept across Africa in the 1960s was predicated on a number of assumptions which have turned out to be false: that British and French parliamentary systems can be unproblematically transplanted to the emergent nation-states; that political parties will essentially reflect class/ideological differences; and that the rule of law, loyal opposition, etc., can take root, leading to the establishment of democratic self-governance. The failure of these assumptions, in the context of neocolonial underdevelopment, set the stage for the emergence of one-party states, the marginalisation of the populace, authoritarian personal rule and the military dictatorships that have plagued the continent from the mid-1960s. From the late 1980s, a new wind of change has been gathering force in Africa in the democratisation of authoritarian state structures. What are the assumptions that underlie this new phase in the evolution of the African state? And to what extent do these assumptions correspond to the reality on the ground?

A common assumption, associated with the political conditionalities of the IMF, is the equation of multipartyism with democratisation. Another assumption, articulated by defenders of the status-quo from Moi to Chirac, suggests that democratisation and multipartyism can only lead to the recrudescence of 'tribalism', an ugly phenomenon which the authoritarian state had done much to suppress. This second assumption raises the question of the relationship between ethnicity and democratisation. This question is all the more important, considering that, for many analysts, African politics is equated with 'tribalism'.

Available evidence on the process of democratisation in Africa so far suggests that there may not be a simple and straightforward relationship between ethnicity and democratisation. Some have suggested, for instance, that the Malawian election of May 1994 revealed a voting pattern along clearly ethnic lines. Much has also been made of the support Eyadema has been able to mobilise from his ethnic base in northern Togo. On the other hand, one could point out that in the controversial June 12, 1993 Presidential Election in Nigeria, Moshood Abiola, a Yoruba from the southwest, defeated Bashir Tofa, a Hausa, in his home base of Kano State. More importantly, the 'tribal' conceptualisation of the process of democratisation ignores the emergence and re-invigoration of organs of civil society, such as trade unions, professional associations, human rights groups and the press, which have given the principal impetus to the democratisation process.

Politicians and neocolonialists like Moi and Chirac raise the spectre of 're-tribalisation' as a means of discrediting the democratisation process. While such an unsavoury manoeuvre, especially in the Kenyan experience, can be seen for what it is, it is also the case that the advocates of multipartyism have simply assumed that political plurality would lead to democracy without giving much thought to intervening variables such as ethnicity, regionalism and religious polarisation. Notions of rights, citizenship and the moral basis of the state, prevalent in the West are implicitly assumed to be applicable to Africa. In many cases, the reality may be different from the assumptions.

There is therefore a need to elaborate the complex relationship between ethnicity and democratisation as the African experience unfolds. By so doing, it should be possible to avoid false hopes, while at the same time addressing real issues. This chapter attempts to do that through an examination of the crises in Zangon Kataf in Kaduna State in northern Nigeria. Central to this analysis will be the conflict over the definition of rights, citizenship, and the ethical basis of the state.

Zangon Kataf: Historical Outline

Zangon Kataf is a Hausa settlement (zango) within a territory occupied by the Kataf, a minority ethnic group in north-central Nigeria. It is the headquarters of the Zangon Kataf Local Government of Kaduna State. Since the latest wave of Kataf/Hausa conflicts in 1992, controversy has raged about the history of the town. It seems clear, however, that the original town was established as a trading post for Hausa merchants en route to the Niger Basin in the early part of the 16th century. While the Hausa of Zangon Kataf and the Kataf tribal polity established economic and commercial relations, they had little in the way of social relations, Zangon Kataf being a wholly Hausa settlement within the Kataf polity. The Hausa settlement was also politically autonomous, being headed by the Sarkin Hausawa. By the end of the 18th century, the settlement became subordinated to Kauru, a larger Hausa settlement within the territory of another ethnic minority in the same region, the Ruruma. Early in the 19th century, Kauru itself became subordinated to Zaria, one of the major Hausa states that constituted the Sokoto Caliphate.

For much of the 19th century, the minority ethnic groups south of Zaria, the Kataf included, were raided for slaves to supply the domestic needs of the Sokoto Caliphate, and for export on both the trans-Saharan and the trans-Atlantic slave routes. From the Kataf point of view, the Hausa community of Zangon Kataf was seen as distinct from the Hausa slave raiders from Zaria. With the imposition of British colonial rule at the turn of the 20th century, however, the Kataf polity was subordinated to the Emir of Zaria, under Lugard's policy of Indirect Rule. Kataf territory became the Katuka District of Zaria Emirate. In 1902, 1904, 1905 and 1907 the Kataf attacked Zangon Kataf, allegedly for colluding with the British in their designs to subjugate the Kataf. The colonial army was called in to suppress the attacks. Subsequently, Zangon Kataf town was moved to its present location in about 1915. For much of the 20th century, especially between 1920 and 1950, there has been a steady influx of Hausa people to Zangon Kataf, primarily from the Emirates of Zaria, Kano, Katsina and Bauchi.

The Crises of 1992

The Zangon Kataf crises of February and May 1992 fall into a general pattern of inter-communal clashes over land and other agricultural resources that have virtually become endemic in the Middle Belt, a region of northern Nigeria lying south of the centralised Islamic states of the Sokoto Caliphate and the Bornu Empire. The region is inhabited largely by minority ethnic groups, most of whom did not have a centralised state system before the imposition of British colonialism. The fact that this area of Nigeria, which has the smallest population density in the country, should also witness the most bloody confrontations over land resources deserves serious study. For our purposes, however, the immediate focus is on the series of clashes in the Southern Kaduna State: the Kasuwan Magani riots in 1980-1981, the Gure/Kahugu riots in Saminaka Local Government Area in 1984, the Lere riots in 1986, and the Kafanchan riots in 1987. This dynamic of communal blood-letting has come to be epitomised in the national consciousness by the very bloody confrontations in Zangon Kataf in 1992.

As in the case of the recent 'Guinea Fowl' war in northern Ghana, when a dispute between two men in a local market over the price of a guinea fowl exposed long-standing ethnic animosities subsequently leading to the death of thousands of people, the Zangon Kataf crises of 1992 started over the construction of a new market by the local government authority. Disagreement between some members of both communities over the issue led to clashes early in February 1992, resulting in a number of fatalities. The Cudjoe Judicial Commission of Inquiry was set up by the Kaduna State Government to investigate the riot. While it was still sitting, tension continued to mount between the two communities. Late in April 1992, the government convened informal meetings with the two communities to cool down tempers. The failure of these efforts was soon apparent. From May 15 and 17, 1992, fresh rioting erupted in Zangon Kataf.

The immediate unfolding of the May riot became the subject of intense controversy, as each community tried to justify its conduct. There are divergent positions as to who started the killings. There is no doubt, however, that most of the victims were the Hausa of Zangon Kataf. There is evidence to suggest that at least 1,536 Hausas were killed in Zangon Kataf. Most of the houses in the town were razed to the ground, and Hausa household property valued at 29,173,850 naira destroyed. It has also been estimated that about 71 motor vehicles and 25 motor cycles and bicycles were destroyed. Estimates of Kataf losses are hard to come by, but they would appear to be much less than those suffered by the Hausa. The intensity of the destruction may be due to the fact that the Middle Belt is the 'labour reserve' from which most of the non-commissioned ranks of the Nigerian Army are recruited. As a consequence, the region contains many ex-service men, many of whom may still have access to fire-arms. It is baffling, though, that the police did not intervene right at the onset of the riot to bring the situation under control; particularly since after the February riot, police vigilance had ostensibly been stepped-up.

As is the case with many of the other communal/religious riots starting from Southern Kaduna State, the Zangon Kataf riot of May 1992 precipitated rioting in other parts of Kaduna State; large-scale rioting broke out in Kaduna, Zaria, Ikara, and Kauru. Kaduna is the state capital, while Zaria and Ikara constitute the Hausa heartland of the state. In Kaduna and Zaria, hundreds of lives were lost, either in the rioting, or in police/military actions that followed. Seven people were reportedly shot dead by the police in Ikara.

Interpreting the Crises

One of the most striking things about the Zangon Kataf riots of 1992 is that they expose the conflicting perceptions of rights, citizenship and the moral basis of the state held by both communities involved in the conflict. Zangon Kataf also illustrates the manner in which the very state that is the target of democratisation can be instrumental in the definition of the process itself.

The Kataf View

The Kataf view, pieced together from diverse sources, is remarkable for its historical sweep of Kataf/Hausa relations, hoping in the process to point out the 'real issues' and the supposed injustices, more historical than immediate, meted out to the Kataf. They attempt to justify their position in the immediate crises within the logic of this history. The argument is that the Kataf have historically welcomed strangers into their midst. These strangers were given clan/communal lands to cultivate, but there was no alienation of the land from the original household, lineage or clan. Individual ownership was not part of the tribal land tenure. Strangers were often absorbed into Kataf society, especially the *Netzit* (Our People) who are the other minority ethnic group of Southern Kaduna State and parts of Plateau State. These groups have very similar historical, cultural, political and demographic characteristics. The argument goes on to suggest that when the Hausa merchants came to the Kataf polity in the 16th century, they were given land to build their settlement, but the rights of ownership over the land remained with the Kataf clans. A mark of this continued ownership, consistent with their traditional tenure system, was their abiding right to harvest the tree crops on the land which they had given to strangers to cultivate. Since most of the Hausa immigrants were traders or craftsmen, they rarely had need of farmland.

Though both communities remained politically and culturally distinct, there was little conflict between them, even when slave raiders from Zaria Emirate launched attacks on the Kataf. The problem began, the Kataf claim, with the imposition of British colonial rule in the early 20th century. While the Emir of Zaria, for regional geo-political reasons, succumbed to colonial imposition without a fight, the Kataf forcefully resisted colonial domination. Against this background, the Kataf were regarded by the British as 'ungovernable'. Given the lack of a centralised state structure, and their traditional religion, they were regarded as 'uncivilised pagans' who were incapable of self-governance. Furthermore, racist colonial anthropology characterised the Kataf as inferior to the lighter-skinned Fulani elite of the Emirates, who were not only monotheists, but had also built up a large empire, the Sokoto Caliphate, complete with a bureaucracy and record-keeping in Arabic.

The Kataf claim that the British were therefore favourably disposed to accept the Zaria claim that the Kataf polity had been 'conquered' by Zaria in pre-colonial times. As far as the Kataf were concerned, although Zaria may lay claim to the political allegiance of the Hausa community of Zangon Kataf through Kauru, that allegiance had nothing to do with the political autonomy of the Kataf, or their ownership of the land on which the town stood. However, as has been stated, the Lugardian policy of Indirect Rule subordinated the Kataf to Zaria Emirate as the Katuka District, with a title-holder from Zaria, the Katukan Zazzau, as District Head. It was the alleged 'collusion' of the Zangon Kataf community with this scheme that led to the series of attacks on the town at the turn of the century; attacks which confirmed the British view of Kataf 'ungovernability'.

With the loss of their traditional clan-based political system and their subjugation to an 'alien' authority, the Kataf claim that they became victims of a series of injustices. They were excluded from the District administration, which became a wholly Hausa affair, right down to the messengers. They were also subjected to various indignities by the 'alien' local administration: cultural denigration by being derogatorily referred to as *arna* (non-Moslems or pagans) and *kabila* (non-Hausa), tyrannical excesses by the Emir's Native Police (*dogarai*), and subjugation to the unsympathetic arbitrariness of the Emir's Alkali courts, which dispensed a form of law based on Islamic principles which were alien to the Kataf. They also complained of excessive taxation, confiscation of their goods for failure to pay, and exclusion from the markets built with Kataf forced labour. They claimed that the ordeal of forced labour was not extended to the Hausas of Zangon Kataf.

Above all, the Kataf complained that the colonial and local administrations encouraged the influx of Hausa settlers to the area, leading to the forcible transfer of Kataf farmlands to new Hausa immigrants. The emergence of large-scale farming in the 1970s intensified this process through various state projects. The intensification of development projects in the country from the 1970s, fuelled by oil-boom petro-dollars, also increased contestation over land rights, as individuals and groups sought to receive the compensation paid by the state for land acquired.

The Kataf claim is that they protested their situation through numerous petitions to the colonial administration, often with the assistance of Christian missionaries who had gained a foothold in the area. After a riot by the Kataf in 1933 and again in 1946, they agitated for the formation of an Independent Tribal Council composed of 'indigenous' — that is Kataf — representatives. These demands were not met, even though they had the support of some colonial administrators. After more rioting in 1953, the principle of including some Kataf in the District Council was accepted, but it was made clear that the district still remained under the Emir. As a result, a few Kataf got into the administration, especially at the Village Head level. The agitation for an Independent Tribal Council continued. On its part, the colonial administration urged the Emir to accept an indigenous District Head, so as not to drive the people of the area into the hands of the anti-colonial Middle Belt movement and their Southern Nigerian supporters.

The appointment of John Tafida, as District Head in Zangon Kataf, a Hausa/Fulani of aristocratic blood from Zaria (*Dan Galadiman Zazzau*) but one who had converted to Christianity due to the influence of Reverend Miller, was aimed at assuaging Kataf resentment. Though his stay was peaceful enough, he was later removed by Zaria and the practice of appointing Moslem Hausa/Fulanis to the District Headship continued. Kataf agitation for an 'indigenous' District Head subsequently led, in 1967, to the transfer of the *Sarkin Yakin Zazzau* from the District and his replacement by the first 'indigenous' (Kataf) District Head, Bala Dauke Gora. He was also conferred with the traditional Zaria title of *Kuyambannan Zazzau*. Considering that the emirate officials from Zaria defined 'indigeneity' in the districts of Southern Kaduna to include the Hausa and Fulani communities of the area and continued to appoint same as 'indigenous' officials, the Kataf and other minority ethnic groups in the area reverted to their old demand for their own independent, 'traditional', chiefdoms in 1974.

The 1976 Local Government Reform created the possibility for the minority ethnic groups of Southern Kaduna State, who nevertheless constituted a huge majority over the Hausa/Fulani communities in the area, to vote in their own people as chairmen of the local government councils. In their view, this development did not address their problem as the elected local government chairmen were incorporated into the Zaria Emirate Council as subordinates of the Emir. Furthermore, all District and Village Heads, though employees of and paid by the local

government, continued to be appointed by and reported directly to the
Emir of Zaria. Though Kataf men were now both Local Government
Chairman and District Head, Kataf disaffection continued to simmer,
fuelled by what they regarded as their continued subordination to Zaria,
and the alleged nepotistic appointment of the minority, but now
'allegedly indigenous', Hausa/Fulani elements from the Southern Kaduna
area to political and other offices in the state and federal governments as
'representatives' of the people of the area. They formed the view that
elements of the local Hausa/Fulani communities were using their wider
connections within the Nigerian state system and the society in general to
continue their effective domination of the Southern Kaduna minority
groups; some even accused the Hausa/Fulani of exhibiting an arrogant
'conqueror's mentality' thanks to their assured external backing. Efforts
to get various state administrations to address Kataf claims were
allegedly frustrated by the administrations' commitment to Hausa
interests.

Such is the context within which the Kataf seek to explain the crisis
over the construction of a market in Zangon Kataf in 1992. They claim
that Kataf exclusion from stall ownership in the Zangon Kataf market led
to agitation, particularly from 1946, for the relocation of the market to a
place less dominated by the Hausa and more accessible to the Kataf. It is
further claimed that a 1961 government-approved lay-out for the
development of Zangon Kataf made provisions for the construction of a
new market. They accuse mercantile interests within the Hausa
community of thwarting all efforts at constructing this new market, since
it would ultimately lead to the weakening of their commercial and
economic 'hegemony'. Even when the Kataf constructed their own
independent Baradawa Kataf Market in the early 1970s, a Hausa
agent-provocateur instigated a fracas in the market, leading to its closure.
From the Kataf point of view, it was the hostility of elements of the
Hausa community to the decision of the local government to move the
market in February 1992 that led to the riots. They claim that it was
elements from the Hausa community that started the killings in both
February and May, and that the first casualties that turned up at local
hospitals were Kataf.

The Kataf argue that it is not only the commercial hegemony of the
Hausa that is at issue, but the very development of their area. They claim
that the Hausa community has consistently refused to release land which
the Hausa allegedly own for the sitting of development projects such as a
Post Office, a Health Centre, a Day Secondary School, and an
agricultural development project. It is claimed that this refusal persisted

even when compensation had been paid. The suggestion is that the Hausa position is dictated by the need to exclude the Kataf from any toe-hold on Zangon Kataf and through that, perpetuate Hausa exclusivity and hegemony.

Since the riots, the Kataf claim that the Hausa community are using their regional and national connections to victimise Kataf community leaders and prominent sons, most of whom, it is claimed, have been sentenced to long terms of imprisonment on trumped up charges by special tribunals set up by the Federal Government to 'teach the Kataf, and through them, other Southern Kaduna minority groups a lesson'. The position of the Federal Government is seen within the context of its long-standing commitment to the interests of the Hausa/Fulani elite, as well as familial ties connecting principal actors in the federal and Kaduna State governments to the Hausa communities of Southern Kaduna State. Zamani Lekwot, the imprisoned retired army general from the Kataf community, is seen as the prime and most prominent victim of this oppressive dynamic.

The Kataf close their case by demanding what is called *social justice*. This can be interpreted to mean a number of things: the right to separate from Zaria Emirate and establish their own chiefdom, the recognition of their land rights over Zangon Kataf, the right to equal and fair treatment before the law, and the freeing of their incarcerated sons.

The Hausa View

Like the Kataf view, the Hausa view is also pieced together from a number of sources, and not necessarily limited to views expressed by only members of the Zangon Kataf community, or the officials of Zaria Emirate Council. For example, after the May 1992 riots spilled over to Ikara and Zaria, the heirs of those killed prepared a memorandum which they submitted to the Cudjoe Judicial Commission of Inquiry. Numerous comments have been made in the mass media by diverse interested groups and individuals. Some strands of this view suggest that the land on which the Hausa settlements in Southern Kaduna State were built were basically no-man's bush (*dajin Allah*) when the settlements were established some centuries ago. Many of the Southern Kaduna ethnic groups are said to have been residing 'in the hills'. These hills may have been sanctuaries from slave-raiding. Others argue that even if the land had belonged to others, the very fact of centuries of continued and effective occupation by the Hausa communities means that those communities have become the owners of the land.

This view is consistent with Hausa land tenure practice. In the specific case of Zangon Kataf, it is suggested that in pre-colonial times, the land on which the town stands was given to the Hausa chief of Kauru by the Hausa chief of Kajuru. Both Kauru and Kajuru are Hausa settlements in Southern Kaduna State.

Another strand of the Hausa view suggests that the blame for Kataf incorporation within Zaria lies with the British colonial administration. It is also argued that agitation against emirate rule is essentially the handiwork of over-zealous Christian missionaries who became prominent in the area, and the mission-educated elite that emerged from missionary activities. It is further claimed that the Hausa/Fulani communities, to the extent that they are also 'indigenous' to the area, have every right to political appointments in the area. It is suggested that the agitation for indigenous chieftaincies can only lead to confusion and the breakdown of law and order, as there are more than 30 ethnic minorities in the area, and that the administrative cost of maintaining numerous chieftaincies would be a drain on the resources of the state government.

Specifically, the 1992 riots were seen as largely the work of 'frustrated' retired army generals and other Kataf elite who were, presumably, jealous of the prosperity of the Hausa community. It is implicitly alleged that these elites armed and instigated their community to perpetrate the rioting. It is alleged that the intention is to annihilate the Hausa and take over their lands; there were also complaints that the Kataf continue to harvest economic tree crops from Hausa farmlands. It is alleged that the police and the army, called in to quell the subsequent rioting in Kaduna, Zaria and Ikara, actually went out of their way to kill innocent Hausas and Moslems, presumably because many of the security personnel were from the minority ethnic groups of the Middle Belt, or were Christians. The Hausa demand for justice is basically that those who killed innocent citizens must be adequately punished by the state, and compensation paid to the victims.

Democratisation and Ethnicity Re-appraised

The aim in this chapter is not to uphold or justify any version of the crises put out by either community; that is a task best left to historians. That is why the claims of both communities have been reported here as 'allegations', with minimal interpretative commentary. Of immediate importance, however, is the fact that both versions expose conflicting notions of fundamental aspects of the Nigerian state. These conflicting notions are implicit in the interpretations of the crises by both communities. It is these conflicting notions, present in the specific case of every African nation-state, rather than the implied relevance of Western political values, that ought to take centre stage in the conceptualisation of the difficult process of African democratisation.

Citizenship

Democracy implies a notion of common and equal citizenship. In fact, advocates of electoral pluralism as an expression of democratisation in Africa assume, if only implicitly, that such is the case in the countries in transit to democracy. What is obvious from the Zangon Kataf case is that there are divergent and even conflicting notions of what citizenship means; the conflict over the definition of 'indigeneity' is nothing but a conflict over the very definition of citizenship. To the Kataf, members of the Hausa community of Zangon Kataf remain 'strangers' or 'settlers', since they are not Kataf. From this point of view, citizenship is defined through the principle of autochthony. It is this definition which informs their agitation for the exclusion of the Hausa community from political representation in the area. On the other hand, the Hausa community defines citizenship in terms of centuries of effective residency.

This conflict over citizenship has a relevance that transcends Zangon Kataf, and draws attention to two salient features of the Nigerian experience: the contradictoriness of the historical process of community formation, and the inadequacy of Nigerian Constitutional provisions on the definition of citizenship rights. Many studies have elaborated the process of community formation in many parts of Nigeria (see Mustapha 1992) characterised by the movement and mingling of groups of people from diverse origins over the centuries, as a consequence of war, commerce or natural calamity.

In most cases, the immigrant groups are absorbed over time into the host community and become fully integrated within it, even though there is a continued consciousness on both sides of their diverse origins. Many communities in the Hausa city of Kano come from Nupe, Yoruba and Kanuri backgrounds (Paden 1970), and similar examples can be cited for places like Lagos, Ibadan, and Ilorin. But the process was/is not only one of inclusion, but also of exclusion. In some cases, especially in the colonial and post-colonial periods, identity boundaries have become more rigid, leading to the exclusion of many immigrants who would otherwise have been absorbed. Zangon Kataf is unique in the sense that in both the pre-colonial and contemporary periods, the dominant tendency has been the logic of exclusion. In other Hausa settler communities in Southern Kaduna State, such as Kachia and Fadan

Chawai, there has been a measure of spatial and even cultural intermingling between hosts and Hausas.

In many parts of Nigeria, there is the same contestation of who is an 'indigene' of an area or a state, and is therefore entitled to full citizenship rights. As this strikes at the root of the notion of a common citizenship, it remains a thorny problem that cannot be glossed over if the process of democratisation is to be rooted in the daily realities of the people. The situation is further compounded by the stipulation in the Nigerian Constitution of 1979 (Section 277) which defines the membership of one of the constituent states of the federation — and through that, the effective rights of individuals at the community level — in terms of the principle of autochthony. This stipulation ignores the historical process of integration, inhibits any contemporary tendency towards integration, and creates a situation of effective dual citizenship in many parts of the country, regardless of how long, and for how many generations the individuals have been resident in the community to which they are not 'indigenous'.

Many Nigerians have, through this stipulation, been reduced to second class citizen in their place of residence in terms of access to education, jobs and political offices. Not even beggars are immune to this divisive orientation; in 1990, the then Lagos State Governor, Raji Rasaki, threatened to deport non-Lagosian beggars to their 'home' states with effect from January 1991 (CDHR 1990:18). This perverted attitude towards indigeneity is what explains the tendency of Nigerians to return to their natal communities to vote in times of elections, or not to vote at all. Only in the December 1990 local government election was residency used as a qualification for candidacy. The constitutional position which bases citizenship on ancestral origin was not, however, changed.

Citizenship rights are often distributed unevenly in most societies, even when a common citizenship is asserted. In the Nigerian experience, however, the very definition of citizenship is contested, in theory and practice, leading to a degree of unevenness which undermines the oft-proclaimed quest for a common nationhood. While electoral pluralism seeks to expand the scope of political choice open to citizens, the reality in many African countries is that a commonly agreed notion of citizenship must first be worked out, taking into account the diverse historical and contemporary issues at stake.

Rights

The question of rights is closely related to that of citizenship. In Zangon Kataf, there is clearly a clash of notions of the right to land and to political office. While the right to political resources can be taken care of through the elaboration of an agreed concept of citizenship, there remains the need to clarify the fundamentals of the right to land. This is particularly important in the Middle Belt and other parts of Nigeria where repeated 'communal clashes' over land make nonsense of even the right to life. In theory in Nigeria, the Land Use Act vests all land in the state, with individuals having only usufruct rights, sometimes backed up by a certificate of occupancy which grants a lease for a specified period. Even before the Act, the colonial administration in Northern Nigeria had nationalised all land not once, but twice (Mustapha 1990). In reality, however, many communities and individuals continue to treat their land as if they have absolute rights of ownership.

The possibility for confusion and conflict is obvious; while the Hausa communities in Southern Kaduna State defend their land rights in terms of concessions obtained from either the colonial or post-colonial states, the Kataf continue to insist on their communal rights, which they seek to assert by harvesting trees on Hausa farmland. At another level, this can be seen as a conflict between individual and collective rights to land. When these conflicting conceptions over land rights correspond to ethnic and religious cleavages, as in Zangon Kataf, the result can be devastating in terms of the socio-political stability of the area. There remains a compelling need to develop an African jurisprudence on land rights (see Mafeje 1991).

Justice

The conflicting demands for justice and social justice in Zangon Kataf calls to mind the Platonic problematic of the definition of justice. As in Plato's Republic, the conflict is really about the very foundations of the state. Can the Hausa community's call for adequate punishment for those who have killed their fellow human beings be questioned? Can the Katafs' demand that historical injustices be corrected be faulted? Which definition of justice should apply to such a conundrum, and what are its implication for the moral basis of the state? And what level or levels of the state are involved? The political level, at which the Kataf claim they are being unfairly tried and jailed, or the institutional level, at which the Hausas of Zaria, Ikara and Kaduna claim that innocent citizens were

killed by anti-riot security forces of Middle Beit origin for being both
Hausas and Moslems?

It is basically in respect to these contentious questions that the Zangon
Kataf crisis intruded upon the national consciousness in 1992. However,
it did so in a highly politicised manner, in which the quest for justice
often played second fiddle to the search for political advantage by both
the government and those groups in society opposed to Babangida's
kleptocratic autocracy. The democratisation process in Nigeria has
continued to subjugate these fundamental questions to partisan political
ends.

Conclusion: Accommodating Democratisation to Ethnicity

While the equation of democratisation with the recrudescence of
'tribalism' is untenable, the assumption that electoral pluralism will usher
in a democratic system must be set against the background of ethnic
conflicts which challenge the very basis of a common citizenship. The
Zangon Kataf crisis suggests that democratisation takes place in a
context of existing conflict over fundamental issues. And such
contestations often dictate an unwholesome agenda for the
democratisation process.

Nigerian society was divided over Zangon Kataf, with little
consideration on either side for a just resolution of the substantive issues
raised. The southern press generally supported the Kataf cause, seeing
the crises as yet another illustration of the Hausa/Fulani drive for
hegemony. On its part, the northern press refused to address the
historical origins of Kataf grievances. And the conduct of the Special
Tribunals set up to try the accused, particularly that of the Okadigbo
Tribunal, cast much doubt on the impartiality of the Babangida
administration. The contestation created an opportunity for the regime to
weaken the united opposition to military dictatorship. Many of these
ethno-religious and regional apprehensions were to re-surface when the
debacle over the June 12 Presidential election erupted in 1993-1994.

If the drive for democratisation is to succeed, there is the need to
address the problems raised by the emphasis on indigeneity and
autochthony in the definition of state citizenship in Nigeria. Ethnic
identities and community boundaries are a problematic reality of African
societies which should be incorporated into the conceptualisation of
democratisation. Zangon Kataf illustrates the possible confusion that can
arise from the use of indigeneity as the sole foundation for determining
citizenship, and efforts should be made to incorporate the principle of
residency.

In the same vein, it is not enough to emphasise individual rights, as libertarians are wont to do. Within the African context, there may be a need to incorporate group rights as well (Mamdani 1992). Such an approach would accommodate the fact that rights to land and citizenship are not always contested at the level of the individual. The Kataf claim to land and the right to establish their own chieftaincy and the Hausa claim to citizenship could be resolved within this context. But this incorporation should take account of both contemporary realities, and possibilities for future broadening of identities, as no identity is fixed for all time. The recent decision by the Constitutional Conference to incorporate the principle of rotational presidency in the Nigerian Constitution appears to address this issue, but as it is only limited to the right to political office, it may only regulate the circulation of a political elite whose integrity has been called into question. More pressing issues of group rights to equal citizenship and collective land rights continue to remain unaddressed.

Appendices

1

Conference Report

Tanimu Abubakar

The CODESRIA National Working Group (NWG), researching on 'Expanding Nigerian Democratic Space' held its conference at the National Institute for International Affairs (NIIA), Lagos between December 15 and 17, 1993. In his welcome address, the coordinator of the NWG, Jibrin Ibrahim, informed the participants that the research network was born out of the need to examine the problems of democratisation in the fast changing national and international context in which Nigeria found itself since the end of the 1980s. The circle of interested individuals discussing the issues were also keenly interested in the changing fortunes of communism and left politics and their impact on democratic struggles, locally and internationally.

The central idea that emerged was the necessity to create a forum in which a broad section of activist groups and individuals could carry out research and discussions on the unfolding issues. The discussions were concretised into a proposal which CODESRIA found worthy of sponsoring through the NWG. The conference, Ibrahim stated, was therefore a culmination of the efforts of individuals, groups, the NWG and CODESRIA. The CODESRIA representative, Ayesha Imam, also gave an address during the opening session in which she explained to the participants the objectives of CODESRIA and an outline of its activities concerning the promotion of research in the social sciences and the humanities in Africa.

The conference began with a keynote address given by Alao Aka-Bashorun, a Lagos-based legal practitioner, former President of the Nigerian Bar Association and the first Chairperson of the Umbrella Human Rights Organisation, Campaign for Democracy. In his speech, Aka-Bashorun focused on the varying seasons of the frustration of national unity and democratic aspirations of the Nigerian people. Following the struggle for independence, Nigerians had the vision that their country would be a great and leading star in Africa. Three decades after independence, Nigeria, and indeed Africa, is ravaged by famine, desertification, civil wars and unprecedented poverty. The problem, Aka-Bashorun added, was that the new African elite that came into power after independence saw itself as the new colonialists of their countries.

On the current political situation in Nigeria, Alao argued that while the exit of the Babangida regime was a welcome development, it was unfortunate that it had been replaced by another military dictatorship. The military, which has been in power for a long long time, has inhibited the actualisation of the yearnings of Nigerians for unity and democracy. For example, the present military regime argued that it was the previous regime that annulled the June 12 1993 General Elections, instead of informing the people of what went wrong with June 12 or paving the road to a genuine democratic settlement. The present military regime has proposed a Constitutional Conference with several no go-areas, a position which cannot help the development of genuine confidence in our people. He added that military dictatorship has always been challenged by progressive forces in Nigeria. For example, the National Consultative Forum was established in 1990 as a plank for organising a Sovereign National Conference, intended to harness the human and material resources of Nigeria for the construction of a democratic state. 'The military', Aka-Bashorun stated, 'is an alien culture and has always failed when used for governance'. The basis for binding a united country and pushing the frontiers of democracy in Alao's view lies in explaining why the election of June 12 was not actualised. 'We spent', he said, 'a lot of resources, both human and material, as well as eight years of our existence to arrive at June 12'. He concluded by calling upon the present military regime to probe the circumstances behind the annulment of June 12 and conduct a referendum on it. Finally, Aka-Bashorun hoped that the conference would provide the theoretical framework for the building of democracy in Nigeria.

I. Part One
Conference Papers

A) First Session

The first paper was presented by Jibrin Ibrahim and was entitled 'On the Expansion of Nigerian Democratic Space'. He argued that central to the notion of expanding democratic space is the reduction or prevention of the monopolisation of power and resources by a few individuals or groups. It therefore involves the empowerment and the autonomisation of the weak, who are also the majority. Nigerian democratic space has been shrinking over the past few decades due to the suppression of democratic aspects of the country's traditions and the entrenchment of anti-democratic ones such as patriarchy from the pre-colonial period and the colonial traditions of autocracy and excessive empowerment of so-called traditional rulers. The military, who have ruled Nigeria for 21 years in the postcolonial period, have added a crass political culture of over-centralisation of power, greed, corruption, theft, and vandalisation of public resources. Power has been transformed into an instrument for profit-making and laws have been turned into a device for protecting ruling vandals.

In this context, the democratisation of society would require a return to basic principles such as is found in, for instance, the Cromwellian and French revolutions: that the people must acquire notions of popular sovereignty and that power belongs to the people and could be wielded by the people and that popular capacity to exercise power could be enhanced. At the formal level, the expansion of democratic space would involve the following — establishment of a multi-party system with no restrictive conditions for the registration of political parties; the development of plural power centres of the type provided for by genuine federalism and parliamentary democracy; and the repeal of military decrees that have negated the rule of law. At the informal level, democrats must strive for the democratisation of civil society by combating patriarchy in the family, enhancing democratic practices in civil and professional organisations and encouraging the proliferation of unrestrained mass media. Human and civil rights must be protected and enhanced at all levels of society.

The second paper by Yusuf Bangura was entitled 'Intellectuals, Economic Reform and Social Change'. The paper starts with a discussion of the problematic about whether the intellectual is a part of the new ruling class or the proletariat. The author then discussed the basic hindrances against the capacity of the Nigerian academician to act as a cohesive force before 1975. This limitation had to do with the impact of bureaucratic power, family background and economic conditions. Academicians emerged as a cohesive force as from 1975 in the context of the general expansion of universities and the increase in economic fortunes in the oil boom era. The need for intellectuals to protect their interests and secure advantages against the bureaucracy led to unionisation, which in turn transformed them into a cohesive force. However, the deepening economic crisis, the paper argued, led to a sharp decline in the conditions of service, funding and autonomy of universities. Academicians responded to this crisis in three main ways:

brain drain or the exit option, collaboration with the state through their associations, and resistance. Some even joined the informal sector.

According to the paper, the overall impact of the economic crisis and the introduction of reform through the Structural Adjustment Programme (SAP) was the emergence of a technocracy which draws its support from the senior academicians, the top military officers, serving and retired, the business and political classes and the bureaucracy. The paper also examined the 'implications of the emergence of technocracy for democracy and took the position that technocrats are more cohesive in conditions of economic growth. Technocracy has also led to the coming into prominence of neo-liberalism which has no theory of state formation and therefore lacks cohesive clues of solving problems of de-institutionalisation. Technocrats thrive under totalitarian conditions and are as such incapable of responding to conflicting interests. They prefer predictability and are thus incapable of giving democracy a chance.

The third paper by Ayesha Imam was on 'Gender and Democratic Discourses in Nigeria'. She defined gender as social relations that determine positions of men and women as they are expressed in power, economics, ideology, etc. In patriarchal societies such as Nigeria, such structured relations have produced a 'regime of truth' that place men on the top of most hierarchies. The general discourses on democracy in Nigeria have been structured along the lines of liberal democratic presumptions, although more radical discourses exist. Both have, in different ways and to different degrees, and occasionally for different reasons, been gender structured, in their ideals and in their practices in such a way as to reproduce gendered inequality in democratic participation. The paper then cited empirical evidence from succeeding regimes which show specific forms of discrimination against women supported and maintained by political parties, governments, etc., on issues such as education, employment opportunities and suffrage. Finally, the author showed various repressive mechanisms used to checkmate women's struggles to eliminate discrimination and broaden participation.

Discussion

The discussion that followed concentrated on the complexity and wide scope of the theme of the expansion of democratic space. One major issue that became central to the debate was that although the military cannot escape responsibility for the restriction of democratic space, they have never been able to rule alone. Technocrats have always been at hand to help them make and implement policies. Even left groups and human rights organisations have at one time or the other fallen into the trap of believing they could use the military as a short cut to achieve their objectives and have always been disappointed. When discussing the problem of democracy, we should take note of the absence, not just of a democratic culture, but also of structures. This dearth inhibits especially women from popular and effective participation in democracy. With regards to the emergence of technocracy, some participants argued that such a theoretical postulation is gloomy since it regards state collaboration as endemic.

The point was also made that the significance of the resistance by the academicians under the Academic Staff Union of Universities should not be exaggerated, it has been a conventional trade union struggle and it is by this very nature a syndicalist action rather than a democratic one. The problem of reform under the Structural Adjustment Programme is more than a democratic problem; it also touches on the New World Order and the problem of regional, economic, social and cultural integration. On the way forward, it was emphasised that the destruction of the centralisation of power that has occurred in the country's body politic and the establishment of a multi-party regime are essential. In addition, democracy needs alternative, multiple and antithetical sources of power and control. The discussion noted, for example, that the limitation of women's participation in the political arena is easily maintained because of their limited influence in the economic sphere.

B) Second Session

The first paper was by Attahiru Jega and was entitled 'The Role of Intellectuals and Academicians in the Struggle for Democracy'. He started with the observation that as a result of a long period of military rule, authoritarianism has been on the ascendance in the country and democratic space has been narrowed. The intensification of the Structural Adjustment Programme, combined with the highly restrictive political transition programme of the Babangida regime, have demarcated the parameters of the democratic space allowed by the state and have at the same time set the agenda for the struggles which surfaced aimed at widening the scope of democracy in Nigeria. Very active vibrant groups have emerged and traditionally conservative groups have been reinvigorated, shaken out of their lethargy by economic deprivations occasioned by SAP. In the process, the struggle for democracy has become intertwined with the struggle for protecting basic rights and privileges.

The paper argued that the intellectuals are a good illustration of the way in which conservative sections of the middle class come to play significant roles in the democratisation process. Intellectuals cannot be simply reduced to a part of the community of technocrats, they play roles on both sides: for and against the people. From the colonial period to around 1975, they collaborated closely with the state, they were accommodative and pro-status-quo and were basically a deluded hybrid with no cohesive socially relevant role. In the oil boom period, the intellectual terrain broadened but the role they played still remained vacillatory, and because it was a period of affluence, intellectuals played a socially irrelevant role. However, since the economic crisis of the 1980s, social contradictions have sharpened. The SAP and the political transition programmes, coupled with shrinking opportunities and space have put the intellectuals at the cross roads of livelihood and social relevance. The rising authoritarianism of the state led them into participating in political struggles for and against specific policies. It was in this context, the paper argued that three categories of intellectuals emerged, viz.: the collaborationists, who became the architects of the social and political engineering policies the state used in its deceptive programme of social improvement and political democratisation, and the democrats, who participated in the democratic struggles against the regime's authoritarian disposition. The role of this category of intellectuals was conditioned by their principles and radical, if not revolutionary ideological orientation as well as their concerns on SAP's 'proletarianisation' of the middle class. Finally, the Academic Staff of Nigerian Universities (ASUU) provided an organised platform for struggles which combined welfare and basic survival issues with broad democratic struggles. In general, opposition motivated by the crisis and commitment facilitated the linkage between the struggle of the academician with that of the wider civil society. The lesson of this linkage is that the necessity for fighting for democracy is an objective task of opposition.

The second paper by Issa Aremu was on 'Trade Unions and Democratic Struggles in Nigeria'. The author examined the complex relationship between trade unions and democratic struggles and argued that democracy has an instrumental value for unions. The objective of expanding the scope of collective bargaining in the workplace is a function of the level of democratic practice at the enterprise and in the wider society. In Nigeria, there is a widening gap between constitutionally guaranteed rights of trade unions and the worsening anti-democratic practices of intolerance by the state and employers alike.

It is therefore in the interest of the unions to overcome obstacles to enjoying legally protected rights and expanding the scope for such rights. The Nigerian state has actively intervened in the administration of the trade union movement in manners that tend to limit democratic space. The existing Nigerian Labour Congress (NLC), was decreed into existence in 1978 after the then military administration banned independent efforts of unionists to form a common centre. The imposition of a single trade union centre is part of the strategy of imposing 'guided democracy'. In March 1988, the government dissolved and reconstituted the NLC. At the level of the enterprise, freedom of association has frequently been denied by police intervention. The paper concluded by arguing that trade unions have asserted their rights to association despite harassment. To further expand these rights, issues to work on include the rights to unionise, to strike, to a living wage as well as the guarantee that laws that protect trade union activities are operative. In addition, the Nigeria Labour Congress and its component unions must practice internal democracy, get embedded in the struggles of civil society and strive to become more effective in democratic struggles.

The subsequent paper by Yahaya Hashim, also on trade unions was entitled 'Disagregating Democracy: Trade Unions and Transition to Democracy'. The presenter started by questioning the widespread notion that civil society is the harbinger of democracy and argued that there is nothing inherently democratic about civil society. Similarly, trade unions are not inherently democratic. There are two sides to the discussion of the role of trade unions in democratic struggle. These are, the role labour plays in the democratisation of society and the democratisation of labour itself. Democracy itself is not a unitary concept. There are different democratic discourses and when they are arbitrarily merged, a lot is lost. There are, for instance, industrial democracy, patriarchal democracy and labour democracy and they could be contradictory. There is therefore the need to disaggregate democracy and relate each component to its arena. He emphasised the importance of democratic struggles for the labour movement especially in an epoch of deep economic crisis.

The fourth paper by Adebayo Olukoshi was on the theme of 'The Left and the Struggle for Democracy in Nigeria'. The paper examines the role played by the Nigerian left, as represented by a host of organisations acting on their own, within existing popular associations, and in alliance with one another in the expansion of democratic space. They have forged platforms' to push the case for the increased democratisation of the country, public accountability, the rule of law and respect for human rights. The basic argument is that although the left continues to be strong

in its advocacy of the economic and social dimensions of the measures
necessary for the creation of a democratic order, a strength that
underscores its continuing influence within and outside the labour
movement, the 1980s brought out clearly numerous problems which
many left organisations and activists continue to have with the political
dimensions of democracy.

From the puritanical and sectarian to the more broad-based, many in
the left displayed a lack of interest in questions of political pluralism, the
rule of law, human rights and the secular status of the state, dismissing
them as bourgeois constitutional values even as they were becoming
germane to the sustenance of popular contestation to the Structural
Adjustment Programme and the restrictive political transition programme
of the Babangida regime. When they did join in the struggle for political
rights, however, many continued to see it as merely a 'tactic' to be
employed in the struggle against the bourgeoisie or a protective
instrument against state repression rather than an integral part of the
struggle for the creation of a new social order in the country. The events
in the Soviet Union and Eastern Europe have not had much impact on
the Nigerian left as many have attributed the decline of the socialist
movement in that part of the world to 'opening up' to bourgeois
economic and political values. The paper concluded on the note, 'it is
inconceivable that the Nigerian Left could ever advance itself and the
society it seeks to change if it does not take more seriously the
democracy question in general and its political components, including the
issue of pluralism'.

Discussion

The participants generally acknowledged the extent to which the papers
explore the complicated nature of the role and place of groups and
associations in democratic struggle. A number of speakers argued that it
was wrong to assume that the left has not been very active in democratic
struggle. On the contrary, the left, has been in the forefront of popular
struggles for democracy. With regards to labour, the discussions raised
the need to examine the experience of labour in partisan politics,
especially with regards to the formation, in 1989, of the Labour Party
and the subsequent alliance forged with the Social Democratic Party
(SDP). There is also the need to trace the history of labour struggles right
from the period of decolonisation. The relative ineffectiveness of labour
in struggle is more closely associated with its tradition of sit-tight
leadership and lack of internal democracy than with trade union goals.
Unions join democratic struggle in moments of crisis. It is, however,

erroneous to assume that there is nothing democratic about civil society because.democracy is sometimes regarded as an end it itself especially in the area of power and allocation of resources. But this does not negate the engagement of various groups in democratic struggles.

The discussion also raised the need for a historical explanation of the categorisation of the intellectuals and of their oscillation. There is thus the need to differentiate between the intellectuals and the intelligentsia, which is a broader concept which could explain more coherently the role of intellectuals right from the colonial period to have gone beyond mere collaboration. The term 'collaborative' is insufficient for explaining the crucial role intellectuals played up to and during the First Republic in parties such the Northern People's Congress and the National Council of Nigerian Citizens. It is typical for intellectuals to be ambivalent but this characteristic is stronger in Africa and this tendency gives credence to the categorisation of intellectuals as collaborative or combative.

C). Third Session
The third session opened with the paper by Bashir Kurfi on 'Ethnicity Citizenship and Democracy: A Zangon Kataf Case Study'. The paper defended the choice of the topic on the grounds that the Zangon Kataf experience has become an important threshold in Nigerian politics and should not be reduced to personalities. The events analysed relate to the attack and destruction of a Hausa/Fulani Muslim community on May 12 1992 in which about 2,000 people lost their lives. Following that, the crisis spilled to surrounding towns and a lot of people were arrested and a judicial panel established. The paper examined what happened in Zango, the role of the state and the predicament of the affected people. The author contended that there is a misconception of the Zango episode because the extent to which the emotions, anger and concerns it has generated has been underestimated. The Zango crisis occurred because of the inclination of both the Hausa/Fulani and Kataf elite to manipulate ethnicity and religion. The paper traced the origins of this manipulation to the hegemonic tussles by various reactionary groups who have no popular base among the people.

The second paper was presented by Femi Falana and was entitled 'Civil Liberties, Human Rights Organisations and the Rule of Law'. The paper argued that from the colonial days Nigerians have enjoyed very little human rights and civil liberties and they have not been ruled in accordance with the law, which in any case, is fashioned without their contribution and is often at variance with their interests. The right to life, the most basic of all rights is not enjoyed by many Nigerians who die of 'hunger and freedom of expression means nothing to millions of illiterate and dehumanised Nigerians. However, it is necessary to pursue the struggle for civil liberties, human rights and the rule of law to expose the ruling class which is restricting these rights and liberties and force them to expand them. The paper stated that 23 years of military rule had messed up the guarantee of civil rights because of the persistent suppression of the constitution and the rule of law. The paper associated the upsurge of human rights groups to the suppression of the rule of law and discusses how the impotence of courts compelled these groups, under the Campaign for Democracy, to enter the political terrain. The paper argued that in the present Nigerian context, human rights will still be denied by the military dictatorship in power and its restoration therefore needs a Sovereign National Conference which could provide an avenue for the discussion of the unequal relationship between the various components of the country. The paper concluded by stating that human rights organisations should be engaged in the campaign for democracy so as to terminate military dictatorship and ensure the justiciability of the rights and liberties of the nation and the people.

The third paper by Jibrin Ibrahim was on the theme 'Democracy and the Transition Programme'. The paper traced the development of Babangida's 'transition programme' and showed that the regime had a clear political project of destroying the democratic potential in Nigeria's social fabric. The programme imposed Babangida's agenda on the political process by among other things, the active encouragement of communal and religious crises so as to create a 'breakdown of security' syndrome as a justification for the perpetuation of military rule and the imposition of a state orchestrated two-party system so as to exclude genuine democrats from the political arena, the de-stabilisation of the country's political class through constant banning and unbanning and the elimination of ideological politics through the reduction of politics to money spending and money-making. These anti-democratic tendencies compelled Nigerians to turn the June 12 elections into a referendum that voted NO to national disintegration, military rule and geo-political domination. The paper further argued that the massive support for Abiola's presidential bid was a declaration for the necessity to share Federal power and to enhance the powers of states and local governments. He concluded by stating that any genuine transition to democratic rule must involve the establishment of civilian supremacy in the country and the confinement of the totalitarian ambitions of the military.

The fourth paper by Y.Z. Ya'u was entitled 'The Mass Media and the Struggle for Democracy: Constraints and Possibilities'. The paper argued that in spite of the enormous constraints faced by the mass media, which are rooted in property relations, media organs have enormous potential in the struggle to expand democratic space in Nigeria. Conscious of this potential, the state has consistently intervened, through repressive laws, harassment of journalists, propaganda, etc., to cripple the progressive media but their efforts have never been completely successful. The Structural Adjustment Programme (SAP), has profoundly affected the mass media; first, media products have been priced out of the reach of the ordinary citizen, second, the media has responded to the crisis by commercialisation and only relaying the news of those who can pay and third, liberalisation has created a situation in which only the rich could own and operate the media. In addition, SAP and the transition programme component of the authoritarian agenda of the Babangida regime substantially reconstituted the character of the structural contest for space between progress (presented by human right groups, students, etc., and their views) and armed populism represented by the regime.

The author concluded that the success or failure of campaigns to force concessions from government was not necessarily dependent on media support, although media coverage had a significant influence. The success of the campaigners was determined by their ability to turn the campaign into a mass movement capable of engaging government in serious confrontation. It was the impact of confrontation that forced the media to identify with popular causes which in turn, helped the cause through increased coverage and enlightenment the media gave. Thus when the movements against SAP and human rights abuses acquired momentum and became popular struggles, the media abandoned their earlier position of cautious reminder to Government about its responsibilities, to become virulent attackers of the human rights abuses of Government and to expose the evils of SAP. The end result was that the Government conceded on both issues. On the other hand, the campaign for a Sovereign National Conference and the one against the Interim Government both failed to become mass based, and they did not attract the media with the same force. The degree to which the newspapers in particular, gave prominence to news from the progressive groups, although in staccato and highly unsystematic manner, is taken as indicators of their potentials and prospect, provided the forces of progress identify clear objectives and are able or prepared to contest grounds with the forces of reaction as far as the propaganda

/conscientisation axis of popular struggle is concerned, which is where the media come in.

The fifth paper by Abubakar Momoh was on 'The Legacy of the Military Rule on Democratisation'. The paper looked at the military in the democratisation process using a historical perspective, that is, it assesses how the military aids or truncates democracy. The paper argued that since its inception in 1914 and through its growth through the colonial era up to 1956, the interest and role of the military has been repression, violence and the support of imperialism. It was, therefore, antithetical to decolonisation. In addition, the recruitment of illiterates and peasants into the military complied with the continuation or recruitment on quota basis cripples the ability of the military to question the status quo and organically relates the officer corp with primordial interests and the state. The paper also states that at independence, in 1960, the politicians had already appreciated the value of the military and that in itself made the military political. The military has since colonialism been used to haunt and intimidate nationalists, and later, the politicians and this drags the military into the logic of accumulation and politicisation. The paper also argued that the military cannot democratise, it can only transit to civil rule. Democratisation is more than handing over power; it involves all interest groups recognising the limits of their own right within a constitutional setting. The author argued that the action of civil society, especially, those of collectives such as the Campaign for Democracy (CD) composed of 42 affiliates, shows that true democracy can only be created by popular will. Unless the military as a *social force* is convinced by 'force of example' that it does not have a monopoly of the use of force, and that the *people's popular will* is superior to their force, we may not get out of the game of musical chairs the military has dragged us into.

Discussions

The discussions were lively and appreciative of the efforts of the presenters in confronting complex and sensitive issues affecting the democratisation process and military rule in Nigeria. It was generally agreed that the Zango Kataf issue, though sensitive, needs to be more rigorously studied. It was also observed that the discourse on the mass media ignored other avenues of expanding the democratic space such as leaflets, music and theatre which have proved effective in mobilisation. On the transition programme, it was argued that military transition should not be confused with democratic transition and that in a militarised setting, the guarantee for ensuring the development of socially relevant democratic values is hindered by authoritarianism. There is therefore, the need to compare the Nigerian experience with those of other countries such as Brazil. On theoretical perspectives, it was observed that the conference was meant to document the authoritarianism of the state and how to defeat it. Too much theory could therefore lead to epistemological paralysis. It was also suggested that the discourse on the rule of law needs to show how a general apathy in the country which inhibits the crystallisation of a common framework of action and analysis has arisen in the country. The civil rights organisations should therefore do more pedagogic work to teach people about their rights.

2

Round Table Discussion on Human Rights

A) Academic Staff Union of Nigerian Universities (ASUU)

ASUU's position was presented by its president, Attahiru Jega. He stated that ASUU has been very much interested in democratisation in the country within the organisation itself. There are two components of the expansion of democracy within ASUU, Rights the internal dimension is oriented to mobilising members to realise the need for active participation in organisational matters, upholding democratic principles and ensuring the democratisation of the mode of the internal governance of the Universities. There are, of course, problems of equitable representation in some of the internal organs of ASUU such as the National Executive Council (NEC) and the National Delegates Conference (NDC) related to the fact that all affiliates, irrespective of the size of their membership and their financial contributions have the same level of representation and the same vote. In addition, there are problems of ideological vacillation such as the one that caused the organisational crisis of 1988. Accountability is also of an important ingredient of ASUU's internal democratisation.

At the national level, the thrust of democratisation is based on ASUU's role as a union of academics, and given this role, there is the need to bring the skill and knowledge of academicians into popular struggles. ASUU makes its contributions in the struggle against authoritarianism through resolutions, communiqués and press conferences. Through these instruments, ASUU has been critical of many policies of the state. More concretely, and at a time when ASUU realised that military rule as a threat, ASUU saw the need for a broad alliance with Democratic Organisations through the Campaign for Democracy (CD) and its local variants. The experiences of ASUU in this regard are revealing in demonstrating the high level of effectiveness of professional organisations in democratic struggles when they are in league with popular forces.

B) Community Action for Popular Participation (CAPP)

Community Action for Popular Participation was represented by its Executive Secretary, Emma Ezeazu. The organisation is a new human rights initiative that was inaugurated in May 1993 with the following objectives:

- The strengthening of popular structures for participation at the local level.
- Empowerment of the poor and powerless to take part in the government of their communities.
- Educational and Action campaigns against community environmental degradation.
- The promotion of women's participation in local government.

The organisation has conducted a series of community based workshops to ascertain the problems of popular participation at the local level and the peculiar needs of the rural areas. The next line of action is to take one of the problems identified and help organise and mobilise the people practically to solve these problems. In addition, CAPP intends to establish 5 pilot Citizen Advisory and Advocacy Units in 5 local areas within the year.

On the working methods of existing human rights organisations in the country, CAPP is of the opinion that they have been more effective in litigation, press campaigns and research, but poor in citizen mobilisation, popular education and organisation. They are also poor in networking among themselves and in most cases are unable to follow up persistently on abuses identified. It was only on the June 12 issues that they made a serious effort to reach out to the citizens in a political way. Currently, the human rights groups are facing credibility problems because of their perceived role in tacitly helping to bring about the present military administration of General Abacha. It is thus not surprising that their integrity is at stake.

C) Campaign for Democracy (CD) and the Struggle for Human Rights and Democracy in Nigeria

The paper was presented by Chima Ubani, the General Secretary of CD who explained that the collective was established in 1991 with the objective of restoring the sovereignty of the Nigerian people. Its strategic aim is the convening of a Sovereign National Conference as a forum for advancing the democratic project in Nigeria. He was of the view that the efforts of the CD so far are essentially an   experience in non-partisan empowerment of civil society as a means of broadening democratic space in Nigeria. The CD is a non-political, non-partisan coalition of human rights and other patriotic organisations as well as individual mass membership organisation with structures at the state and national levels. The organisation contributed immensely to the campaign to ouster the Babangida dictatorship and its surrogate Interim Government. It helped teach major lessons on what can be achieved in terms of broadening the Nigerian democratic space through non-partisan empowerment of civil society.

Yet, the derailment of the recent democratic struggles through conspiracy of the political elite and the military raises a few issues about the need to define the stake of such mass pressure groups as the CD in the quest for power. Until this relationship is carefully defined and understood, it may not be possible for the patriotic forces within the CD to transcend pressure group politics and effect fundamental changes in power relations and in the economic, political and cultural circumstances of the oppressed classes in our society they are seeking to mobilise.

D) The Committee for the Defence of Human Rights (CDHR) and the Democratic Project

The CDHR Report was presented by Osagie Obayuwana. He argued that the CDHR which was formed in 1989 takes its point of departure from the parameters set in the African Charter for Popular Participation in Development and Transformation which rests on the premise that nations cannot be built and the economic and political issues facing countries like Nigeria cannot be resolved without popular support and full participation of the people. Essentially popular participation is a fundamental right, the people must fully and effectively participate in taking decisions which affect their lives at *all levels* and at *all times*. So conceived, the concept of democratic space goes beyond the role of the people as a whole in the nation's political life, important as that is. It embodies a set of principles for conflict resolution and decision making; a way of doing things which should govern interpersonal relationships, in the home, affording space for the realisation of women's and children's rights; in the school environment, allowing for enjoyment of democratic rights by students, in the work place, and in the running of mass organisations.

Given this generalisation of the concept of democratic space, there is the need to characterise *what obtains in Nigeria* now that needs to be expanded. For the CDHR, the situation in Nigeria is characterised by military usurpation of power, an exclusion of students from decision making process within the school environment, women are generally kept out of decision making in the home, workers have hardly any say about what is done at the work place and finally, the role of rank and file members of organisations (trade unions, nongovernmental organisations, etc.) in decision making is highly constrained. A major factor in the question of expanding democratic space is that of the level of consciousness of target groups historically denied participatory rights. This is the reason why we of the CDHR place a lot of emphasis on public enlightenment and the reorientation of the populace to combat illiteracy and apathy in the quest to enforce opinion and public accountability.

Historically, the CDHR has carried out investigations, exposed human rights abuses, defended victims of violations. It has also utilised symposia, seminars, leaflets, posters, etc., as well as entered into correspondence, issued press statements, instituted court actions, written petitions and appeared before panels, etc. The organisation has put in place a system of networking with other organisations both local and international. To expand the democratic space in Nigeria it shall continue to do what it has been doing, hoping that it can obtain a greater level of operational efficiency. If that succeeds, CDHR shall have mobilised Nigerian and world opinion to restrain the state in Nigeria from what has turned out to be incessant raids on its offices, seizure of its material and equipment and arrest and detention of its leaders and staff.

E) The Role of the Nigerian Union of Journalists (NUJ) in Expanding Nigeria's Democratic Space

The position of the NUJ was presented by Chom Bagu, their Deputy General Secretary. He opined that in modern democracies, the press places a fundamental role of holding Government responsible and accountable for its acts of commission or omission. Undemocratic and corrupt governments have therefore been eager to control and co-opt the press through among others, bribery and force. The NUJ was formed in 1955 and it has the mandate to defend press freedom and the rights of journalists, and also to improve the economic well-being of journalists. In its work, it has had to wage struggles against anti-press laws, attack the detention of journalists, closure of media houses and confiscation of publications. It also negotiates for wages and terms of employment for its members. It is currently engaged in the campaign against anti-press laws and public harassment of journalists. It has established a press freedom committee which issues press freedom reports and campaigns against abuses. It is also working on a draft Freedom of Information Act and a campaign against corruption among journalists. Its problems are mainly that of internal democracy and accountability.

F) National Association of Nigerian Students (NANS) and the Democratic Space Project

The NANS President, Naseer Kura presented their position paper. He argued that the organisation has a militant political profile and has played a 'democratic vanguard' role, at least since 1986. From that time, the organisation has moved from economistic or welfare struggles and focused on struggles related to the historical essence of the neocolonial state in general and the SAP regime of Babangida in particular. This type of intervention has paid off in the context of the rising consciousness against the specific manifestations of the neo-liberal project of the Nigerian state and its foreign backers. While recognising the room for improvement, especially of an organisational and tactical nature, NANS remains committed to its internal principles of democratic organisation and the pursuit of democratic struggles at the national level.

G) Women in Nigeria (WIN) and the Democratic Project

The WIN report was presented by Glory Kilanko, the Organisation's Coordinating Secretary. WIN was established in 1982 with the self defined task of organising women to fight for their full social and economic rights in the family, in the work place and in the society in general, as a necessary part of the continuing struggle to create and develop a just society for all. In this regard, WIN has since its formation been in the vanguard of political agitation and campaigns to evolve a humane democratic dispensation in the country that will uplift the lot of Nigerian Women in particular and the poor masses of our people in general. Over this period, WIN has, as part of its overall mandate, articulated positions on how particular policies or programme of government affects women and the oppressed strata of society as a whole. Hence right from the inception of the Structural Adjustment Programme (SAP) in 1986-7, WIN was among the first group to draw attention to the terrible consequence the policy will have for the average Nigerian household, and the Nigerian economy at large.

In 1986, WIN coordinated the WOMEN input into the national debate on what the future political direction of the country should be. Central to the demand of the women who participated in this debate was the necessity to redress the gross imbalance in representation of women in policy decisions in the country. In fact to redress this, under the subheading on: 'Structure of Government and Forms of Representations'

WIN had specifically called for 50 per cent of all places in legislative and executive bodies to be reserved for women who form at least half of the population. On philosophy of government, WIN held that the only assurance for social justice, progress, self reliance and economic buoyancy was popular democracy. WIN similarly called for the expansion of democracy to include the grassroots majority, and the right of all to participate in the control and management of our country's economic resources. WIN was part of the civil society coalition that resisted General Babangida's plot to making himself life-president of Nigeria. The organisation pursued a principled campaign to ensure that the military regime respect the will of the Nigerian people who went to the polls on June 12 and in a remarkably free and fair election gave mandate to the Social Democratic Party (SDP) flag-bearer in the presidential elections. In the series of protests organised under the Campaign for Democracy (CD) umbrella, WIN played key roles in mobilising market women and men to lock-up their stores while the protests lasted. In virtually all the places where the protest took place, WIN cadres were actively in the front-line. WIN has been and is still committed to a democratic society which gives concrete meaning to the existence and material well-being of both men and women in the country. Hence our support for the call for a Sovereign National Conference, to address the issues that have prevented Nigeria from advancing forward.

H) The Role of the Constitutional Rights Project (CRP) in the Struggle for Democracy

The CRP position was presented by Babatunde Olugboji. In broad terms, the CRP, as the name implies, is all about rights: rights are freedom of expression, association, and unencumbered judiciary, a society where human rights are respected, where the rule of law prevails, where political, economic, democratic and all fundamental rights are guaranteed. CRP seeks to create awareness on the rights of Nigerians, sensitise them to their fundamental rights and work towards the empowerment of people to exercise these rights. The CRP is a non-governmental organisation with an observer status with the African Commission on Human and People's Rights. It fulfils its mission by engaging in activities designed to:

- Ensure that legislation affecting the rights of Nigerians conform to international standards;
- Monitor institutions whose activities impact on the rights of citizens. These institutions include the judiciary, security agencies (police, state

security services, directorate of military intelligence, etc.), the electoral agency, the press, etc.; and

• Provide legal assistance to victims of human rights abuses.

Since the CRP was established in 1990, it has provided assistance to several victims of human rights abuse. For example, in 1991, CRP challenged the detention of Mrs. Dora Mukoro wife of a coup suspect who had been detained without trial for more than nine months under the State Security (Detention of Persons) Decree 2 of 1984. Her 'offence' was being married to an alleged illegal coup plotter who escaped arrest. The pregnant woman was held in custody before the matter could be heard. CRP, through its various publication also seeks to enhance human rights and promote democratic ideals and ensure a conducive environment in which democracy can thrive. The publications include Constitutional Rights News, a regular newsletter and Constitutional Rights Journal a specialised well-researched quarterly, published since 1990. CRP has also published three book length reports:

• The Bill Process and Human Rights in Nigeria (1992)

• The Crisis of Press Freedom in Nigeria (1993)

• Human Rights Practices in Nigerian Police (1993)

CRP recognises the importance of creating a forum for Nigerians to discuss issues relating to democracy and human rights, hence, the organisation, from time-to-time, organises workshops and seminars. In November 1993, CRP hosted a widely acclaimed Constitutional Conference on Contemporary National Issues in Abuja. About 50 experts and representatives of interest groups deliberated on Nigerian federalism, revenue allocation, ethnicity and democracy, justice, law and order among other issues. The communiqué issued at the end of the conference has become a reference point for many prominent Nigerians. It condemned the military coup of November 17, 1993 and agreed on the need to convene a constitutional conference for Nigeria to work out a constitutional basis for the country's future.

Discussions

The discussions generally acknowledged the fact that while the earlier papers expressed, in the main, an essentially theoretical concern, the Round Table on Human Rights demonstrates the centrality of practice in the struggle. The conference has thus provided an ample opportunity for the enunciation of the relationship between theory and practice. It was however, observed that the conference runs short of achieving the above-named ideal by its failure to invite ordinary people, the masses, to discuss their experiences in the struggle. It was observed that the issues raised by the various human rights struggles, especially in the context of deepening poverty and alienation. These forms of struggles are also limited by their ignoring the fact that, for instance, the pursuit of the right for employment cannot be enforceable without industrialisation of the country.

One other limitation of the struggle for human and civil rights is uneven permeation of the struggles in the north and south of Nigeria simultaneously. This handicap is attributed to elite vacillation, opportunism and hypocrisy of leadership and the emersion of struggle in primordial discourse which discourages effective participation especially from the north. There is also the need for the human rights groups to introduce a harmonious ideological political discourse that goes beyond the tenets of liberalism. The promotion of gender issues, tolerance of other views, solidarity, internal democracy and sincere leadership were presented in the discussions as crucial to the capacity of human rights organisations to expand the democratic space. These virtues are all the more crucial in light of the planned constitutional conference.

The discussion gave due prominence to the nature and sources of funding the human rights organisations depend upon. It was strongly felt that the source of funding the organisations, just as the ownership structure of the mass media, raise not only the question of patronage but also the organisations. The representatives of the human rights organisations explained the fact that their sources of funding are limited to levies, philanthropic donations and a cone-in-while assistance from credible international organisations. Funds raised from those sources are generally judiciously used and accounted for. The discussions recognised the fact that sources of funding the human rights organisations are inadequate and the limited funds at the disposal of these organisations leaves them vulnerable. This vulnerability in itself poses a great danger to the capacity of the human rights organisations to perform effectively.

The discussions also focused on the centrality of mobilisation and consciousness in the struggle for expanding the democratic space. It was observed that mobilisation is crucial and methods of achieving it adopted by the human rights organisations are elite-based, and therefore need to be re-considered and broadened. Finally, the conference provided a forum for the invited organisations to discuss some of their problems in tête-à-tête.

3

National Working Group Communiqué

The National Working Group (NWG) on the 'Expansion of Nigerian Democratic Space' is an ad hoc research network sponsored by the Council for the Development of Social Science Research in Africa (CODESRIA). It has the specific objective of investigating and documenting the role of the state, social institutions and civil and democratic associations in expanding democratic space at all levels of the Nigerian polity and society.

At the conference at the Nigerian Institute of International Affairs (NIIA), Lagos in December 1993, researchers and the 15 interest groups and mass organisations participating noted as follows:

1. That democracy cannot be confined to the transition to civil rule, voting or elections;

2. That democracy has intra-organisational and extra-organisational (national) components;

3. That democratic governance is a process of continuous expression of autonomous popular decision-making that comes about through constant struggle. It involves the institutionalisation of rules and procedures that allow freedom of expression and diversity of opinion;

4. That the Nigerian military has arrogated to themselves the right to 'democratise' the country and this is an obstacle to the realisation of genuine democracy. Unfortunately, some technocrats, especially a group within the intelligentsia, have been willing accomplices;

5. That issues relating to women, children and minority ethnic groups have not been properly addressed by most organisations interested in the expansion of democratic space;

6. That the shrinking of democratic space through militarism, repression, harsh economic policies and the greed of the ruling class in grabbing state resources for themselves have created and/or intensified communal and religious clashes;

7. That the political class has not demonstrated enough conviction and commitment to democratic struggle and are partly responsible for the current return country of the military; and

8. That those Nigerians who claim to believe in respect for human rights and enthronement of democracy, and yet advocate for military intervention as a result of the political problems surrounding the annulment of the June 12 elections, have demonstrated opportunism and lack of faith in popular struggle.

The Conference then resolved:

1. That the military as an interest group among several other competing groups has no right to arrogate to itself the task of supervising the transition to democratic rule.

2. That in the interest of promoting genuine democracy and expansion of democratic space:

    a) All associations and interest groups must democratise their internal decision-making structures; and

    b) Civil society through popular will should increase its efforts to determine the tenor and direction of the democracy project;

3. That while the Constitutional Conference proposed by the current military junta may be one way of starting to address the problems of democratisation and popular participation, it is not broad enough and cannot substitute for the Sovereign National Conference that pro-democracy advocates have been struggling for.

4. That democracy is a learning process that has to be nurtured through civility, moderation, tolerance and the spirit of accommodating other people's views.

5. That minorities and other oppressed groups should strive and promote their specific interests through practical involvement in national and grassroots organisations.

6. That democratic, human rights and mass organisations should formulate their activities in such a way so as to ensure that issues affecting both women and men as human beings and citizens are given equal attention, and that women are represented at all levels of their practices.

7. That for there to be mass participation in the expansion of democratic space, the current social and economic hardship occasioned by the structural adjustment programme must be alleviated.

8. And that the military have no right to rule, no legitimacy and no competence in governance. The Abacha Administration should therefore immediately vacate office and hand power to a Sovereign National Conference.

Bibliography

Abbas-Ibrahim, J., 1992, 'Memorandum by Heirs of Those Killed and Others Injured by the Armed Police and Soldiers on 20th May, 1992 at Ikara and Zaria Local Government Areas', submitted to Zangon Kataf (Market) Riot and Subsequent Riots Judicial Commission of Inquiry, 23 June.

Abdel-Kadr, S., 1988, *Egyptian Women in a Changing Society, 1899-1987*, L. Rienner, USA/UK.

Abdulraheem, Tajudeen and Olukoshi, Adebayo O., 1986, 'The Left in Nigerian Politics and the Struggle for Socialism', *Review of African Political Economy*, no. 37, December.

Academic Staff Union of Universities (ASUU), 1986a, *ASUU and the 1986 Education Crisis in Nigeria*, Zaria.

Academic Staff Union of Universities (ASUU) 1986b, 'Professor Jibrin Aminu and the Crisis in Nigerian Education', *The Guardian* August 31.

Adam, H. M., 1992, 'Somalia: Militarism, Warlordism or Democracy', *Review of African Political Economy*, no. 54.

Adekanye, J. Bayo, 1978, 'On the Theory of Modernising Soldier; A Critique', *Current Research on Peace and Violence*, vol. III, no. 1.

Adekanye, J. Bayo, 1981, *Nigeria in Search of a Stable Civil-Military System*, Westview Press, Boulder.

Adekanye, J. Bayo, 1985, 'The Politics of the Post-Military State in Africa', in Clapham, Christopher and Philip, George (eds.), *The Political Dilemmas of Military Regimes*, Croomheld, London.

Adekanye, J. Bayo, 1989, 'The Recruitment Policy: Its Sources and Impact on the Nigerian Military', in Ekeh P. P., and Osaghae E. E. (eds.), *Federal Character and Federalism in Nigeria Heinemann*, Ibadan.

Adekanye, J. Bayo, 1992, 'The Military as a Problem in Comparative Political Analysis', *Nigerian Journal of International Affairs*, vol. 8, no. 1.

Agbaje, Adigun, 1990, 'In Search of Building Blocks. The State, Civil Society, Voluntary Action and Grassroots Development in Africa', *Africa Quarterly*, vol.30, Nos. 3/4.

Aguda, T. Akinola, 1986, *The Crisis of Justice*, Eresu Hills Publishers, Akure.

Ake, Claude, 1990, 'The Case for Democracy', African Governance in the 1990s, The Carter Centre.

Ake, Claude, 1991, *Manchean Dialectics: The State Project and its Decivilising Mission in Africa*, ISS, The Hague.

Alemika, E. E. O., 1992, *Protection and Realisation of Human Rights in Africa*.

Althach, G. Philip, 1991, 'Student Politics and Culture', *Higher Education*, vol. 22. no. 2.

Amadiume, I. 1987, *Male Daughters, Female Husbands*, Zed Books, London.

Amadiume, I., 1990, 'Contemporary Women's Organisations, Contradictions and Irrelevance in the Struggle for Grassroots Democracy in Nigeria', paper presented to CODESRIA seminar on Social Movements, Social Transformation and the Struggle for Democracy in Africa, Tunis, May 21-23.

Amidu, Ado and Ekeocha, O., 1988, 'Communiqué Issued at the end of Eight Annual Convention of NANS', University of Ilorin, July 22-23.

Amin, Samir, 1990, 'The Issue of Democracy in the Contemporary Third World', paper for CODESRIA symposium on Academic Freedom, Research and the Social Responsibility of the Intellectual in Africa, Kampala.

Amin, Samir, 1993, 'History as Iconoclast: A Short Comment', *CODESRIA Bulletin*, No 2.

Aminu, Jibrin, 1986, *Quality and Stress in Nigerian Education*, University of Maiduguri and Northern Nigeria Publishing Company, Maiduguri and Zaria.

Amuta, Chidi, 1992, *Prince of the Niger: The Babangida Years*, Tamus, Lagos.

Ananaba, Wogu, 1969, *The Trade Union Movement in Nigeria*, C. Hurst, London.

Andrae, G. and Beckman, B., 1991, 'Textile Unions and Industrial Crisis in Nigeria: Labour Structure, Organisation, and Strategies', in Brandell, I. (ed.), *Workers in Third World Industrialisation*, London, MacMillan.

Andrae, G. and Beckman, B., 1992, 'Labour Regimes and Adjustment in the Nigerian Textile Industry', paper presented to workshop on The State, Structural Adjustment and Changing Social and Political Relations in Africa, Scandinavian Institute of African Studies, Uppsala.

Anyang' Nyong'o, P. (ed.), 1987, *Popular Struggles for Democracy in Africa*, Zed, London.

Anyang' Nyong'o, P., 1988, 'Political Instability and the Prospects for Democracy in Africa', *Africa Development*, Nos. 13.1 and 13.3.

Ardigo, Achille, 1985, 'Sociabilité et démocratie' in Leca J. and Papini R. (eds.), *Les Democraties: Sont-elles Gouvernables?*, Economica, Paris.

Aremu, Issa, 1990, 'Moscow: Though Cheap, No More Free Lunch' in *Textile Workers*, Kaduna.

Avineri, S., 1968, *The Social and Political Thought of Karl Marx*, Cambridge University Press.

Awe, B., 1989, 'Nigerian Women and Development in Retrospect' in Parpart J. L. (ed.), *Women and Development in Africa: Comparative Perspectives*, Dalhousie University.

Awe, B. (ed.), 1992, *Nigerian Women in Historical Perspective*, Sankore/Bookcraft, Ibadan.

Awe, B., (undated), *The National Commission for Women: Policy and Program Focus*, unpub., NCW, Abuja.

Ayandele, E. A., 1974, *The Educated Elite in Nigerian Society*, Ibadan.

Ayu, Iyorchia, 1986, *Essays in Popular Struggle: Fela, Students Patriotism, Nicaraguan Revolution*, Oguta: Zim Pan African Publishers.

Babatope, E., 1989, *Awo's Great Life Battles*, Friends Foundation Publishers Limited.

Badran, M., 1988, 'Dual Liberation: Feminism and Nationalism in Egypt, 1875-1925', *Feminist Issues*, Spring.

Bakke, E. Wight., 1966, Mutual Survival: The Goal of Unions and Management, Archon Books, Hamden, 1966.

Bangura, Y., 1986, 'Structural Adjustment and the Political Question', *Review of African Political Economy*, no. 37.

Bangura, Y., 1989, 'Authoritarian Rule and Democracy in Africa: A Theoretical Discourse', UNRISD Discussion Paper no. 18.

Bangura, Y., 1993, 'Intellectuals, Economic Reform and Social Change', Conference Paper, Holland.

Bangura, Y. and Beckman, B., 1993, 'African Workers and Structural Adjustment: A Nigerian Case Study' in Olukoshi A. (ed.), *The Politics of Structural Adjustment in Nigeria*, James Currey, London.

Bayart, Jean-Francois, 1986, 'Civil Society in Africa' in Chabal, Patrick (ed.), *Political Domination in Africa: Reflections on the Limits of Power*, Cambridge University Press, London.

Beckman, B., 1987, 'The Military as Revolutionary Vanguard: A Critique' in Olugbemi, Stephen O. (ed.), *Alternative Political Futures for Nigeria*, Nigerian Political Science Association, Lagos.

Beckman, B., 1989, 'Whose Democracy: Bourgeois versus Popular Democracy', *Review of African Political Economy*, no. 45/46.

Beckman, B., 1990, 'Structural Adjustment and Democracy: Interest Group Resistance to Structural Adjustment and the Development of the Democracy Movement in Africa', research proposal, Stockholm University, Department of Political Science.

Beckman, B., 1992, 'Empowerment or Repression? The World Bank and the Politics of Adjustment', in Gibbon, P., Bangura Y. and Ofstad A. (eds.), *Authoritarianism, Democracy and Adjustment: The Politics of Economic Reform in Africa*, Scandinavian Institute of African Studies, Uppsala.

Beckman, B., 1993a, 'The Liberation of Civil Society: Neo-Liberal Ideology and Political Theory', *Review of African Political Economy*, no. 58.

Beckman, B., 1993b, 'The Politics of Labour and Adjustment: The Experience of the Nigeria Labour Congress', *CODESRIA Seminar*, Dakar.

Beckman, B. and Jega, A., 1994, 'Scholars and Democratic Politics in Nigeria', paper to conference on 'Knowledge and Development' organised by the Norwegian Association of Development Research (NFU), Tromsö.

Benjamin, M., 1990, 'History of the Minimum Wage Law', *Philippine Journal of Labour and Industrial Relation*, vol. XII, no. 1.

Bereday, George, 1958, *Public Education in America: A New Interpretation on Purpose and Practice*, New York, Harper.

Bobbio, N., 1987, *The Future of Democracy*, Polity Press, Oxford.

Bonat, Z. A., 1992, 'Intercommunal and Religious Crises in Kaduna State: Their Historical Origins and Contemporary Forms', Draft Research Report.

Boro, Isaac, 1982, *The Twelve Day Revolution*, Idodo Umeh Publishers, Benin City.

Braveman, Harry, 1974, 'Labour and Monopoly Capital: The Degradation of Work in the Twentieth Century', Monthly Review Press, New York and London.

Buijtenhuijs, R., 1990, 'Democratisation and Participation in Africa South of the Sahara', in Sub-Saharan Africa Beyond Adjustment, Africa seminar, Maastricht.

Chazan, N., 1989, 'Gender Perspectives on African States', in Parpart and Staudt (eds.), *Women and the State in Africa*, L. Rienner, USE and UK.

Choi, Hyaeweol, 1991, 'The Societal Impact of Student Politics in Contemporary South Korea', Higher Education, vol. 22 no. 2.

Civil Liberties Organisation (CLO), 1990, *Decree 2: A Special Publication of the CLO*, March.

Clegg, et al., 1986, 'Weber: Economic Class and Civil Status' in *Their Class Politics and The Economy*, London, Routledge and Kegan Paul.

Clegg, H. A., 1975, 'Pluralism in Industrial Relations', *The British Journal of Industrial Relations*, vol. XIII, no. 3.

Coleman, J. S., 1986, *Nigeria: Background to Nationalism*, University of California Press, Berkeley.

Committee for the Defence of Human Rights (CDHR), 1990, *Annual Report on Human Rights Situation in Nigeria*, Lagos.

Crisp, Jeff, 1984, *The Story of an African Working Class: Ghanaian Miners' Struggles 1870-1880*, Zed Books, London.

Crouch, Colin, 1982 (ed.), *Trade Union: The Logic of Collective Action*, Fontana Paperbacks.

Dahl, Robert, 1994, 'A Democratic Dilemma: System Effectiveness versus Citizen Participation', *Political Science Quarterly*, vol. 109, no. 1.

Dare, L. O., 1991, 'The Praetorian Trap: The Problems and Prospects of Military Disengagement', Inaugural Lecture Series 94, Obafemi Awolowo University Press.

Daura, Mamman, 1971, 'Editing a Government Newspaper in Northern Nigeria', in Stokke, O. (ed.), *Reporting Africa*, Scandinavian Institute of African Studies, Uppsala.

Dawn, 1988, *Development Crises and Alternative Visions: Third World Women's Perspectives*, Earthscan.

Decalo, Samuel, 1976, *Coups and Army Rule in Africa*, Yale University Press, New Haven.

Dennis, C., 1987, 'Women and the State in Nigeria: The Case of the Federal Military Government', in Afshar H. (ed.), *Women, State and Ideology*, MacMillan.

Diamond, L., 1988, 'Nigeria: Pluralism, Statism and the Struggle for Democracy', in Diamond, Linz and Lipset, (eds.), *Democracy in Developing Countries*, vol. 2, Africa, Lynne Rienner Publishers, Boulder.

Dike, Enwere, 1990, 'Nigeria: The Political Economy of the Buhari Regime', *Nigerian Journal of International Affairs*, vol. 16, no. 2.

Diop, M. C. and Diouf, M., 1991, 'Statutory Political Successions: An Afterword', *CODESRIA Bulletin*, no. 3.

Djilas, M., 1957, *The New Class: An Analysis of the Communist System*, Praeger; New York.

Doornbos, M., 1990, 'The African State in Academic Debate: Retrospect and Prospect in Beyond Adjustment', Africa Seminar, Maastricht.

Dudley, B. J., 1973, *Instability and Political Order: Politics and Crisis in Nigeria*, Ibadan University Press, Ibadan.

Dunlop, J., 1958, *Industrial Relations Systems*, Southern Illinois Press.

Ekwe-Ekwe, Herbert, 1985, 'The Nigerian Plight: Shagari to Buhari', *Third World Quarterly*, vol. 7, no. 3.

Erd, R. and Scherrer, C., 1985, 'Unions Caught Between Structural Competition and Temporary Solidarity: A Critique of Contemporary Marxist Analysis of Trade Unions in Germany', *British Journal of Industrial Relations*, vol. XXIII.

Essien-Ibok, A., 1982 (eds.), *Towards a Progressive Nigeria*, Kano.

Eze, Osita, 1984, *Human Rights in Africa - Some Selected Problems*, NIIA and MacMillan, Lagos.

FNV, 1991, *Moving Borders: Women and the Trade Unions in Netherlands*, Amsterdam.

Fashoyin, T., 1984, 'Trade Unionists and the Quality of Work: Perspective from Nigeria', *Labour and Society*, vol. 9 no. 3.

Fashoyin, T., 1985, *The Structure and Scope of the Trade Union Movement in Nigeria: Trade Union and Industrial Relations Management - A Manual.*

Fawehinmi, Gani, 1991, 'Denial of Justice Through Ouster of Courts Jurisdiction in Nigeria', *Journal of Human Rights Law and Practice*, vol. 1, no. 2.

Federal Republic of Nigeria (FRN), 1975, *The Dawn of A New Era*, Government Printer, Lagos.

Federal Republic of Nigeria (FRN), 1987, *Report of the Political Bureau*, Government Printer, Lagos.

Federal Government of Nigeria (FGN), 1986, *Government White Paper on the Commission of Inquiry into the Student Crisis at A.B.U. Zaria*, Federal Government Press, Lagos.

Federal Government of Nigeria (FGN), 1989, *Decree no. 47, Student Union Activities (Control and Regulation)*, Federal Government Press, Lagos.

Finer, Samuel, E., 1975, *The Man on Horseback: The Role of the Military in Politics*, Harmondsworth, Penguin Books.

First, Ruth, 1975, *The Barrel of a Gun*, Allan Lane, The Penguin Press.

Fox, Alan, n.d., 'Collective Bargaining, Flanders and The Webbs', *The British Journal of Industrial Relations*, vol. VIII, no. 2.

Frank, R. A., 1988, 'Gramsci's Theory of Trade Unionism', Rethinking Marxism, vol. 1.

Goldthorpe, John, et.al., 1968, *The Affluent Worker: Industrial Attitudes and Behaviour*, University Press Cambridge.

Gouldner, Alvin, W., 1979, *The Future of Intellectuals and the Role of the New Class*, Oxford University Press.

Gravin, Roger, 1985, *On the History of Trade Unionism With Special Reference to Nigeria: Trade Union and Industrial Relations Management in Nigeria - A Manual.*

Gutteridge, W. F., 1975, *Military Regimes in Africa*, Metheun, London.

Harris, K., 1982, *Teachers and Classes: A Marxist Analysis*, Routledge and Kegan Paul, London.

Harrod, J., 1977, *The Ideology of the International Labour Organisation Towards Developing Countries in The Impact of International Organisation on Legal and Institutional Change in Developing Countries*, New York.

Harrod, J. (ed.), 1986, *Social Relations of Production, System of Labour Control and Third World Trade Unions*, Zed Press, London.

Harrod, J., 1987, *Power, Production, and the Unprotected Worker*, New York, Columbia University, University Press.

Hashim, Y., 1987, *State Intervention in Trade Unions: A Nigerian Case Study 1975-1978*, ISS, The Hague.

Hoffman, John, 1988, *State, Power and Democracy*, Wheat Sheaf Books, Sussex.

Hughes, A. and Cohen, R., 1971, *An Emerging Nigerian Working Class: The Lagos Experience, 1887-1939*, University of Birmingham Press, Birmingham.

Huntington, Samuel, P., 1957, *The Soldier and the State*, Harvard University Press, Cambridge.

Huntington, Samuel, P., 1968, *Political Order in Changing Societies*, Yale University Press, New Haven.

Hutchful, E., 1989, 'Military and Militarism in Africa: A Research Agenda', *CODESRIA Working Paper*, no. 31, Dakar.

Hutchful, E., 1991, 'Reconstructing Political Space Militarism and Constitutionalism in Africa' in Shivji, Issa G. (ed.), *State and Constitutionalism: An African Debate on Democracy*, SAPES, Harare.

Hutchful, E., 'African Marxism and the Gender Question', in *Gendering African Social Science*, CODESRIA, Dakar, forthcoming.

Hyden, G. and Bratton, M., 1992, *Governance and Politics in Africa*, Lynne Rienner Publishers, Boulder.

Hyman, Richard, 1974, *Industrial Relations: A Marxist Introduction*, Macmillian Press.

ICFTU, 1988, *The Challenge of Change*, 14th World Congress, Brussels.

ICFTU, 1989, *Trade Union Rights, Survey of Violations*, Brussels.

ICFTU, 1991, *BFTU/ICFTU PanAfrican Conference on Democracy, Development and the Defence of Human and Trade Union Rights Gaborone*, July.

Ibrahim, J. and Pereira, C., 1993, 'On Dividing and Uniting: Ethnicity, Racism and Nationalism in Africa', paper for International Development Information Network, CLACSO, Buenos Aires.

Ibrahim, Rufai, 1981 (ed.), *The Example of Bala Mohammed*, Gaskiya, Zaria.

Ibrahim, Jibrin, 1983, 'The Political Economy of Mass Communications in Nigeria: A Case Study of the Daily Times and New Nigerian', M.Sc. Thesis, Zaria.

Ibrahim, Jibrin, 1986, 'The Political Debate and the Struggle for Democracy in Nigeria', *Review of African Political Economy*, no. 37.

Ibrahim, Jibrin, 1990, 'Succession politique et crispation sociale au Nigeria: 1987-1988', *Année Africaine*, Pedone, Bordeaux.

Ibrahim, Jibrin, 1992, 'Expanding Democratic Space: An African and Nigerian Discussion' mimeo, Zaria.

Ibrahim, Jibrin, 1992, 'From Political Exclusion to Popular Participation: Democratic Transition in Niger Republic' in Caron, B. Gboyega A. and Osaghae E. (eds.), *Democratic Transition in Africa*, CREDU, Ibadan.

Ibrahim, Jibrin, 1993, 'History as Iconoclast: Left Stardom and the Debate on Democracy', *CODESRIA Bulletin*, no. 1, 1993 and 'History as Iconoclast: A Rejoinder', no. 2.

Ibrahim, Jibrin, 1993, 'Transition to Civil Rule: Sapping Democracy' in Olukoshi, A. O. (ed.), *The Politics of Structural Adjustment in Nigeria*, James Currey, London.

Imam, Ayesha, 1985, 'Ideological Manipulation, Political Repression and African Women', *AAWORD Occasional Paper Series 2*.

Imam, Ayesha, 1993, 'If You Don't Do These Things For Me I Won't Do Seclusion For You', PhD Thesis, Sussex.

Jaafar, N. and Onoja, A., 1993, 'NANS Position on the June 12 Election', *The Guardian*, July 16.

Jayawardena, K., 1986, *Feminism and Nationalism in the Third World*, Zed Press, London.

Jega, A. M., 1988, 'The Labour Movement and Popular Democratic Struggles in Nigeria', Mahmoud Tukur Memorial Symposium, Zaria, November.

Jega, A. M., 1990, 'The Influence of Class Actors in Nigeria's Transition Process', Conference on Democratic Transition and Structural Adjustment, Stanford University, August.

Jega, A. M., 1992, 'Growth and Innovation in the Nigerian Universities: A Critical Perspective', 15th Committee of Vice-Chancellors Seminar, Bauchi, April.

Jega, A. M., 1993, 'Professional Associations and Structural Adjustment' in Olukoshi, A. (ed.), *The Politics of Structural Adjustment in Nigeria*, James Currey, London.

Kasfir, N., 1976, *The Shrinking Political Arena*, University of California Press, Berkeley.

Kuti, Beko Ransome, 1973, 'The Chicken has Come Home to Roost', Text of a Press Conference by Campaign for Democracy, Lagos, June 17.

Leca, Jean, 1986, 'Individualisme et citoyenneté' in Birnbaum P. and Leca J. (eds.), *Sur L'Individualisme*, Presse de la Fondation Nationale des Sciences Politiques, Paris.

Legum, Colin, 1990, 'The Coming of Africa's Second Independence', *The Washington Quarterly*, Winter.

Levy, Daniel, 1991, 'The Decline of Latin American Student Activitism', *Higher Education*, vol. 22, no. 2.

Leys, Colin, 1994, 'Confronting the African Tragedy', *New Left Review*, no. 204.

Lukham, Robin, 1971, *The Nigerian Military: A Sociological Analysis of Authority and Revolt 1960-1967*, Cambridge University Press, Cambridge.

Lukman, Salisu, 1989, 'Text of a Press Conference', Lagos, May 12.

Macpherson, C. B., 1972, *The Life and Times of Liberal Democracy*, Oxford University Press, Oxford.

Madunagu, Edwin, 1980, *The Tragedy of the Nigerian Socialist Movement and Other Essays*, Centaur Press, Calabar.

Mafeje, A., 1991, 'African Households and Prospects for Agricultural Revival in Sub-Saharan Africa', Working Paper 2/91, CODESRIA, Dakar.

Mafeje, A., 1993, 'On "Icons" and African Perspectives on Democracy: A Commentary on Jibrin Ibrahim's Views', *CODESRIA Bulletin*, no. 2.

Mainguwa, A., 1987, 'Guidelines on Reactivation of Student Union Activities', Ahmadu Bello University, Zaria.

Mamdani, M., 1990, 'State and Civil Society in Contemporary Africa: Reconceptualising the Birth of State Nationalism and the Defeat of Popular Movements', *Africa Development*, vol. XV, Nos. 3/4.

Mamdani, M., 1990, 'The Social Basis of Constitutionalism in Africa', *Journal of Modern African Studies*, no. 28 (3).

Mamdani, M., 1992, 'African Democratic Theory and Democratic Struggles', *Seventh General Assembly*, CODESRIA, Dakar.

Mannheim, H., 1972, *The Pioneers in Criminology*, Montclair, Petterson Smith.

Mba, Nina, 1989, 'Kaba and Khaki: Women and the Militarised State in Nigeria', in Parpart J. and Staudt K., (eds.), *Women and the State in Africa*, Lynne Rienner, Boulder and London.

Meagher, K., 1990, *Socialist Reforms and Implication for Trade Unions in Developing Countries in The Textile Worker*, Kaduna, Nigeria.

Medard, J. F., 1991, *Les Etats d'Afrique*, Karthala, Paris.

Mkandawire, T., 1988, 'Comments on Democracy and Political Instability', *Africa Development*, vol. XIII, no. 3.

Mkandawire, T., 1991, 'Crisis and Adjustment in Sub-Saharan Africa' in Ghai D. (ed.), *The IMF and the South*, Zed, London.

Mohammed, Abubakar Sokoto, 1986, 'The Struggle for Democratic Rights and Socialism in Nigeria', paper for Conference on Popular Struggles in Africa, ROAPE in association with the Centre of African Studies, University of Liverpool, September 26-28.

Momoh, Abubakar, 1991, 'The 1989 Constitution and The Nigerian Toiling Masses', *Journal of Constitutional and Parliamentary Studies*, vol. XXV, Nos. 1-4.

Momoh, Abubakar, 1992, 'The Philosophical and Ideological Foundations of the Transition to Civil Rule in Nigeria' in Caron, B. Gboyega, A. and Osaghe E. O. (eds.), *Democratic Transitions in Africa*, CREDU, Ibadan.

Morera, E., 1990, 'Gramsci and Democracy,' *Canadian Journal of Political Science*, vol. XXIII, No. I.

Mouffe, Chantal, 1992, 'Democratic Politics Today' in Mouffe, C. (ed.), *Dimensions of Radical Democracy: Pluralism, Citizenship, Community*, Verso, London.

Muazzam, Ibrahim, 1982, 'The PRP-Imoudu and the Politics of Realignment: A Call to March Separately But Strike Together', mimeo, Kano.

Muazzam, Ibrahim, 1992, 'Against Pragmatic and Reformist Illusion', mimeo, Kano.

Munoz, Carlos, 1989, *Youth, Identity, Power: The Chicano. Movement*, London, Verso.

Musa, S. A., 1982, 'The Place and Role of Nigerian Universities in National Politics', in Baike, A. (ed.), *Higher Education and Development in the Context of the Nigerian Constitution*, University of Benin, Benin-City.

Mustapha, A. R., 1985, 'Critical Notes on the National Question: Practical Politics and the People's Redemption Party', (mimeo), Zaria.

Mustapha, A. R., 1986, 'The National Question and Radical Politics in Nigeria', *Review of African Political Economy*, no. 37, December.

Mustapha, A. R., 1990, 'Peasant Differentiation and Politics in Rural Kano: 1900-1987', D.Phil. Thesis, University of Oxford.

Mustapha, A. R., 1992, 'Identity Boundaries, Ethnicity and National Integration in Nigeria', research report, *CODESRIA Network on Ethnic Conflicts in Africa*, Dakar.

Mzirag, G., 1989, 'Organising Women for Change: The Experience of Women in Tanzania Since Independence' unpub MA research paper, Institute of Social Studies, The Netherlands.

Naanen, Ben, 1995, 'Oil Producing Minorities and the Restructuring of Nigerian Federalism: The Case of the Ogoni People', *Journal of Commonwealth and Comparative Politics*, vol. 33, No 1.

National Association of Nigerian Students (NANS), 1982, *Nigerian Students Charter of Demands*, Ibadan, Iva Valley Press.

National Association of Nigerian Students (NANS), 1988, 'NANS Travails, Successes and Challenges', Publicity Bureau.

National Association of Nigerian Students (NANS), 1990, 'Communiqué Issued at the End of Emergency Meeting', Rivers State University of Technology, Port Harcourt, April 7-8.

National Association of Nigerian Students (NANS), 1990, 'Communiqué Issued at the End of 23rd Senate Meeting', Bayero University, Kano.

National Association of Nigerian Students (NANS), 1991, 'NANS Call' in Nkinyangi, A. (1991) 'Student Protests in Sub-Saharan Africa', *Higher Education*, vol. 22, no. 2.

National Commission for Women, 1992, *Annual Report*, Abuja.

National Commission for Women, 1992, *Partners in Development*, September 1992 issue, Abuja.

National Consultative Forum on National Conference, 1990, *Agenda for Democracy*, Lagos.

National Directorate of Employment, 1990, *Digest of Education Statistics*, Lagos.

National Universities Commission, 1977, *Report of the Academic Planning Group*, Lagos.

National Univefsities Commission, 1982, *Twenty Years of University Education in Nigeria*, Lagos.

National Universities Commission, 1983, *Annual Reports*, Lagos.

Nigerian Labour Congress (NLC), 1984, *Social and Economic Viewpoint*, Lagos.

Nigerian Labour Congress (NLC), 1986, *Memorandum on New Minimum Wage*, Lagos.

Nnoli, Okwudiba, 1984, 'Musical Chairs and the Cheers For the Music', *Studies in Politics and Society*, no. 2, October.

Nwabueze, B. O., 1973, *Constitutionalism in the Emergent States*.

Nzongola-Ntalaja, 1987, *Revolution and Counter-Revolution in Africa*, London, Zed Books.

O'Donnell, G. A. *et al.*, 1986, *Transitions from Authoritarian Rule: Prospects for Democracy*, John Hopkins University Press, Baltimore.

Offe, Claus *et al.*, 1985, *Two Logics of Collective Action: Disorganised Capital*, Polity Press, Cambridge.

Ogunkoya, Michael, O., 1989, *Report of The Administration of the Nigeria Labour Congress*, Printed by the Federal Government of Nigeria Printer Lagos.

Olagunju, T. and Oyovbaire, S., 1989 (eds.), *Foundations of a New Nigeria: The IBB Era*, Precision Press, Lagos.

Olagunju, T. and Oyovbaire, S., 1991 (eds.), *For Their Tomorrow, We Gave Our Today: Selected Speeches of IBB*, vol. 2, Sefari Books, St. Helier.

Oldfield, Adrain, 1990, 'Citizenship: An Unnatural Practice', *The Political Quarterly*, vol. 61 no. 2.

Olson, Mancur, 1982, *The Logic of the Rise and Decline of Nations*, Yale University Press.

Olukoshi, Adebayo and Abdulraheem, Tajudeen, 1985, 'Nigeria Crisis Management under the Buhari Administration', *Review of African Political Economy*, no. 34, December.

Olukoshi, Adebayo, O., 1988, 'Associational Life During the Nigerian Transition to Civilian Rule', (mimeo), Lagos.

Olukoshi, Adebayo, O., 1991, 'Nigerian Marxist Responses to the Formation of the Nigerian Labour Party (NLP)' in Neugebuer, Christian, (ed.), *Philosophy, Ideology and Society in Africa*, Peter Lang, Frankfurt.

Olukoshi, Adebayo, O., 1992, 'The State and the Civil Liberties Movement in Nigeria', (mimeo), Lagos.

Olukoshi, Adebayo, O., 1993, 'The Current Transition From Military Rule in Nigeria', paper presented to the Workshop on Experiences of Political Liberalisation in Africa, Centre for Development Research, Copenhagen, June 3-4.

Olusanya, Gabriel, 1982, *The West African Student's Union and the Politics of Decolonisation 1925-1958*, Ibadan, Daystar Press.

Omu, Fred, 1978, *The Press and Politics in Nigeria: 1880-1937*, Longman, London.

Oshiomhole, A., 1993, 'Welcome Address at the Commissioning of 15 Units of Buses and Operations of Kaduna Depot', NUTGTWN, Kaduna.

Osoba, Segun, 1993, 'Crisis of Accumulation and Democratic Misadventure in Nigeria: A Retrospective and Perspective Analysis', *Ife Journal of History*, vol. 1, no. 1, Jan-June.

Othman, S., 1984, 'Classes, Crises and the Coup: The Demise of Shagari's Regime', *African Affairs*, vol. 83.

Otobo, Dafe, 1988, *State and Industrial Relations in Nigeria*, Malthouse Press Lagos.

Otu, O., 1990, 'The Better Life Program for Rural Women in Nigeria: A Great Leap Forward in National Development', unpub paper, Ahmadu Bello University, Zaria, Nigeria.

Owolabi, A. Olayiwola, 1992, 'The Military and Democratic Transition: An Analysis of the Transition Programme of the Babangida Administration' in Caron, B. Gboyega A. and Osaghae E. (eds.), *Democratic Transition in Africa*, CREDU, Ibadan.

Oyediran, Oyeleye, 1988-1989, 'The Gospel of the Second Chance. A Comparison of Obasanjo and Babangida Military Disengagement in Nigeria', *Quarterly Journal of Administration*, vol. XXIII no. 1.

Paden, J., 1970, 'Urban Pluralism, Integration and Adaptation of Communal Identity in Kano, Nigeria', in Cohen R. and Middleton, J. (eds.), *From Tribe to Nation in Africa*, Chandler Publishing Co., Scranton.

Parpart, J. and Standt, K., 1989 (eds.), *Women and the State in Africa*, L. Rienner.

Patterson, Orlando, 1994, 'Freedom, Slavery and the Modern Construction of Rights' lead paper for Conference on Democracy: Popular Precedents, Practice, Culture, University of Witwatersrand, Johannesburg, July.

Perry, L., 1984, *Intellectual Life in America*, New Delhi.

Phillips, Anne, 1991, *Engendering Democracy*, Polity Press, Cambridge.

Pittin, R., 1984, 'Documentation and Analysis of the Invisible Work of Invisible Women: A Nigerian Case Study', *International Labour Review*, vol. 123, no. 4, July-August.

Pye, Lucian, 1990, 'Political Science and the Crisis of Authoritariansm', *American Political Science Review*, vol. 84, no. 1.

Ramaswany, E. A., 1991, *Do We Need Trade Unions?*, ISS, The Hague.

Ramaswany, E. A., 1991, *Participation: What about the Union?*, ISS, The Hague.

Ricard, Alain, 1986, *Wole Soyinka ou l'ambition democratique*, Abidjan.

Rousseau, J. J., 1966, *Du Contrat Social*, Flammarion, Paris.

Rudebeck, Lars, 1992 (ed.), *When Democracy Makes Sense: Studies in the Democratic Potential of Third World Popular Movements*, Uppsala, AKUT.

Russell, D. E. H., 1990, *Lives of Courage: Women for a New South Africa*, Virago.

Sachkonye, L., 1989, 'The Debate about Democracy in Contemporary Zimbabwe', *Review of African Political Economy*, no. 45/46.

Samatar, A. I., 1994 (ed.), *The Somali Challenge: From Catastrophe to Renewal*, Lynne Reinner, Boulder.

Sandbrook, R., 1988, 'Liberal Democracy in Africa: A Socialist-Revisionist Perspective', *Canadian Journal of African Studies*, vol. 22, no. 2.

Sarup, M., 1992, *Education, State and Crisis: A Marxist Perspective*, Routledge and Kegan Paul, London.

Schmitter, P. C., 1995, 'More Liberal, Preliberal, or Postliberal', *Journal of Democracy*, vol. 6, No. 1.

Shawalu, R., 1990, *The Story of Gambo Sawaba*, Echo Communications, Jos.

Shettima, A. K., 1989, 'Women's Movement and Visions: The Nigeria Labour Congress Women's Wing', *Africa Development*, XIV 3.

Shettima, A. K., 1993, 'Structural Adjustment and the Student Movement in Nigeria', *Review of African Political Economy*, no. 56.

Shettima, A. K. (undated), 'Constitutional Development, Party Politics and Prospects for Women in Nigeria's Third Republic', unpublished paper, University of Maiduguri.

Shils, E., 1968, International Encyclopaedia of the Social Sciences IESS.

Shils, E., 1991, 'The Virtue of Civil Society', *Government and Opposition*, vol. 26, no. 1.

Shivji, Issa, 1989, 'The Pitfalls of the Debate on Democracy', *CODESRIA Bulletin*, vol. XIII no. 4.

Shivji, Issa, 1989, *The Concept of Human Rights in Africa*, CODESRIA, Dakar.

Sithole, M., 1994, 'The Democratisation Process in Africa: Is the Second Wind of Change Any Different From the First', paper for CODESRIA/Rockefeller Reflections Programme, Dakar.

Sow, Fatou, 1994, 'The Role of Gender Analysis in the Future of Social Sciences in Africa', *CODESRIA Bulletin*, no. 2.

Stanton, I., 1990 (ed.), *Mothers of the Revolution*, Baobab Books, Harare.

Stephan, A., 1988, *Rethinking Military Politics: Brazil and the Southern Core*, Princetown, Princetown University Press.

Stephan, A., 1990, 'On the Tasks of a Democratic Opposition', *Journal of Democracy*, vol. 1, no. 2 (Spring).

Thomas, H., 1990, 'Labour and Work in Small Scale Enterprises', Working Paper Series no. 79, Institute of Social Studies.

Tokumboh, M. A., 1985, *Labour Movement in Nigeria: Past and Present*, Literamed Publication, Lagos.

Tongo, A., 1990, 'Better Life for Rural Women', paper presented at the 4th International Interdisciplinary Congress on Women, Hunter College, New York.

Toyo, Eskor, 1985, 'An Open Letter to the Nigerian Left', *Review of African Political Economy*, no. 32, April.

Traore, Eno. Edet, 1982, 'Realists, Trotskyites and Anarchists', (Mimeo), Lagos.

Tsikata, E., *Gender Analysis and the State in Ghana: Some Preliminary Issues in Gendering African Social Science*, CODESRIA, Dakar, forthcoming.

Tukur, M. M., 1990, 'The Intellectual and Anti-Imperialist Struggle in Asia, Latin America and Africa', in Abubakar T. (ed.), *The Essential Mahmud Tukur*, ABU Press, Zaria.

Turner, Terisa, 1978, 'Commercial Capitalism and the 1975 Coup', in Panterbrick K. (ed.), *Soldier and Oil: The Political Transformation of Nigeria*, London, Frank Cass.

Turner, T., 1976, 'Multinational Corporations and the Instability of the Nigerian State', *Review of African Political Economy*, no. 5.

Ukpabi, C., 1987, *Mercantile Soldiers in Nigerian History*, Gaskiya Corporation, Zaria.

Ukpabi, C., 1987, *The Origins of the Nigerian Army*, Gaskiya Corporation, Zaria.

Urdang, S., 1979, *Fighting Two Colonialisms: Women in Guinea Bissau*, Monthly Review Press, NY/London.

Urdang, S., 1989, *And Still They Dance: Women, War and the Struggle for Change in Mozambique*, Earthscan, London.

Uviegbara, E. E., 1976, *Trade Unions Law in Nigeria*, Ethiope Publishing Corporation, Ring Road, Benin City, Nigeria.

Walker, C., 1982, *Women and Resistance in South Africa*, Onyx Press, London.

Wamba-dia-Wamba, E., 1992, 'Africa in Search of a New Historical Mode of Politics', paper for CODESRIA General Assembly Conference on Democratisation Processes in Africa, Dakar.

Waterman, P., 1973, 'Communist Theory in The Nigeria Trade Union Movement', Occasional paper, ISS, The Hague.

Waterman, P., 1975, *Conservation Among Nigerian Workers*, ISS, The Hague.

Waterman, P., 1990, *Social Movement Unionism. Beyond Economic and Political Unionism*, ISS., The Hague.

Waters, Malcolm, 1989, 'Citizenship and the Constitution of Structural Social Inequality', *International Journal of Comparative Sociology*, vol. XXX (3-4).

Welch, Claude E., 1970, (ed.), *Soldier and State in Africa*, Evanston, Illinois, Northwestern University Press.

Welch, Claude, E., 1987, *No Farewell to Arms? Military Disengagement From Politics in Africa and Latin America*, London, West View Press.

West Africa Magazine, 1989, 'Voices of Abuja', 20-26 November.

Women in Nigeria (WIN), 1985a, *Women and the Family: Proceedings of the Second Annual WIN Conference*, CODESRIA, Dakar.

Women in Nigeria (WIN), 1985b, *Women in Nigeria Today*, Zed Press, London.

Women in Nigeria (WIN), 1985c, *The WIN Document: Conditions of Women in Nigeria and Policy Recommendations to 2,000 AD*, Zaria, Nigeria.

World Bank, 1989, *Sub-Saharan Africa From Crisis to Sustainable Growth, A Long-Term Perspective Study*, Washington.

World Bank, 1991, *World Development Report 1991, The Challenge of Development*, Washington.

Yahaya, Shehu et al., 1991 (eds.), *Perestroika in Eastern Europe and Europe 1992: Implications for Africa*, Department of Economics, Bayero University, Kano.

Zasha, J., 1985, 'The State and Trade Unions', *Nigerian Journal of Political Science*, vol. 4, Nos. 1 and II.

Index

A

Abacha regime 62-63, 74, 180, 198-200
Abiola, M.K.O. 73, 119-120
Aborishade, F. 123
Academic Staff Union of Universities
(ASUU) 11, 53, 148-151, 175
academics 145
  See also intellectuals
Achebe, Chinua 10
Action Group (AG) 4-5, 157-158
Adefarasin, Mrs 87
Adelugba, Mrs F.M. 109
advertising 105-108
African Alternative to SAP (AASAP) 115
African Concord 111, 115, 124
African Guardian 113
African Mail 8
African Training and Research Centre for
Women (ACTRW) 80
Aguiyi-Ironsi, Mrs Victoria Nwanyiocha 89
Ahmadu Bello University (ABU) 112
Aikhomu, Mrs Rebecca 89
Air Transport Services Employers of
Nigeria 54
Ajasa, Sir Kitoye 8
Akerele, Mrs Kofo Bucknor 93
Akilu, Col. Halilu 13
Akinrade, Chief 85
Akinrinade, Chief Janet 84
Alfa, Ibrahim 69
Ali Must Go campaign 133
Alliance for Democratic Rights (ADR)
138, 140
Aminu, Jibril 148
Anglo-African 8
Armed Forces Ruling Council 51
Association of Advertising Practitioners of
Nigeria (AAPN) 105
Association of Democratic Lawyers of
Nigeria (ADLN) 13
Association of Furniture, Fixture and Wood
Workers Employers of Nigeria 54
associations 25-28, 30
  See also institutions, interest groups,
professional associations, trades unions

authoritarianism 57
Awa, Professor Eme 70
Awe, Professor 94
Awolowo 4, 58
Azikiwe, Nnamdi 4, 8, 58

B

Babangida regime 50-54, 61, 118
  and corruption 62-63
  and democracy 66-67, 70-74, 143
  and human rights 196-198
  and intellectuals 148-151
  and the left 163-164
  and political parties 53, 67-70
  and women 87-88
Babangida, General Ibrahim 61, 66-67
Babangida, Mrs Maryam 88-91, 93-95
Bafyau, Paschal 54
Balewa, Tafawa 2, 12
ballot systems 71-72
  See also elections
barrack culture 58
Bello, Ahmadu 12
Better Life for Rural Women Programme
(BLP) 89-95
Bornu Youth Movement (BYM) 6, 65
Boro, Major Isaac 6
bourgeoisie 43, 48, 59, 156
Buhari regime 61
Buhari, Hajiya Sefinatu 88

C

Caliphate Oligarchy 7
Campaign for Democracy (CD) 54-55, 119,
138-141, 164, 198, 200
Campbell, Horace 8
censorship 8
  See also repression
centralisation 63-64
Centre for Women and Development 95
Chiroma, Ali 54
Citizen 105, 119
citizenship 16-17, 215-217
  See also rights
civil liberties 13, 18, 159, 162-165,

www.ingramcontent.com/pod-product-compliance
Lightning Source LLC
Chambersburg PA
CBHW061004280326
41935CB00009B/830